Shelby Foote

THE CIVIL WAR

A NARRATIVE

THE CIVIL WAR

A NARRATIVE

2

★ ★ ★

FORT DONELSON
TO MEMPHIS

40th Anniversary Edition

BY SHELBY FOOTE
AND THE EDITORS OF TIME-LIFE BOOKS,
ALEXANDRIA, VIRGINIA

All these were honoured in their generations,
and were the glory of their times.

There be of them,
that have left a name behind them,
that their praises might be reported.

And some there be, which have no memorial;
who are perished, as though they had never been;
and are become as though they had never been born;
and their children after them.

But these were merciful men,
whose righteousness hath not been forgotten.

With their seed shall continually remain
a good inheritance,
and their children are within the covenant.

Their seed standeth fast,
and their children for their sakes.

Their seed shall remain for ever,
and their glory shall not be blotted out.

Their bodies are buried in peace;
but their name liveth for evermore.

— ECCLESIASTICUS XLIV

Contents

★ ★ ★

★

Prologue

As the first year of the Civil War drew to a close, both sides, having hoped for a short war, were beginning to realize that they were in for a long struggle. It had taken years to come to blows and now it appeared it would take a protracted fight to win independence, as the South hoped, or to restore the Union, as the North intended.

Decades of sectional strife and failed compromises concerning the rights of states versus those of the federal government, trade and tariffs, and the existence and expansion of slavery, and finally, the election of an antislavery President in the fall of 1860, led seven states to secede. The eight-decade-old House was divided. After Fort Sumter yielded to Charleston's guns in April 1861, the call to battle on both sides was answered with exuberance. Four more southern states seceded. Unionists and Confederates alike rushed to arms.

Smaller in territory and population, with fewer natural resources and railways and little in the way of manufacturing, the South, when compared to its northern adversary, seemed at a disadvantage. Confederate President Jefferson Davis and his military commanders opted for a defensive war — a war in which the enemy would have to attack in its effort to take them back into the Union fold. Behind their defensive line, the Confederates had shorter communications routes and thus were better able to shuttle men and matériel to meet threats wherever they might arise. They also sent emissaries to Europe in search of foreign recognition of their new Confederacy, hoping for political and physical support.

Thus, although the South had fired the first shot, the North was forced to be the aggressor. As Lincoln and his advisers began massing their forces to reunite the nation, Union General-in-Chief Winfield Scott proposed an overall strategy: a Union blockade of the South's Atlantic and Gulf coasts, cutting off supplies from, and preventing shipments of cotton and other goods to, foreign lands; capture of the Mississippi River; and application of constant military pressure along the land boundary between the two adversaries. By incircling the Confederacy, and eventually strangling it, Scott thought he could bring the South under control with little need for major battles and bloodshed. But hot-headed politicians and a short-sighted public ridiculed Scott's proposal, referred to now as the "Anaconda Plan," and demanded a decisive attack to end the war quickly. Both plans ultimately were adopted: the Union would combine the stranglehold of the serpent and the piercing thrust of the fencer to bring the Confederates to bay.

Almost a year into the conflict it appeared, paradoxically, that the strategies of both sides were working, at least in part, fairly well. The defending Confederates had stopped the attacking Yankees at Big Bethel, Manassas, and Ball's Bluff in Virginia, and at Belmont and Wilson's Creek in Missouri. The southern heartland remained independent. While Union overland offensives into the Confederacy had been thwarted, Scott's Anaconda seemed to be succeeding. The Federals had captured staging areas around the Confederate coast, Ship Island in the Gulf of Mexico, Hatteras Inlet and Port Royal Sound on the Atlantic coast; had kept the border states of Kentucky, Missouri, Delaware, and Maryland from seceding; had controlled northwestern Virginia; and had taken Fort Henry in Tennessee. To date, neither side held an advantage over the other.

However, as the anniversary of Fort Sumter came and went, things began to turn sour for the Confederacy. Richmond would receive news of one setback after another. Internationally, Britain and France were still balking at recognition of the new nation. While neither rejected the idea completely, the South could expect no help from them any time soon.

Out west, after taking Fort Henry in February 1862, northern forces would capture Fort Donelson, securing Kentucky for the Union. The Federal victory at Pea Ridge, Arkansas, would do the same for Missouri. The Confederacy's drive up the Rio Grande in New Mexico to secure the Far West for its cause would end in defeat. The Confederate repulse at Shiloh and the subsequent evacuation of Corinth would give the Federals at least tentative possession of western Tennessee, and the Union's assaults on New Orleans, Island Ten, and Memphis would go a long way toward sealing off the Mississippi from southern use.

In the East, the stalemate after Manassas seemed to hold. But soon, growing Union strength would force the Confederates to evacuate the Centreville/Manassas area. Southern hopes would rise when the iron clad C.S.S. *Virginia* attacked the Federal fleet in Hampton Roads. But those hopes would be dashed the following day when the U.S.S. *Monitor* appeared, and in a revolution in naval warfare, ironclad against ironclad, the two would battle to a draw.

As if these setbacks were not enough, large Federal forces were gathering on the York-James peninsula, apparently for a massive assault on Richmond itself.

★　★　★

Shelby Foote

*General Ulysses Grant,
on horseback (center), oversees
the Federal attack on Fort
Donelson, atop the distant ridge,
on February 15, 1862.*

Donelson—
The Loss of Kentucky

1862 ★ ★ ★ ★ ★ **Grant was not alone in his belief** that he could "take and destroy" the Cumberland fortress; Albert Sidney Johnston thought so, too. When word of the fall of Henry reached his headquarters at Bowling Green next day, he relayed the news to Richmond, adding that Fort Donelson was "not long tenable." In fact, such was his respect for the promptness and power with which the ironclads had reduced their first objective, he wrote that he expected the second to fall in the same manner, "without the necessity of [the Federals'] employing their land force in coöperation."

All the events he had feared most, and with good cause, had come to pass. Right, left, and center, his long defensive line was coming apart with the suddenness of a shaky split-rail fence in the path of a flood. His right at Mill Springs had been smashed, the survivors scattering deep into Tennessee while Buell inched toward Bowling Green with 40,000 effectives opposing Hardee's 14,000. The loss of Henry and its railroad bridge, with Federal gunboats making havoc up the river to his rear, had split his center from his left, outflanking Columbus and Bowling Green and rendering both untenable. When Donelson fell, as he expected in short order, the gunboats would continue up the Cumberland as they had done up the Tennessee, forcing the fall of Nashville, his main depot of supplies, and cutting off the Army of Central Kentucky from the southern bank.

★

This left him two choices, both unwelcome. With his communications disrupted and his lines of reinforcement snapped, he could stand and fight against the odds, opposing two converging armies, each one larger than his own. Or he could retreat and save his army while there was time, consolidating south of the river to strike back when the chance came. Whichever he did, one thing was clear: the choice must be made quickly. All those sight-drafts he had signed were coming due at once. The long winter's bluff was over. The uses of psychological warfare were exhausted. He was faced now with the actual bloody thing.

He called at once a council of war to confer with his two ranking generals. One was Hardee, commander of the center, whose prominent forehead seemed to bulge with knowledge left over from what he had packed into the *Tactics*. The other was Beauregard. The hero of Sumter and Manassas had arrived three days ago; but there were no fifteen regiments in his train, only a handful of staff officers. Davis had long since warned that he could spare no more soldiers,

---

The long winter's bluff was over. The uses of psychological warfare were exhausted. He was faced now with the actual bloody thing.

---

and he meant it. But apparently he could spare this one, whom many considered the finest soldier of them all, and by sparing him solve the double problem of removing the Creole's busy pen from the proximity of Richmond and silencing those critics who cried that the President had no thought for the western front.

Beauregard had come to Kentucky believing that Johnston was about to take the offensive with 70,000 men. When he arrived and learned the truth he reacted with a horror akin to that of Crittenden at Zollicoffer's rashness, and like Crittenden he at first proposed an immediate withdrawal. By the time of the council of war, however, he had managed to absorb the shock. His mercurial spirits had risen to such an extent, in fact, that the news of the fall of Henry only increased his belligerency. At the council, held in his hotel room on the afternoon of the 7th —the general was indisposed, down with a cold while convalescing from a throat operation he had undergone just before leaving Virginia—he proposed in a husky voice that Johnston concentrate all his troops at Donelson, defeat Grant at that place, then turn on Buell and send him reeling back to the Ohio.

Johnston shook his head. He could not see it. To give all his attention to Grant would mean abandoning Nashville to Buell, and the loss of that

★

transportation hub, with its accumulation of supplies, would mean the loss of subsistence for his army. Even if that army emerged victorious at Donelson—which was by no means certain, since Grant might well be knocking at the gate already, his invincible ironclads out in front and his numbers doubled by reinforcements from Missouri and Illinois—it would then find Buell astride its communications, possessed of its base, twice its strength, and fresh for fighting. Johnston's army was all that stood between the Federals and the conquest of the Mississippi Valley. To risk its loss was to risk the loss of the Valley, and to lose the Valley, Johnston believed, was to lose the war in the West. It was like the poem about the horseshoe nail: Fort Henry was the nail.

Beauregard at last agreed. Along with Hardee he signed his name approving the document by which Johnston informed Richmond that, Henry having fallen and Donelson being about to fall, the army at Bowling Green would have to retreat behind the Cumberland. For the present at least, Kentucky must be given up.

Preparations for the evacuation began at once. Four days later, with Buell still inching forward, the retrograde movement began. The garrison at Donelson was expected to hold out as long as possible, keeping Grant off Hardee's flank and rear, then slip away, much as Tilghman's infantry had slipped away from Henry, to join the main body around Nashville. Beauregard was up and about by then, helping all he could, but Johnston had a special use for him. Columbus, being outflanked, must also be abandoned. Severed already from headquarters control, it required a high-ranking leader who could exercise independent command. That meant Beauregard. After a final conference with Johnston, who reached Nashville with the van of his army one week after the council of war at Bowling Green, he started for Columbus. His instructions empowered him to give up that place, if in his judgment it was necessary or advisable to do so, then fall back to Island Ten, where the Mississippi swung a lazy S along the Tennessee line, and to Fort Pillow, another sixty air-line miles downriver.

Charged with the conduct of a retreat, the Creole's spirits flagged again. His heart was heavy, he wrote to a friend in Virginia; "I am taking the helm when the ship is already on the breakers, and with but few sailors to man it. How it is to be extricated from its present perilous condition, Providence alone can determine."

★ ★ ★   *S*outheast of Columbus, the gloom was no less heavy for being fitful. During the week since the fall of its sister fort across the way, the atmosphere at Donelson had been feverish, with a rapid succession of brigadiers hastening preparations for the attack which each believed was imminent.

First had come the fugitives from Henry, shamefaced and angry, with lurid details of the gunboats' might and the host of Federals whose trap they had eluded. Brigadier General Bushrod Johnson assumed command the following day, an Ohio-born West Pointer who had left the army to teach school in Tennessee and, liking it, offered his services when that state seceded. Two days later, on the 9th, Gideon Pillow arrived from Clarksville. Relying on "the courage and fidelity of the brave officers and men under his command," he exhorted them to "drive back the ruthless invaders from our soil and again raise the Confederate flag over Fort Henry. . . . Our battle cry, 'Liberty or death.'" Simon Buckner marched in from Russellville next day. All this time, John B. Floyd was hovering nearby with his brigade; Johnston had told him to act on his own discretion, and he rather suspected the place of being a trap. By now Pillow had recovered from his notion of launching an offensive, but he wrote: "I will never surrender the position, and with God's help I mean to maintain it." Encouraged by this show of nerve, Floyd arrived on the 13th. Donelson's fourth commander within a week, he got there at daybreak, in time to help repulse the first all-out land attack. Grant's army had come up during the night.

The Federals were apt to find this fort a tougher nut than the one they had cracked the week before. Like Henry, it commanded a bend in the river; but there the resemblance ceased. Far from being in danger of inundation, Donelson's highest guns, a rifled 128-pounder and two 32-pounder carronades, were emplaced on the crown of a hundred-foot bluff. Two-thirds of the way down, a battery mounting a 10-inch columbiad and eight smooth-bore 32-pounders was dug into the bluff's steep northern face. All twelve of these pieces were protected by earthworks, the embrasures narrowed with sandbags. Landward the position was less impregnable, but whatever natural obstacles stood in the path of assault had been strengthened by Confederate engineers.

To the north, flowing into the river where the bluff came sheerly down, Hickman Creek, swollen with backwater, secured the right flank like a bridgeless moat protecting a castle rampart. The fort proper, a rustic sort of stockade affair inclosing several acres of rude log huts, was designed to house the garrison and protect the water batteries from incidental sorties. It could never withstand large-scale attacks such as the one about to be launched, however, and the engineers had met this threat by fortifying the low ridge running generally southeast, parallel to the bend of the river a mile away. Rifle pits were dug along it, the yellow-clay spoil thrown onto logs for breastworks, describing thus a three-mile arc which inclosed the bluff on the north and the county-seat hamlet of Dover on the south, the main supply base. At its weaker and more critical points, as for instance where Indian Creek and the road from Henry pierced its center, chevaux-de-frise were improvised by felling trees so that they lay with their tops outward, the branches interlaced and sharpened to impale attacking troops. All in all, the line was strong and adequately manned. With the

★

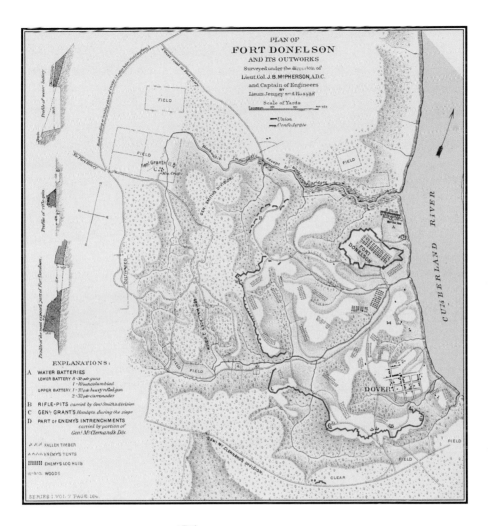

*This Federal army map shows
the initial Confederate defenses and Union
troop deployments around Fort Donelson.*

arrival of Floyd's brigade there were 28 infantry regiments to defend it: a total of 17,500 men, including the artillery and cavalry, with six light batteries in addition to the big guns bearing riverward.

Floyd had experienced considerable trepidation on coming in, but his success in repulsing attacks against both ends of his line that morning restored his spirits and even sent them soaring. "Our field defenses are good," he wired Johnston. "I think we can sustain ourselves against the land forces." As for his chances against the ironclads, though his batteries turned back a naval reconnaissance that afternoon, he felt less secure. He wired Johnston: "After two hours' cannonade

★

the enemy hauled off their gunboats; will commence probably again."

He was right. Steaming four abreast against his batteries next day, they did indeed commence again. When the squat black bug-shaped vessels opened fire, the cavalry commander Bedford Forrest turned to one of his staff, a former minister. "Parson, for God sake pray!" he cried. "Nothing but God Amighty can save that fort." Floyd emphatically agreed. In fact, in a telegram which he got off to Johnston while the gunboats were bearing down upon him, he defined what he believed were the limits of his resistance: "The fort cannot hold out twenty minutes."

★ ★ ★   **G**rant had predicted the immediate fall of Donelson to others beside Halleck. On the day the gunboats took Fort Henry he told a reporter from Greeley's *Tribune*, who stopped by headquarters to say goodbye before leaving to file his story in New York: "You had better wait a day or two....I am going over to capture Fort Donelson tomorrow." This interested the journalist. "How strong is it?" he asked, and Grant replied: "We have not been able to ascertain exactly, but I think we can take it." The reporter would not wait. On the theory that a fort in the hand was worth two in the brush, he made the long trip by river and rail to New York, filed his story—and was back on the banks of the Cumberland before Grant's campaign reached its climax.

The initial delay was caused by a number of things: not the least of which was the fact that on the following day, the 7th, in pursuance of his intention to "take and destroy" the place on the 8th, Grant reconnoitered within a mile of the rifle pits the rebels were digging, and saw for himself the size of the task he was undertaking. To have sent his army forward at once would have meant attacking without the assistance of the gunboats, which would have to make the long trip down the Tennessee and up the Cumberland to Donelson. Besides, the river was still rising, completing the shipwreck of Henry and threatening to recapture from Grant the spoils he had captured from Tilghman, so that his troops, as he reported in explanation, were "kept busily engaged in saving what we have from the rapidly rising waters."

There was danger in delay. Fort Donelson was being reinforced; Johnston might concentrate and crush him. But Grant was never one to give much weight to such considerations, even when they occurred to him. Meanwhile, his army was growing, too. Intent on his chance for command of the West—for which he had already recommended himself in dispatches announcing the capture of Henry and the impending fall of Donelson—Halleck was sending, as he described it, "everything I can rake and scrape together from Missouri." Within a few days Grant was able to add a brigade to each of his two divisions. On second thought, with 10,000 more reinforcements on the way in transports and Foote's ironclads undergoing repairs at Cairo, he believed that he had more to gain from waiting than from haste. So he waited. All the same, in a letter written on the 9th he declared that he would "keep the ball moving as lively as possible." Hearing that Pillow, whose measure he had taken at Belmont, was now in command of the fort, he added: "I hope to give him a tug before you receive this."

By the 11th he was ready to do just that. Unit commanders received that morning a verbal message: "General Grant sends his compliments and requests to see you this afternoon on his boat." That this headquarters boat was called the *New Uncle Sam* was something of a coincidence; "Uncle Sam" had been Grant's Academy nickname, derived from his initials, which in turn were accidental. The congressional appointment had identified him as Ulysses Simpson Grant, when in fact his given name was Hiram Ulysses, but rather than try to untangle the yards of red tape that stood in the way of correction — besides the risk of being nicknamed "Hug" — he let his true name go and took the new one: U. S. Grant. There were accounts of his gallantry under fire in Mexico, and afterwards his colonel had pointed him out on the street with the remark, "There goes a man of fire." However, even for those who had been alongside him at Belmont, these things were not easy to reconcile with the soft-spoken, rather seedy-looking thirty-nine-year-old general who received his brigade and division commanders aboard the steamboat.

Almost as hard to believe, despite the whiskey lines around his eyes, were the stories of his drinking. Eight years ago this spring, the gossip ran, he had had to resign from the army to avoid dismissal for drunkenness. So broke that he had had to borrow travel money from his future Confederate opponent Simon Buckner, he had gone downhill after that. Successively trying hardscrabble farming outside St Louis and real-estate selling inside it, and failing at both, he went to Galena, Illinois, up in the northwest corner of the state, and was clerking in his father's leather goods store — a confirmed failure, with a wife out of a Missouri slave-owning family and two small children — when the war came and gave him a second chance at an army career. He was made a colonel, and then a brigadier. "Be careful, Ulyss," his father wrote when he heard the news of the fluke promotion; "you're a general now; it's a good job, don't lose it."

He was quiet, not from secretiveness (he was not really close-mouthed) but simply because that was his manner, much as another's might be loud. In an army boasting the country's ablest cursers, his strongest expletives were "doggone it" and "by lightning," and even these were sparingly employed. "In dress he was plain, even negligent," one of his officers remarked; yet it was noted — "in partial amendment," the witness added — that "his horse was always

★

a good one and well kept." All his life he had had a way with horses, perhaps because he trusted and understood them. His one outstanding accomplishment at the Academy had been the setting of a high-jump record on a horse no other cadet would ride. There was an unbuttoned informality about him and about the way he did things; but it involved a good deal more of reticence than congeniality, as if his trust and understanding stopped at horses.

The conference aboard the *New Uncle Sam*, for instance, was as casual as the summons that convened it. What the participants mainly came away with was the knowledge that Grant had told them nothing. He had wanted to find out if

Grant, shown at left in an early 1850s photo, added to his fame as a daring horseman in a race through enemy fire during the Mexican War (below).

they were ready to move out, and apparently he believed he could determine this better by listening than by talking or even asking. He sat and smoked his long-stem meerschaum, appearing to get considerable satisfaction from it, and that was all. The council of war ("calling it such by grace," one participant wrote) broke up and the officers dispersed to their various headquarters, where presently they received the written order. Yet even this was vague. Stating only that the march would begin "tomorrow," it gave no starting time and no exact details of attack. "The force of the enemy being so variously reported," it closed, ". . . the necessary orders will be given in the field."

Whatever qualms the troop commanders might be feeling as a result of all this vagueness, the troops themselves, being better accustomed to mystification from above, were in high spirits as the march got under way around mid-morning of Lincoln's birthday. With one quick victory to their credit — in celebration of which, they knew, the folks at home were already ringing church bells — they looked forward to another, even though it did not give promise of being quite so bloodless as the first. Besides, the sun was out and the air was cool and bracing. They were enjoying the first fine weather they had known since boarding the transports at Paducah nine days back.

The column was "light," meaning that there were no wagons for tents or baggage, but the adjective did not apply for the men in ranks, each of whom carried on his person two days' rations and forty rounds of ammunition, in addition to the normal heavy load for winter marching. Glad to be on the move, however burdened, they stepped out smartly, with the usual banter back and forth between the various candidates for the role of company clown. Once clear of the river lowlands, they entered a hilly, scrub-oak country that called for up-and-down marching, with pack straps cutting first one way, then another. Presently, as the sun rose higher and bore down harder, and perhaps as much from sheer elation at being young and on the march as from discomfort, they began to shed whatever they thought they could spare. The roads were littered in their wake with discarded blankets and overcoats and other articles not needed in fair weather.

Grant shared his men's high spirits. He now had under his command over twice as many men as General Scott had employed in the conquest of Mexico: 15,000 in the marching column, 2500 left on call at Henry, available when needed, and another 10,000 aboard the transports, making the roundabout river trip to join the overland column on arrival. Undiscouraged at being already four days past his previous forecast as to the date the fort would fall, in a telegram to Halleck announcing the launching of the movement ("We start this morning . . . in heavy force") he essayed another, but with something more of caution as well as ambiguity: "I hope to send you a dispatch from Fort Donelson tomorrow." Whether this meant from in*side* the fort or just in *front* of it, the words would make pleasant reading for the President on his birthday, in case Halleck passed them along (which he did not). But Grant, who perhaps did not even know it was Lincoln's birthday, had his mind on the problem at hand. He must get to the fort before he could take it or even figure how to take it.

He got there a little after noon, the skirmishers coming under sniper fire at the end of the brisk ten-mile hike, and threw his two divisions forward, approaching the spoil-scarred ridge along which the defenders had drawn their curving line of rifle pits. Beyond it, gunfire boomed up off the river: a welcome sound, since it indicated that the navy had arrived and was applying pressure against the Confederate rear. The Second division, led by Grant's old West Point commandant C. F. Smith, turned off to the left and took position opposite the northern half of the rebel arc, while the First, under

Thin-faced, crowding fifty, with sunken eyes and a long, knife-blade nose, a glistening full black beard and the genial dignity of an accomplished orator, he had exchanged a seat in Congress for the stars of a brigadier.

John A. McClernand, filed off to the right and prepared to invest the southern half, where the ridge curved down past Dover.

McClernand was a special case, with a certain resemblance to the man whose birthday the investment celebrated. An Illinois lawyer-politician, Kentucky-born as well, he had practiced alongside Lincoln in Springfield and on the old Eighth Circuit. From that point on, however, the resemblance was less striking. McClernand was not tall: not much taller, in fact, than Grant: but he *looked* tall, perhaps because of the height of his aspirations. Thin-faced, crowding fifty, with sunken eyes and a long, knife-blade nose, a glistening full black beard and the genial dignity of an accomplished orator, he had exchanged a seat in Congress for the stars of a brigadier. In addition to the usual patriotic motives, he had a firm belief that the road that led to military glory while the war was on would lead as swiftly to political advancement when it ended. Lincoln had already shown how far a prairie lawyer could go in this country, and McClernand, whose

★

eye for the main chance was about as sharp as Lincoln's own, was quite aware that wars had made Presidents before — from Zachary Taylor, through Andrew Jackson, back to Washington himself. He intended to do all he could to emerge from this, the greatest war of them all, as a continuing instance. So far as this made him zealous it was good, but it made him overzealous, too, and quick to snatch at laurels. At Belmont, for example, he was one of those who took time out for a victory speech with the battle half won: a speech which was interrupted by the guns across the river and which, as it turned out, did not celebrate a conquest, but preceded a retreat. He needed watching, and Grant knew it.

What was left of the 12th was devoted to completing the investment. The gunboat firing died away, having provoked no reply from the fort. Grant sent a message requesting the fleet to renew the attack next morning as a "diversion in our favor," and his men settled down for the night. Dawn came filtering through the woods in front of the ridge, showing once more the yellow scars where the Confederates had emplaced their guns and dug their rifle pits. They were still there. Pickets began exchanging shots, an irregular sequence of popping sounds, each emphasizing the silence before and after, while tendrils of pale, low-lying smoke began to writhe in the underbrush. Near the center, Grant listened. Then there was a sudden clatter off to the right, mounting to quick crescendo with the boom and jar of guns mixed in. McClernand had slipped the leash.

His attack, launched against a troublesome battery to his front, was impetuous and headlong. Massed and sent forward at a run, the brigade that made it was caught in a murderous crossfire of artillery and musketry and fell back, also at a run, leaving its dead and wounded to mark the path of advance and retreat. Old soldiers would have let it go at that; but there were few old soldiers on this field. Twice more the Illinois boys went forward, brave and green, and twice more were repulsed. The only result was to lengthen the casualty lists — and perhaps instruct McClernand that a battery might appear to be exposed, yet be protected. The clatter died away almost as suddenly as it had risen. Once more only the pop-popping of the skirmishers' rifles punctuated the stillness.

Presently, in response to Grant's request of the night before, gunboat firing echoed off the river beyond the ridge. To the north, Smith tried his hand at advancing a brigade. At first he was successful, but not for long. The brigade took its objective, only to find itself pinned down by such vicious and heavy sniper fire that it had to be withdrawn. The sun declined and the opposing lines stretched about the same as when it rose. All Grant had really learned from the day's fighting was that the rebels had their backs up and were strong. But he was not discouraged. It was not his way to look much at the gloomy side of things. "I feel every confidence of success," he told Halleck in his final message of the day, "and the best feeling prevails among the men."

The feeling did not prevail for long. At dusk a drizzling rain began to fall. The wind veered clockwise and blew steadily out of the north, turning the rain to sleet and granular snow and tumbling the thermometer to 20° below freezing. On the wind-swept ridge the Confederates shivered in their rifle pits, and in the hollows northern troops huddled together against the cold, cursing the so-called Sunny South and regretting the blankets and overcoats discarded on the march the day before. Some among the wounded froze to death between the lines, locked in rigid agony under the soft down-sift of snow. When dawn came through, luminous and ghostly, the men emerged from their holes to find a wonderland that seemed not made for fighting. The trees wore icy armor, branch and twig, and the countryside was blanketed with white.

Grant was not discomforted by the cold. He spent the night in a big feather bed set up in the warm kitchen of a farmhouse. But he had worries enough to cause him to toss and turn—whether he actually did so or not—without the weather adding more. The gunboat firing of the past two days had had none of the reverberating violence of last week's assault on Henry, and this was due to something beside acoustic difficulties. It was due, rather, to the fact that there was only one gunboat on hand. The others, along with the dozen transports bearing reinforcements, were still somewhere downriver. Their failure to arrive left Grant in the unorthodox position of investing a fortified camp with fewer troops than the enemy had inside it. During the night he sent word back to Henry for the 2500 men left there to be brought forward. That at least would equalize the armies, though it was still a far cry from the three-to-one advantage which the tactics books advised. They arrived at daybreak, and Grant assigned them to Smith, one of whose brigades had been used to strengthen McClernand. Doubtless Grant was glad to see them; but then even more welcome news arrived from the opposite direction. The fleet had come up in the night and was standing by while the transports unloaded reinforcements.

Presently these too arrived, glad to be stretching their legs ashore after their long, cramped tour of the rivers. Grant consolidated them into a Third division and assigned it to Lew Wallace, one of Smith's brigade commanders, who had been left in charge at Henry and had made the swift, cold march to arrive at dawn. A former Indiana lawyer, the thirty-four-year-old brigadier wore a large fierce black mustache and chin-beard to disguise his youth and his literary ambitions, though so far neither had retarded his climb up the military ladder. Grant put this division into line between the First and Second, side-stepping them right and left to make room, and thickening ranks in the process.

Along that snow-encrusted front, with its ice-clad trees like inverted cutglass chandeliers beneath which men crouched shivering in frost-stiffened garments and blew on their gloveless hands for warmth, he now had three divisions facing the Confederate two, eleven brigades investing seven, 27,500 troops in blue opposing 17,500 in gray. They were not enough, perhaps, to assure a successful all-out assault; he was still only halfway to the prescribed three-to-one advantage, and after yesterday's bloody double repulse he rather doubted the wisdom of trying to storm that fortified line. But now at last the fleet was up, the fleet which had humbled Henry in short order, and that made all the difference. Surely he had enough men to prevent the escape of the rebel garrison when the ironclads started knocking the place to pieces.

Shortly after noon — by which time he had all his soldiers in position, under orders to prevent a breakout — he sent word to the naval commander, requesting an immediate assault by the gunboats. Then he mounted his horse and rode to a point on the high west bank of the Cumberland, beyond the northern end of his line, where he would have a grandstand seat for the show.

★ ★ ★ **F**oote would have preferred to wait until he had had time to make a personal reconnaissance, but Grant's request was for an immediate attack and the commodore prepared to give it to him. He had done considerable waiting already, a whole week of it while the armorers were hammering his ironclads back into shape. All this time he had kept busy, supervising the work, replenishing supplies, and requisitioning seafaring men to replace thirty fresh-water sailors who skedaddled to avoid gunboat duty. Nor were spiritual matters neglected. Three days after the Henry bombardment he attended church at Cairo, where, being told that the parson was indisposed, Foote mounted to the pulpit and preached the sermon himself. "Let not your heart be troubled" was his text: "ye believe in God, believe also in me."

Next day, having thus admonished and fortified his crews, he sent one ironclad up the Cumberland — the *Carondelet*, a veteran of Henry — while he waited at Cairo to bring three more: the flagship *St Louis*, another Henry veteran, and the *Pittsburg* and the *Louisville*, replacements for the *Cincinnati*, which remained on guard at the captured fort, and the hard-luck *Essex*, which had been too vitally hurt to share in a second attempt at quick reduction. It took the commodore two more days to complete repairs, replace the runaway sailors, and assemble his revamped flotilla, including two of the long-range wooden gunboats and the twelve transports loaded with infantry reinforcements. Then on the 13th he went forward, southward up the Cumberland in the wake of the *Carondelet*, whose skipper was waiting to report on his two-day action when Foote arrived before midnight at the bend just north of Donelson.

The report had both its good points and its bad, though the former were predominant. On the first day, when the *Carondelet* steamed alone against the fort, firing to signal her presence to Grant, who was just arriving, there was no reply from the batteries on the bluff. The earthworks seemed deserted, their frowning guns untended. All the same, the captain hadn't liked the looks of them; they reminded him, he said later, "of the dismal-looking sepulchers cut into the

*Federal gunboats blaze away in
an unsuccessful attempt to silence Fort
Donelson's upper batteries.*

rocky cliffs near Jerusalem, but far more repulsive." He retired, answered only by
echoes booming the sound of his own shots back from the hills, and anchored for
the night three miles downstream. It was strange, downright eerie. Next morning,
though, in accordance with a request from Grant, who evidently had not known
there was only one gunboat at hand, he went forward again, hearing the landward
clatter of musketry as McClernand's attack was launched and repulsed.

On this second approach, the *Carondelet* drew fire from every battery
on the heights. Under bombardment for two hours, she got off 139 rounds and
received only two hits in return. This was poor gunnery on the enemy's part, but
one of those hits gave the captain—and, in turn, the commodore—warning of
what a gun on that bluff could do to an ironclad on the river below. It was a 128-
pound solid shot and it crashed through a broadside casemate into the engine
room, where it caromed and ricocheted, ripping at steam pipes and railings,

knocking down a dozen men and bounding after the others, as one of the engineers said, "like a wild beast pursuing its prey." Shattering beams and timbers, it filled the air with splinters fine as needles, pricking and stabbing the sailors through their clothes, though in all the grim excitement they were not aware of this until they felt the blood running into their shoes. The *Carondelet* fell back to transfer her wounded and attend to emergency repairs, but when the racket of another land assault broke out at the near end of the line, she came forward again, firing 45 more rounds at the batteries, and then drew off unhit as the clatter died away, signifying that Smith's attack, like McClernand's, had not succeeded.

Aboard the flagship, Foote had the rest of the night and the following morning in which to evaluate this information. Then came the request for an immediate assault. As Grant designed it, the fleet would silence the guns on the bluff, then steam on past the fort and take position opposite Dover, blocking any attempt at retreat across the river while it shelled the rebels out of their rifle pits along the lower ridge; whereupon the army would throw its right wing forward, so that the defenders, cut off from their main base of supplies and barred from retreat in either direction, could then be chewed up by gunfire, front and rear, or simply be outsat until they starved or saw the wisdom of surrender. The commodore would have preferred to have more time for preparation—time in which to give a final honing, as it were, to the naval blade of the amphibious shears—but, for all he knew, Grant had special reasons for haste. Besides, he admired the resolute simplicity of the plan. It was just his style of fighting. Once the water batteries were reduced, it would go like clockwork, and the example of Henry, eight days back, assured him that the hard part would be over in a hurry. He agreed to make the assault at once.

One thing he took time to do, however. Chains, lumber, and bags of coal—"all the hard materials in the vessels," as one skipper said—were laid on the ironclads' upper decks to give additional protection from such plunging shots as the one that had come bounding through the engine room of the *Carondelet*. This done, Foote gave the signal, and at 3 o'clock the fleet moved to the attack, breasting the cold dark water of the river flowing northward between the snow-clad hills, where spectators from both armies were assembling for the show. One was Floyd, who took one look at the gunboats bearing down and declared that the fort was doomed. Another was Grant, who said nothing.

They came as they had come at Henry, the ironclads out in front, four abreast, while the brittle-skinned wooden gunboats *Tyler* and *Conestoga* brought up the rear, a thousand yards astern. At a mile and a half the batteries opened fire with their two big guns, churning the water ahead of the line of boats, but Foote did not reply until the range was closed to a mile. Then the flagship opened with her bow guns, echoed at once by the others, darting tongues of flame and steaming steadily forward, under orders to close the range until the batteries were silenced. Muzzles flashing and smoke boiling up as if the bluff itself were ablaze, the Confederates stood to their guns, encouraged by yesterday's success against the *Carondelet*, just as Henry's gunners had been heartened by turning back the *Essex* on the day before their battle. The resemblance did not stop there, however. After the first few long-range shots, as in the fallen fort a week ago, the big 128-pounder rifle on the crest of the bluff—the gun that had scored the only hit in two days of firing—was spiked by its own priming wire, which an excited cannoneer left in the vent while a round was being rammed. This left only the two short-range 32-pounder carronades in the upper battery and the 10-inch columbiad and eight smooth-bore 32-pounders in the lower: one fixed target opposing four in motion, each of which carried more guns between her decks than the bluff had in all, plus the long-range wooden gunboats arching their shells from beyond the smoke-wreathed line of ironclads.

Foote kept coming, firing as he came. At closer range, the *St Louis* and *Pittsburg* in the middle, the *Carondelet* and *Louisville* on the flanks, his vessels were taking hits, the metallic clang of iron on iron echoing from the surrounding hills with the din of a giant forge. But he could also see dirt and sandbags flying from the enemy embrasures as his shots struck home, and he believed he saw men running in panic from the lower battery. The Confederate fire was slackening, he afterwards reported; another fifteen minutes and the bluff would be reduced.

It may have been so, but he would never know. He was not allowed those fifteen minutes. At 500 yards the rebel fire was faster and far more effective, riddling stacks and lifeboats, sheering away flagstaffs and davits, scattering the coal and lumber and scrap iron on the decks. The sloped bulwarks caused the plunging shots to strike not at glancing angles, as had been intended, but perpendicular, and the gunboats shuddered under the blows. Head-on fire was shucking away side armor, one captain said, "as lightning tears the bark from a tree." At a quarter of a mile, just as Foote thought he saw signs of panic among the defenders, a solid shot crashed through the flagship's superstructure, carrying away the wheel, killing the pilot, and wounding the commodore and everyone else in the pilot house except an agile reporter who had come along as acting secretary.

The *St Louis* faltered, having no helm to answer, and went away with the current, out of the fight. Alongside her, the *Pittsburg* had her tiller ropes shot clean away. She too careened off, helmless, taking more hits as she swung. The *Louisville* was the next to go, struck hard between wind and water. Her compartments kept her from sinking while her crew patched up the holes, but then, like her two sister ships, she lost her steering gear and wore off downstream. Left to face the batteries alone, at 200 yards the *Carondelet* came clumsily about, her forward compartments logged with water from the holes punched in her bow, and fell back down the river, firing rapidly and wildly as she went, not so much in hopes of damaging the enemy as in an attempt to hide in the smoke from her own guns.

★ ★ ★ *H*igh on the bluff, the Confederates were elated. In the later stages of the fight they enjoyed comparative immunity, for as the gunboats closed the range they overshot the batteries. Drawing near they presented easier targets, and the cannoneers stood to their pieces, delivering hit after hit and cheering as they did so. "Now, boys," one gunner cried, "see me take a chimney!" He drew a bead, and down went a smokestack. One after another, the squat fire-breathing ironclads were disabled, wallowing helplessly as the current swept them northward, until finally the *Carondelet* made her frantic run for safety, firing indiscriminately to wreathe herself in smoke. The river was deserted; the fight was over quite as suddenly as it started. The flagship had taken 57 hits, the others about as many. Fifty-four sailors were casualties, including eleven dead. In the batteries, on the other hand, though the breastworks had been knocked to pieces, not a man or a gun was lost. The artillerists cheered and tossed their caps and kept on cheering. Fort Henry had shown what the gunboats could do: Fort Donelson had shown what they could not do.

★

The Confederate commander was as jubilant as his gunners. When the tide of battle turned he recovered his spirits and wired Johnston: "The fort holds out. Three gunboats have retired. Only one firing now." When that one had retired as well, his elation was complete.

It was otherwise with Grant, who saw in the rout of the ironclads a disruption of his plans. Mounting his horse, he rode back to headquarters and reported by wire to Halleck's chief of staff in Cairo: "Appearances indicate now that we will have a protracted siege here." A siege was undesirable, but the rugged terrain and the bloody double repulse already suffered in front of the fortified ridge caused him to "fear the result of an attempt to carry the place by storm with raw troops." Meanwhile, he reported, he was ordering up more ammunition and strengthening the investment for what might be a long-drawn-out affair. Disappointed but not discouraged, he assured the theater commander: "I feel great confidence . . . in ultimately reducing the place."

★ ★ ★ *G*lorious as the exploit had been, Floyd's elation was based on more than the repulse of the flotilla. Since the night before, he had had the satisfaction of knowing that he had successfully accomplished the first half of his primary assignment, his reason for being at Donelson in the first place: he had kept Grant's army off Hardee's flank during the retreat from Bowling Green. Johnston was in Nashville with the van, and Hardee was closing fast with the rear, secure from western molestation. Now there remained only the second half of Floyd's assignment: to extract his troops from their present trap for an overland march to join in the defense of the Tennessee capital.

This was obviously no easy task, but he had begun to plan for it at a council of war that morning, when he and his division commanders decided to try for a breakout south of Dover, where a road led south, then east toward Nashville, seventy miles away. Pillow's division would be massed for the assault, while Buckner's pulled back to cover the withdrawal. Troop dispositions had already begun when the ironclads came booming up the river. By the time they had been repulsed, the day was too far gone; Floyd sent orders canceling the attack and calling another council of war. No experienced soldier himself, he wanted more advice from those who were.

The two who were there to give it to him were about as different from each other as any two men in the Confederacy. Pillow was inclined toward the manic. Addicted to breathing fire on the verge of combat, flamboyant in address, he was ever sanguine in expectations and eager for desperate ventures, the

*Gideon Pillow,
second in command
at Fort Donelson,
proposed that the
Confederates break
out through the
Yankee lines.*

more desperate the better. Buckner was gloomy, saturnine. Not much given to seeking out excitement, he was inclined to examine the odds on any gamble, especially when they were as long as they were now. Some of the difference perhaps was due to the fact that Pillow the Tennessean was fighting to save his native state — his country, as he called it — while Buckner the Kentuckian had just seen his abandoned. And their relationship was complicated by the fact that there was bad blood between them, dating from back in the Mexican War, when Buckner had joined not only in the censure of Pillow for laying claim to exploits not his own, but also in the laughter which followed a report that had him digging a trench on the wrong side of a parapet.

Between these two, the confident Pillow and the cautious Buckner, Floyd swung first one way, then another, approaching nervous exhaustion in the process. The indecision he had displayed in West Virginia under Lee was being magnified at Donelson, together with his tendency to grow flustered under pressure. Just now, however, with the rout of the Yankee gunboats to his credit, he was inclined to share his senior general's expectations. Adjourning the council, he announced that the breakout designed for today would be attempted at earliest dawn tomorrow. Even the gloomy Buckner admitted there was no other way to save the army, though he strongly doubted its chances for success.

All night the generals labored, shifting troops for the dawn assault.

★

Pillow massed his division in attack-formation south of Dover, while Buckner stripped the northward ridge of men and guns to cover the withdrawal once the Union right had been rolled back to open the road toward Nashville. Another storm came up in the night, freezing the soldiers thus exposed. Yet this had its advantages; the wind howled down the shouts of command and the snowfall muffled the footsteps of the men and the clang of gunwheels on the frozen ground. No noise betrayed the movement to the Federals, huddled in pairs for warmth and sleep beyond the nearly deserted ridge. As dawn came glimmering through the icy lacework of the underbrush and trees, Pillow sent his regiments forward on schedule, Forrest's cavalry riding and slashing on the flank.

They met stiff resistance, not because the Yankees were expecting this specific attack, but because they were well-disciplined and alert. For better than three hours the issue hung in raging doubt, the points of contact clearly marked by bloodstains on the snow. Running low on ammunition, McClernand's men gave way, fought out, and as they fell back, sidling off to the left and exposing in turn the right flank of Wallace, Pillow saw that he had achieved his objective. The Nashville road was open. He paused to send a telegram to Johnston: "On the honor of a soldier, the day is ours!"

However, having paused he took stock, and it was as if the telegram had used up his last ounce of energy and hope, both of which had formerly seemed boundless. For now a strange thing happened: he and Buckner exchanged roles. Now it was Pillow who was pessimistic, fearing a counterattack against his flank while moving through the gap, and Buckner who was ebullient, declaring that the success should be exploited by ramming the column through. He had brought his soldiers forward to hold the door ajar; he could do it, he said — and in fact he insisted on doing it. When Pillow, standing on seniority, ordered him back to his former position, he refused to go. It was nearing noon by now, and all this time the road was standing open.

While the generals stood there wrangling, Floyd arrived. Smooth-shaven, with a pendulous underlip, he stood between them, looking from one to the other while they appealed to him to settle the dispute. At first he agreed with Buckner and told him to stay where he was, holding the escape hatch ajar. Then Pillow took him aside and he reversed himself, ordering both divisions back into line on the ridge. The morning's fight had gone for nothing, together with the bloodstains on the snow.

★ ★ ★   **E**lsewhere along the curving front, practically stripped of Confederate troops for the breakthrough concentration — the sector formerly held by Buckner's whole division, for example, had been left in charge of a single regiment with fewer than 500 men — the lines across the way were strangely silent. To the Southerners, widely spaced along the ridge, this seemed a special dispensation of Providence. Actually, however, the basis for the respite, though unusual, was entirely natural.

Before daylight that morning Grant had received a note from Flag Officer Foote, requesting an interview. The wounded commodore was going back downriver for repairs, both to his worst-hit vessels and to himself, and he wanted to talk with Grant before he left. Grant rode northward to meet him aboard the flagship. Having, he said later, "no idea that there would be any engagement on land unless I brought it on myself," he left explicit orders that his division commanders were not to move from their present positions. Baffled by the wintry trees and ridges, the three-hour uproar of Pillow's assault on the opposite end of the line reached him faintly, if at all. He rode on. Hard pressed, McClernand was calling for help which Grant's orders prohibited Wallace and Smith from sending, though the former, on his own responsibility, finally sent a

Now that the rebels had stopped shoving, they stopped running, but as they stood around in leaderless clumps, empty cartridge boxes on display as an excuse for having yielded, they gave little evidence of wanting to regain what they had lost.

brigade which helped to blunt the attack when his own lines were assailed. Grant knew nothing of this until past noon, when, riding back from the gunboat conference, he met a staff captain who informed him, white-faced with alarm, that McClernand's division had been struck and scattered into full retreat. Grant put spurs to his horse.

Speed was impossible on the icy road, however, even for so skillful a horseman as Grant. It was 1 o'clock before he reached the near end of his line, where he found reassurance in the lack of excitement among the troops of Smith's division. Even Wallace's men, already engaged in part, showed fewer signs of panic than the captain who had met him crying havoc. McClernand's, next in sight, were another matter. They had been ousted from their position, taking some rough handling in the process, and they showed it. Now that the rebels had stopped shoving, they stopped running, but as they stood around in leaderless clumps, empty cartridge boxes on display as an excuse for having yielded, they gave little evidence of wanting to regain what they had lost.

★

There was a report that Confederate prisoners had three days' cooked rations in their haversacks. Some took this as proof that they were prepared for three days of hard fighting, but Grant had a different interpretation. He believed it meant that they were trying to escape, and he believed, further, that they were more demoralized by having failed in a desperate venture than his own men were by a temporary setback. "The one who attacks first now will be victorious," he said to his staff, "and the enemy will have to be in a hurry if he gets ahead of me."

He told McClernand's men, "Fill your cartridge boxes, quick, and get into line. The enemy is trying to escape and he must not be permitted to do so." This worked, he said later, "like a charm. The men only wanted someone to give them a command." To the wounded Foote went a request that the gunboats "make appearance and throw a few shells at long range." He did not expect them to stage a real attack, he added, but he counted on the morale effect, both on his own troops and the enemy's, of hearing naval gunfire from the river. Reasoning also that the rebels must have stripped the ridge to mass for the attack on the south, he rode to the far end of the line and ordered Smith to charge, advising him that he would find only "a very thin line to contend with."

This was what Smith had been waiting for, and for various reasons. His bright blue eyes and oversized snowy mustache standing out in contrast to his high-colored face, he was Regular Army to the shoe-soles, the only man in the western theater, one of his fellow officers said, who "could ride along a line of volunteers in the regulation uniform of a brigadier general, plume, chapeau, epaulets and all, without exciting laughter." Like many old-army men, since that army had been predominantly southern in tone, he was suspected of disloyalty; but Smith, who had been thrice brevetted for bravery in Mexico, was not disturbed by these suspicions. "They'll take it back after our first battle," he promised. And now, with that first battle in progress, he got his troops into line, gave them orders not to fire until the rebel abatis had been cleared, and led them forward. High on his horse, the sixty-year-old general turned from time to time in the saddle to observe the alignment and gesture with his sword, the bullets of the sharpshooters twittering round him. "I was nearly scared to death," one soldier afterwards said, "but I saw the old man's white mustache over his shoulder, and went on."

They all went on, through the fallen timber and up the ridge, where they drove back the regiment Buckner had left to man the line. All that kept them from storming the fort itself was the arrival of the rest of Buckner's division, which Floyd had ordered back. On the right, McClernand's rallied men hurried the retirement of Pillow, reoccupying the ground they had lost. Wallace took a share in this, shouting as he rode along the line of his division, "You have been wanting a fight; you have got it. Hell's before you!" Two of the battered ironclads reappeared around the bend in answer to Grant's request, lobbing long-range shells to add to the Confederate confusion.

In what remained of the short winter afternoon, since saying, "The one who attacks first now will be victorious," Grant saw his army not only recover from the morning's reverses, but breach the line of rebel intrenchments as well. By daylight there would be Union artillery on the ridge where Smith had forced a lodgment. The fort, the water battery, Dover itself: the whole Confederate position would be under those guns. It was not going to be a siege, after all.

★ ★ ★ **T**his was realized as well by the commanders inside the fort, swinging once more from elation to dejection, as it was by those outside. At the council of war, held late that night in the frame two-story Dover Inn, the prime reaction was consternation. Pillow and Buckner had reverted to their original roles. The former had thrown off his gloom, the latter his ebullience, and each accused the other of having failed to exploit the morning's gains. Pillow declared that he had halted only to send his men back after their equipment; he was ready to cut his way out in earnest, all over again. Buckner said that stopping, for whatever reason, had been fatal; the Federals had restored the line, and his men were too dispirited to make another assault. Floyd was as usual in the middle, looking from one to the other as the recriminations passed him.

This time, though, he sided more with Buckner; Smith's guns were on the ridge by now, waiting for dawn to define the targets. Forrest, who was present in his capacity as cavalry commander, reported that a riverside road was open to the south, though icy backwater stood waist-deep where it crossed a creekbed. However, the army surgeon—who had yet to learn just how tough a creature the Confederate soldier could be, despite his grousing—advised against using the flooded road, predicting that such exposure would be

Soon after John Floyd ceded command of Donelson, President Davis removed him from Confederate service.

fatal to the troops. Then too, there was a report that Grant had received another 10,000 reinforcements. Floyd already believed his men were outnumbered four-to-one, and as far as he was concerned that settled the matter. Only one course remained: to surrender the command.

Whatever their differences at this final conference, he and Pillow were agreed at least on the question of personal surrender. Neither would have any part of it, and each had his reasons. Floyd had been indicted for malfeasance in office as Secretary of War. The charge had been nol-prossed but it might very well be reopened in a wartime atmosphere. Besides, it was a matter of general belief in the North that he had diverted federal arms and munitions to southern arsenals on the eve of secession. To surrender would be to throw himself on a mercy which he considered nonexistent. Pillow's was a different case, but he was no less determined to avoid captivity. Having sworn that he would never surrender, he intended to keep his oath. He agreed by now as to the necessity for surrender of the army, but like Floyd he refused to be included. His battle cry was "Liberty or death," and he chose liberty.

Buckner felt otherwise. He accepted the facing of possible charges of treason as one of the hazards of waging a revolution. Also, he had done the Federal commander certain personal services, including the loan of money when Grant was on his way home from California in disgrace, and this might have a happy effect when the two sat down together to arrange terms for capitulation. He would surrender the army, and himself as part of it, along with all the others who had fought here and been worsted. The necessary change of commanders was effected in order of rank:

"I turn the command over, sir," Floyd told Pillow.

"I pass it," Pillow told Buckner.

"I assume it," Buckner said. "Give me pen, ink and paper, and send for a bugler."

This colloquy omitted a fourth member of the council. Bedford Forrest rose up in his wrath. "I did not come here for the purpose of surrendering my command," he declared. Buckner agreed that the cavalryman could lead his men out if the movement began before surrender negotiations were under way.

Forrest stamped out into the night, followed by Floyd and Pillow, while Buckner composed his note to Grant: "In consideration of all the circumstances governing the present situation of affairs at this station, I propose to the commanding officer of the Federal forces the appointment of commissioners to agree upon the terms of capitulation of the forces and fort under my command, and in that view suggest an armistice until twelve o'clock today." He signed it, "Very respectfully, your obedient servant."

Buckner's men by no means shared his gloom. Except for the regiment overrun by Smith's division, they had whipped the Yankees on land and water each time they had come to grips. Rested from the previous day's exertions, they expected a renewal of the fight. Consequently, the bugler going forward to sound the parley and the messenger bearing Buckner's note and a white flag of truce had trouble getting through the lines. At last they did, however. The bugle rang out, plaintive in the frosty night, and men of the northern Second division received them and gave them escort back to the division commander. Smith read the note and set out at once through the chill predawn darkness for the farmhouse which was army headquarters.

Grant was snug in his feather bed when Smith came in saying, "There's something for you to read." During the reading the old soldier crossed to the open fire and stroked his mustache while warming his boots and backside. Grant gave a short laugh. "Well, what do you think of it?" he asked. Smith said, "I think, no terms with the traitors, by God!" Grant slipped out of bed and drew on his outer garments. Then he took a sheet of tablet paper and began to write. When he had finished he handed it to Smith, who read it by firelight and pronounced abruptly, "By God, it couldn't be better."

*Nathan Bedford Forrest leads
his Confederate troopers through an icy backwater during their escape from Donelson.*

Confederate Simon Bolivar Buckner surrendered Fort Donelson to his friend and fellow West Pointer, Ulysses Grant.

Once more the truce party crossed the lines, headed now in the opposite direction as they picked their way to the Dover Inn, where Buckner was waiting to learn Grant's terms. There had been considerable bustle in their absence. A steamboat had arrived in the night, bringing a final batch of 400 reinforcements who landed thus in time to be surrendered. Floyd commandeered the vessel for the evacuation of his brigade, four regiments from his native Virginia and one from Mississippi, the latter being assigned to guard the landing while the others got aboard. The first two regiments of Virginians had been deposited safely on the other shore; the boat had returned and the second pair were being loaded when word came from Buckner that surrender negotiations had been opened; all who were going must go at once. Floyd hurried aboard with his staff and gave the signal and the steamboat backed away, leaving the Mississippians howling ruefully on the bank.

Pillow had been less fortunate. The best transportation he could find was an abandoned scow, with barely room for himself and his chief of staff, and they were the only two from his command who got away in the night. Forrest, on the other hand, took not only all of his own men, but also a number of infantrymen who swung up behind the troopers, riding double across low stretches where the water was "saddle-skirt deep," as Forrest said. He believed the whole army could have escaped by this route, the venture he had urged at the council of war, only to be overruled. "Not a gun [was] fired at us," he reported. "Not an enemy [was] seen or heard."

★

Sitting and waiting was the harder task, and it was Buckner's. The first Confederate general to submit a request for surrender terms from an opponent, he knew what condemnation was likely to be heaped upon his head by his own people, who would see only that he had ordered his men to lay down their arms in the face of bloody fighting. Yet he took some consolation, and found much hope, in the fact that those terms would come from an old West Point comrade whom he had befriended in another time of trial, when the tide of fortune was running the other way. The truce messenger returned at last and handed him Grant's reply:

> *H*^d *Qrs. Army in the Field*
>
> *Camp near Donelson, Feby 16th*
>
> *Gen. S. B. Buckner,*
>
> *Confed. Army,*
>
> *Sir: Yours of this date proposing Armistice, and*
>
> *appointment of Commissioners, to settle terms of*
>
> *Capitulation is just received. No terms except an*
>
> *unconditional and immediate surrender can be accepted.*
>
> *I propose to move immediately upon your works.*
>
> > *I am Sir: very respectfully*
> >
> > *Your obt. sevt.*
> >
> > *U. S. GRANT*
> >
> > *Brig. Gen.*

This was not at all what Buckner had expected by way of return for favors past. Neither generous nor chivalrous, even aside from personal obligations, such "terms" — which were, in effect, hardly terms at all — were a far cry from those extended by Beauregard ten months ago at Sumter, back in what already seemed a different war entirely, when Anderson was allowed to salute his flag and march out under arms while the victors lined the beaches and stood uncovered to watch him go. Yet there was nothing Buckner could do about it; Floyd and Pillow had left — which might have been considered good riddance except that the former had taken four-fifths of his brigade, lengthening the odds — and Forrest was gone with his hard-hitting cavalry, which otherwise might have covered a retreat. All that remained was for Buckner to make a formal protest and submit. This he did, informing Grant that the scattering of his own troops, "and the overwhelming forces under your command, compel me, notwithstanding the brilliant success of the Confederate arms yesterday, to accept the ungenerous and unchivalrous terms which you propose."

By now it was broad open daylight. Receiving the message, Grant rode forward, past white flags stuck at intervals along the rebel line, into Dover where he found Lew Wallace already sharing a cornbread-and-coffee breakfast with the Confederates at the inn. He joined the friendly discussion, and when Buckner remarked that if he had been in charge during the fighting, the Federals would not have got up to Donelson as easily as they had done, Grant replied that if such had been the case, "I should not have tried it the way I did." Then he took over the inn as his own headquarters. Before sending Buckner north, however, he sought to make amends by offering his prisoner, who had done the same for him when the degrees of fortune and misfortune were reversed, the use of his purse. The Kentuckian declined it.

This flag of the 18th Tennessee was among the dozens of Confederate colors surrendered to the Federals at Fort Donelson.

The actual surrender was accomplished without formality. One northern correspondent observed a marked difference between rebels from the border states and those from farther south. Moving among them he noted that the former "were not much sorry that the result was as it was," while "those from the Gulf states were sour, not inclined to talk." This only applied to the enlisted men, however. Without exception, he found the officers "spiteful as hornets." By journalistic license, another reporter deduced from what he saw that the common people of the South cared very little which way the war ended, so long as it ended soon.

Sullen or friendly, spiteful or morose, men who had been shooting at each other a few hours ago now mingled on the field for which they had fought. Indeed, the occasion was so informal that some Confederates strolled unchallenged through the lines and got away. Bushrod Johnson, who was among those who made off in this manner, later declared: "I have not learned that a single one who attempted to escape met with any obstacle." Apparently Grant, who at this one stroke had captured more prisoners than all the other Union generals combined, did not particularly care. "It is a much less job to take them than to keep them," he said laconically. As for Pillow, he need not have been in such a hurry to escape, Grant told Buckner. "If I had captured him, I would have turned him loose. I would rather have him in command of you fellows than as a prisoner."

★ ★ ★   Throughout the North, church bells rang in earnest this Sunday morning, louder even than they had done for Fort Henry, ten days back. Men embraced on the streets and continued to celebrate into the night by the glare of bonfires. The shame of Bull Run was erased. Indeed, some believed they saw in the smashing double victory the end of armed rebellion, the *New York Times* remarking: "After this, it certainly cannot be materially postponed. The monster is already clutched and in his death struggle."

The nation had a new hero: U. S. Grant, who by an accident and a coincidence of initials now became "Unconditional Surrender" Grant. People had his message to Buckner by heart, and they read avidly of his life and looks in the papers: the features stern "as if carved from mahogany," the clear blue eyes (or gray, some said) and aquiline nose, the strong jaw "squarely set, but not sensual." One reporter saw three expressions in his face: "deep thought, extreme determination, and great simplicity and calmness." Another saw significance in the way he wore his high-crowned hat: "He neither puts it on behind his ears, nor draws it over his eyes; much less does he cock it on one side, but sets it straight and very hard on his head." People enjoyed reading of that, and also of the way he "would gaze at anyone who approached him with an inquiring air, followed by a glance of recollection and a grave nod of recognition." On horseback, they read, "he sits firmly in the saddle and looks straight ahead, as if only intent on getting to some particular point." The words "square" and "straight" and "firm" were the ones that appeared most often, and people liked them. Best of all, perhaps, they enjoyed hearing that Grant was "the concentration of all that is American. He talks bad grammar, but talks it naturally, as much as to say, 'I was so brought up, and if I try fine phrases I shall only appear silly.'"

To them the whole campaign was an absolute marvel of generalship, a superb combination of simplicity and drive, in welcome contrast to all that had gone before in the West and was continuing in the East. They did not dissect it in search of flaws, did not consider that Grant had started behind schedule, that men had frozen to death because of a lax discipline which let them throw away coats and blankets in fair weather, that individual attacks had been launched without coördination and been bloodily repulsed, nor that the commanding general had been absent from his post for better than six critical hours while one of his divisions was being mauled, the other two having been barred by his own orders from lending assistance. They saw, rather, the sweep and slam-bang power of a leader who marched on Wednesday, skirmished on

Thursday, imperturbably watched his fleet's repulse on Friday, fought desperately on Saturday, and received the fort's unconditional surrender on Sunday. Undeterred by wretched weather, the advice of the tactics manuals, or the reported strength of the enemy position, he had inflicted about 2000 casualties and suffered about 3000 himself—which was as it should have been, considering his role as the attacker—and now there were something more than 12,000 rebel soldiers, the cream of Confederate volunteers, on their way to northern prison camps to await exchange for as many Union boys, who otherwise would have languished in southern prisons under the coming summer sun. People saw Grant as the author of this deliverance, the embodiment of the offensive spirit, the man who would strike and keep on striking until this war was won. Fifteen years ago, during a lull in the Mexican War, he had written home to the girl he was to marry: "If we have to fight, I would like to do it all at once and then make friends." Apparently he still felt that way about it.

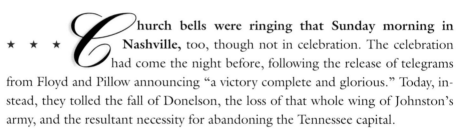

★ ★ ★ *C*hurch bells were ringing that Sunday morning in Nashville, too, though not in celebration. The celebration had come the night before, following the release of telegrams from Floyd and Pillow announcing "a victory complete and glorious." Today, instead, they tolled the fall of Donelson, the loss of that whole wing of Johnston's army, and the resultant necessity for abandoning the Tennessee capital.

All morning the remnants of Hardee's 14,000, reduced to less than two-thirds of that by straggling and sickness during the icy retreat from Bowling Green, filed through the city, harrowing the populace with accounts of Buell's bloodthirsty hordes closing fast upon their rear. Thus began a week of panic. Previously the war had seemed a far-off thing, over in Virginia or across the Mississippi or a hundred miles north in Kentucky. They had been too busy, or too confident, to fortify even the river approaches. Now that it was upon them with the abruptness of a pistol shot in a theater, they reacted variously. Some wept in numb despair. Others proposed to burn the city, "that the enemy might have nothing of it but the ashes." Terrified by a rumor that Buell's army and Foote's gunboats would converge upon the city at 3 p.m. to shell it into submission, they milled about, loading their household goods onto carts and wagons. By that time a special train had left for Memphis, with Governor Harris and the state archives aboard. Later that afternoon, the Yankee soldiers and gunboats not having appeared, the mayor informed the crowd in the Public Square that Johnston had promised to make no stand in Nashville. He himself would go out to meet the Federals and surrender the city before they got there, the mayor told the frantic populace. Meanwhile they should calm their fears and stay at home. As a final mollification, he promised to distribute among them all the Confederate provisions that could not be removed by Johnston's army.

This appeal to the greed of the people, while effective, was to have its consequences. Nashville warehouses were bulging with accumulated supplies, and it was Johnston's task—though he had opposed this placing of all the army's eggs in one basket—to save what he could before the Federals got there. Next morning, when Floyd and his brigade (minus the Mississippians) arrived by steamboat, Johnston put him in charge, while he himself continued the retreat with Hardee's men. Floyd took over the railroads, commandeered what few wagons remained, and in general did what he could. The panic had lessened somewhat since the nonarrival of the Federals, but a lurid glare against the northern sky and the clang of firebells in the night caused its resurgence until the people learned that the reflection, which they had feared might be from torches carried by an army of Yankee incendiaries, was from the hulls of two unfinished Confederate gunboats ordered burned in the yards.

Next day Floyd continued his efforts to save the stores. It was unpleasant work, the citizens growing more mutinous every hour—especially after the destruction, over their protest, of their two fine bridges across the Cumberland. Floyd was greatly relieved when Forrest arrived from Donelson on Wednesday, under orders to assist him in the salvaging of government supplies: so relieved, in fact, that next morning he marched his brigade away, and left the task to Forrest and his troopers.

Instructed to stay there one more day, unless Buell arrived sooner, Forrest stayed four. His iron hand snatched order out of chaos. Rifling machinery and other ordnance equipment, rare items in the Confederacy, were sent from the gun foundry to Atlanta. A quarter-million pounds of bacon and hundreds of wagonloads of clothing, flour, and ammunition were hauled to the railroad station for shipment south. The people, seeing this new efficiency and remembering that they had been promised what was left, sought to interfere by gathering in front of the warehouses. Forrest appealed to their patriotism, and when that did not work, ordered his mounted men to lay about with the flat of their sabers, which worked better. One large mob, in front of a warehouse on the Public Square, was dispersed by the use of fire hoses squirting ice-cold muddy water from the river, and as one of the crowd remembered it later, this had "a magical effect."

All day Thursday and Friday and Saturday, Forrest and his troopers worked, on into Sunday morning, when blue pickets appeared on the north bank of the river. Mindful of his instructions to leave Nashville an open city, Forrest fell back through the suburbs, marching to join Johnston and Hardee, who by now were at Murfreesboro, forty miles southeast. The Army of Central Kentucky—or what was left of it, anyhow—would have to find a new name.

★

Union troops form for a dress parade in Nashville in early March 1862, only a few days after they occupied the city.

Nashville's "Great Panic," as it was called thereafter, had lasted precisely a week, though by way of anticlimax one ignominy remained. True to his promise to the people, the mayor got in a rowboat and crossed the river to deliver the city into the hands of the Yankees before they opened fire with their long-range guns. He found no guns, however, and few soldiers: only half a squad of cavalry and one Ohio captain, who, after some persuasion, agreed to receive the surrender of the city, or at any rate not to attack it. The mayor returned and announced this deliverance to the citizens, who thus were relieved of a measure of their fears—most of which had been groundless in the first place. Buell was still a long way off, toiling down the railroad and the turnpike, repairing washed-out bridges as he came. Grant remained at Donelson, receiving reinforcements. Before the end of the week he had upwards of 30,000 men in four divisions, one of which had been advanced to Clarksville. "Nashville would be an easy conquest," he wrote Halleck's chief of staff, "but I only throw this out

as a suggestion. . . . I am ready for any move the general commanding may order." The general commanding ordered nothing; Grant stayed where he was.

Buell, in fact, did not reach Nashville until Wednesday, though several outfits had come on ahead. A reporter with one of the earliest wrote of what they found. All the stores and most of the better homes were closed; the State House was deserted, the legislators having fled with the governor to Memphis, which had been declared the temporary capital. The correspondent found the door of the leading hotel bolted, and when he rang there was no answer. He kept on ringing, with the persistency of a tired and hungry man within reach of food and a clean bed. At last he was rewarded. A Negro swung the door ajar and stood there smiling broadly. "Massa done gone souf," he said, still grinning.

★ ★ ★

★

*Confederate Texans, guarding the
Potomac River during the winter
of 1861-1862, attend to camp chores
by washing clothes, chopping wood,
and baking cornbread.*

T W O

Gloom; Manassas Evacuation

1862 ★ ★ ★ ★ ★ ★ Inauguration day broke cold and sullen in Richmond, with a scud of cloud that promised and then delivered rain, first a drizzle, then a steady downpour, hissing and gurgling in the gutters and thrumming against roofs and windowpanes. Davis rose early, as was his custom. Not due at the ceremonies until 11.30, he walked first to his office for an hour of the paperwork which filled so large a share of his existence, then back home. His wife, coming to warn him that the dignitaries were waiting to escort him to the Capitol, found him alone on his knees in the bedroom, praying "for the divine support I need so sorely." That too had been his custom since his first inauguration a year ago, under a cloudless Alabama sky.

The procession formed in the old Virginia Hall of Delegates, then moved out onto Capitol Square where a canopied platform had been set up alongside the equestrian statue of Washington, whose birthday this was. Grouped about the President-elect were cabinet officers, admirals and generals, governors and congressmen, newspaper representatives and members of various benevolent societies. Beside him stood Vice President Stephens, undersized and sickly, huddled in layers of clothes and resembling more than ever a mummified child. Asked once to define true happiness, Stephens had replied without hesitation, "To be warm." He was not happy now, presumably, for a cold rain fell in sheets, blown under the canopy by intermittent gusts of northern wind. When the Right Reverend John Johns, Episcopal Bishop of Virginia, raised his arms to pronounce the invocation, his lawn sleeves hung limp and his heavy satin vestments were splotched with wet. Close-packed, the crowd stood and took its drenching, conscious of being present at a historic occasion. Some held strips of canvas or worn carpet over their heads, but there were enough umbrellas to give the square what one witness called "the effect of an immense mushroom bed." They could hear few of the words above the impact of the rain. They saw Davis take the oath, however, and they knew they had a permanent President at last.

Davis's second inauguration occurred in Richmond, in the shadow of this statue of George Washington, shown here in 1858.

When he bent forward to kiss the Book a shout went up. Then they quieted. The drumming of the rain was loud as he turned to address them.

He was thinner and even more austere in appearance, the cheekbones brought into greater prominence and the eyes sunk even deeper in their sockets; "singularly imposing," one witness found him today, albeit with "a pallor painful to look upon." He wore a suit of black for the ceremonies instead of his customary gray, so that to Mrs Davis he seemed "a willing victim going to his funeral pyre." Her thoughts had been directed into such channels by an occurrence on the way. Observing that the carriage moved at a snail's pace, accompanied by a quartet of black-suited Negro footmen wearing white cotton gloves, she asked the coachman, to whom she had left the arrangements, what it meant. He told her, "This, ma'am, is the way we always does in Richmond at funerals and sichlike."

A year ago there had been no talk of funerals; "joyous" was the word Davis had used to describe the atmosphere on the day of his first inaugural. It was not so now. The outlook was as different as the weather. Nor did he assume a falsely joyous manner on this second occasion of taking the oath as President of the Confederacy. After referring to the birthday of the Virginian who looked out from his bronze horse nearby, he once more outlined and defended the course of events which had led to secession, characterizing the North as barbarous and expressing scorn for the "military despotism" which had "our enemies" in its grip. All this was as it had been before, but soon he passed to words that touched the present:

"A million men, it is estimated, are now standing in hostile array and waging war along a frontier of thousands of miles. Battles have been fought, sieges have been conducted, and although the contest is not ended and the tide for the moment is against us, the final result in our favor is not doubtful. We have had our trials and difficulties. That we are to escape them in the future is not to be hoped. It was to be expected when we entered upon this war that it would expose our people to sacrifices and cost them much, both of money and blood. But the picture has its lights as well as its shadows. This great strife has awakened in the people the highest emotions and qualities of the human soul. It was, perhaps, in the ordination of Providence that we were to be taught the value of our liberties by the price we pay for them. The recollection of this great contest, with all its common traditions of glory, of sacrifice and blood, will be the bond of harmony and enduring affection amongst the people, producing unity in policy, fraternity in sentiment, and just effort in war."

An invocation had opened the proceedings. Now another closed them. Davis lifted his hands and eyes to heaven as he spoke the final words. "My hope is reverently fixed on Him whose favor is ever vouchsafed to the cause which is just. With humble gratitude and adoration, acknowledging the Providence which has so visibly protected the Confederacy during its brief but eventful career, to Thee, O God, I trustingly commit myself and prayerfully invoke Thy blessing on my country and its cause."

Under the spell of that closing prayer, the people dispersed in silence and good order, "as though they had attended divine service," one remarked. Later, however, away from the magic of his voice and presence, they doubted that there was "unity in policy" or "fraternity in sentiment" or "just effort" in the prosecution of the war. Prompted by hostile editors, whose critiques of the address came out in their papers the following day—along with the news from Donelson and Nashville announcing the loss of Kentucky and most of Tennessee—they began to consider not only what he had said, but also what he had not said. He had outlined no future policy for raising the blockade, whose pinch was already being felt, or for overcoming the recent military reverses. Though his words were obviously spoken as much for foreign as for domestic ears, he had not foretold international recognition or the receiving of assistance from abroad. Except in vague and general terms, including the closing appeal to the Almighty, he had announced no single plan for coming to grips with the host of calamities they knew were included in his admission that "the tide for the moment is against us."

The fact that he refrained from explicit mention of these reverses did not mean that the people were unaware of them. They knew all too well that even a bare listing would have doubled the length of his address. Foremost among the disappointments, at least to men who took a long view of the chance for victory, was the failure of Confederate diplomacy. Original computations had shown that, before spring, England would have begun to suffer from the cotton famine which would bring her to her knees. Yet the looms and jennies, spinning away at the surplus bulging the warehouses, had not slowed. Ironically, the shortage there was not in cotton, but in wheat, the result of a crop failure in the British Isles. They were buying it now by the shipload from the North, which had harvested a bumper crop with its new McCormick reapers: another example of what it meant to fight a race of "pasty-faced mechanics."

Back at the outset, Southerners had predicted that the great Northwest—meaning Michigan, Wisconsin, Minnesota, and Iowa, along with northern Illinois and Indiana—would be pro-Confederate because of its need for an outlet to the Gulf of Mexico. Some who lived there had thought so, too. The Detroit *Free Press* had declared at the time: "If troops shall be raised in the North to march against the people of the South, a fire in the rear will be opened against such troops, which will either stop their march altogether or wonderfully accelerate it." But events had not worked out that way at all. The men of Grant's army were mostly from that region, and they had been accelerated, not by any "fire in the rear," but rather by an intense concern that the Union be preserved. Then too, instead of working an economic hardship, as the Southerners had predicted, the war had provided the farmers of the area with a new and profitable market for their wheat. The Northwest had not only stood by the Union; it was growing rich from having done so.

To some Confederates, this one among the many was the greatest disappointment of them all. The main hope of redress was that foreign intervention would be won by the new team of professional diplomats, Mason and Slidell, who had made a spectacular entry into the field. Yet here, too, there was disappointment. After serving the South so well from their cells in Boston Harbor, they were proving far less useful now in freedom at their posts. They stepped onto the London railway platform as if into obscurity, unwelcomed and unnoticed save by the late friendly *Times*, which announced their arrival with the following observations: "We sincerely hope that our countrymen will not give

> *"The British public has no prejudice in favor of slavery, which these gentlemen represent. What they and their secretaries are to do here passes our experience. They are personally nothing to us. They must not suppose, because we have gone to the verge of a great war to rescue them, that they are precious in our eyes."*
>
> — London *Times*

these fellows anything in the shape of an ovation. The civility that is due to a foe in distress is all that they can claim. The only reason for their presence in London is to draw us into their own quarrel. The British public has no prejudice in favor of slavery, which these gentlemen represent. What they and their secretaries are to do here passes our experience. They are personally nothing to us. They must not suppose, because we have gone to the verge of a great war to rescue them, that they are precious in our eyes."

Bitter as it was for Mason to see himself and his partner referred to as unprecious "fellows," the reception he received from the Foreign Minister dampened his spirits even more. Ushered into the presence, he was about to present his credentials when his lordship checked him: "That is unnecessary, since our relations are unofficial." Icily polite, but disinclined to enter into any discussion of policy, the most Earl Russell ventured was the hope that Mason

*In this cartoon, France's Napoleon III
(left) follows Queen Victoria's lead
by refusing to recognize the Confederacy.*

would find his visit "agreeable." In parting he did not express the hope that they might meet again. This was the treatment Yancey had broken under, and the Virginian took it scarcely better, reporting: "On the whole it was manifest enough that his personal sympathies were not with us."

Slidell, continuing his voyage across the channel, also encountered conditions which had plagued his predecessor. Unlike Mason, he had no difficulty in securing audiences. He got about as many as he wanted, and Eugénie was obviously charmed—a fact which he reported with some pride—but Napoleon would only repeat what he had said before: France could not act without England. That was the crux of the matter. The Crimean War had been a struggle between West and East, which the West had won, and now in the normal course of events, as demonstrated by history, the victors should have turned upon each other for domination of the whole. Yet it had not worked out that way. There was no such tenuous balance as had obtained at the time of the American Revolution, bringing France to the assistance of the Colonies. On the contrary, the *entente* remained strong, drawing its strength from the weakness of Napoleon, whose shaky finances and doubtful popularity would not allow him to risk bringing all of Europe down on his unprotected back. Slidell could only inform his government of these conditions. It began to seem that, economically and politically — so far at least as Europe was concerned — the South had chosen the wrong decade in which to make her bid for independence.

Like others who took the long view, seeing foreign intervention as the one quick indisputable solution to the Confederacy's being outnumbered and outgunned and outmachined, Davis received this latest news from abroad with whatever grace and patience he could muster. He could wait — though by the hardest. Meantime he had other, more immediate problems here at home, within his own official family: in evidence of which, as even the short-view men could see, the chief post in his cabinet was vacant. The Secretary of State had left in a huff that very week.

At the time when he accepted the appointment, Hunter had announced that he intended to be a responsible and independent official, not just "the clerk of Mr Davis." As Virginia's favorite-son candidate at the Democratic convention of 1860, he had his political dignity to consider. Besides, in the early days of the secession movement, when it was thought that the Old Dominion would be among the first to go, he had been slated for the presidency of the impending Confederacy. Virginia had held back and he had missed it; but there was still the future to keep his eye on, and his dignity to be maintained. The result was a personality clash with Davis, a build-up of bad feeling which reached a climax during a general cabinet discussion of the military situation. When Hunter expressed an opinion on the subject, Davis told him: "Mr Hunter, you are Secretary of State, and when information is wished of that department it will be time for you to speak." The Virginian's resignation was on the presidential desk next morning.

Davis of course accepted it. He made no appointment to fill the post immediately, however. Vacant for a week at the time of the inauguration, it would remain so for three more. The man he had in mind was too deeply embroiled in other matters, filling another cabinet position, to be considered available just yet. And this was one more item which might have been included in any listing of reverses.

As Secretary of War, the rotund, smiling Judah P. Benjamin had been under fire almost since the day of his appointment: not under actual bombardment from the enemy beyond the gates, but rather from the plain citizens and congressmen within, whose ire was aroused by his summary treatment of the nation's military heroes, coming as they did under the jurisdiction of his department. Benjamin had no such notion as Hunter's concerning the duties of his post. As head of the War Department he considered himself quite literally the President's secretary for military affairs, and it did not irk him at all to be tagged "the clerk of Mr Davis." The field of arms was one of the few that had not previously engaged the interest of this myriad-minded man, whereas Davis, a West Pointer and a Mexican War hero, had been the ablest Secretary the Federal War

Department ever had. Benjamin's duty, as he saw it—and here the two men's concepts coincided—was to execute the will and, if necessary, defend the actions of his Commander in Chief. Besides, he saw Davis's needs, the desire for warmth behind his iciness, the ache for understanding behind his stiff austerity. Judah  Benjamin was one of the few who perceived this, or at any rate one of the few—like Mrs Davis—who acted on it, and in doing so he not only made himself pleasant; in time he also made himself indispensable. That was his reward. He gained the President's gratitude, and with it the unflinching loyalty which Davis always gave in return for loyalty received.

He saw Davis's needs, the desire for warmth behind his iciness, the ache for understanding behind his stiff austerity. Judah Benjamin was one of the few who perceived this, or at any rate one of the few—like Mrs Davis—who acted on it, and in doing so he not only made himself pleasant; in time he also made himself indispensable.

Whatever he lacked in the knowledge of arms as a profession, he brought to his job a considerable facility in the handling of administrative matters. Unlike Walker, who had fumed and stewed in tangles of red tape and never got from under the avalanche of army paperwork, Benjamin would clear his desk with dispatch, then sit back smiling, ready for what came next. What came next, as often as not, was an opportunity for exercising his talent in dialectics. Here his skill was admittedly superior—"uncanny," some called it, and they spoke resentfully; for by the precision of his logic he could lead men where they would not go, making them seem clumsy in the process. In taking up his superior's quarrels with the generals on the Manassas line—which seemed to him one of the duties of his post—he gave full play to his talents in this direction, undeterred by awe for the military mind. That was what had caused Beauregard to reach for his pen in such a frenzy, writing with ill-concealed irony of the pity he felt, "from the bottom of my heart," for any man who could not see "the difference between *patriotism*, the highest civic virtue, and *office-seeking*, the lowest civic occupation." It was Benjamin he meant. But in making the charge the general entered a field where his fellow Louisianian was master; and presently he went West.

Even more vulnerable in this respect, though banishment did not follow so close on the heels of contention, was Joseph E. Johnston. After Johnston's protest at being outranked, and Davis's quick slash in reply, Benjamin took up the cudgel for his chief. Johnston was a careless administrator, and whenever he lapsed in this regard, the Secretary took him to task with a letter that prickled his sensitive pride. Infuriated, the general would reply in kind, only to be brought up short by another missive which proved him even further in the wrong. A later observer wrote that Benjamin treated the Virginian as if he were "an adversary at the bar," but sometimes it was worse; he dealt with him as if he were a prisoner in the dock. Johnston's outraged protests against such treatment did him no more good than Beauregard's had done. Once when the Creole complained to Davis that the Secretary's tone was offensive and that he was being "put into the strait jackets of the law," the President replied: "I do not feel competent to instruct Mr Benjamin in the matter of style. There are few whom the public would probably believe fit for the task." As for the second objection, "You surely do not intend to inform me that your army and yourself are outside the limits of the law. It is my duty to see that the laws are faithfully executed and I cannot recognize the pretensions of anyone that their restraint is too narrow for him."

Exalted thus at the expense of those who attempted to match wits with him, Benjamin continued to maintain order at headquarters and to ride herd on recalcitrants among the military. Then, unexpectedly, he ran full tilt into a man who had no use for dialectics, who stood instead on his own ground and gave the Secretary his first check. T. J. Jackson, called "Stonewall" since Manassas, had been promoted to major general in the fall and assigned to command a division in the Shenandoah Valley, from which strategic location he had proposed that he be reinforced for an all-out invasion of the North. Having just rejected a similar proposal from Beauregard at Centreville, the Administration would send him no reinforcements, but attached to his command the three brigades of W. W. Loring, the one professional in the quartet who had tried the patience and damaged the reputation of R. E. Lee in West Virginia. Told to accomplish what he could with this total force of about 9000, Jackson launched on New Year's Day a movement designed to recover the counties flanking the western rim of the Valley theater.

The first phase of the campaign went as planned. Marching in bitter midwinter weather, Jackson's men harried the B & O Railroad, captured enemy stores, and in general created havoc among the scattered Federal camps. This done, Stonewall stationed Loring's troops at Romney, on the upper Potomac, and took the others back to Winchester, thirty-odd miles eastward, to begin the second phase. Just what that would have been remained a mystery, for Jackson was a most secretive man, agreeing absolutely with Frederick II's remark, "If I thought my coat knew my plans I would take it off and burn it." He did say, however, that he left the attached brigades on outpost duty because his own were better marchers and could move more swiftly toward any threatened point. Loring's volunteers did not subscribe to this. Rather, it was their belief that Stonewall was demented. (They saw various symptoms of this — including the fact that he never took pepper in his food, on grounds that it gave him pains in his left leg.) And so were his men, for that matter, since they had a habit of cheering him on the march. Exposed as they were to the elements and the possible swoop of Federal combinations, Loring and his officers petitioned the War Department to withdraw them from their uncomfortable position. On the next to last day of January, Jackson received the following dispatch signed by Benjamin: "Our news indicates that a movement is being made to cut off General Loring's command. Order him back to Winchester immediately."

Jackson promptly complied with the order. Acknowledging its receipt and reporting its execution, the next day he addressed the War Department: "With such interference in my command I cannot expect to be of much service in the field," wherefore he asked to be returned to his teaching job at V.M.I., or else "I respectfully request that the President will accept my resignation from the army." The letter went through channels to Johnston, who forwarded it regretfully to Richmond. He too had been by-passed, and he told Benjamin: "Let me suggest that, having broken up the dispositions of the military commander, you give whatever other orders may be necessary."

Eventually the trouble was smoothed over and Jackson's resignation returned to him, Governor Letcher and various congressmen exerting all the pressure of their influence, but not before violent recriminations had been heaped on the head of the smiling Secretary, especially by Stonewall's fellow officers. Tom Cobb of Georgia, a brigadier in the Virginia army, stated flatly: "A grander rascal than this Jew Benjamin does not exist in the Confederacy and I am not particular in concealing my opinion of him." Nor were others particular in that respect, their fury being increased when Loring was promoted in mid-February and taken from under the stern control of Jackson, who had recommended that he be cashiered.

Benjamin kept smiling through it all, though by then the indestructibility of his smile was being tested even further. Previous recriminations had come mainly from army men, outraged at his interfering in tactical matters. Now he was being condemned by the public at large, and for a lack of similar interference.

Down on the North Carolina coast, set one above the other, Albemarle and Pamlico Sounds were divided by a low-lying marshy peninsula. At its

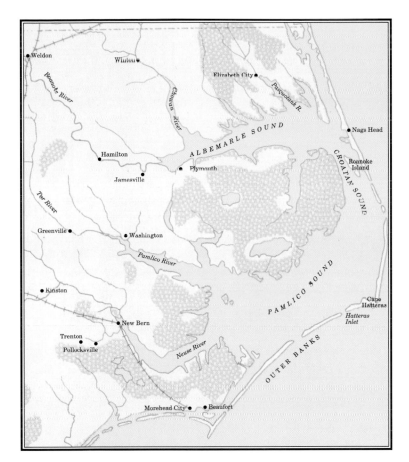

Tiny Roanoke Island sits like a cork between Albemarle and Pamlico Sounds, protecting the upper North Carolina coast.

eastern tip, where the jut of land approached the narrow sands of the breakwater guarding the coast from the gales that blew so frequently off Hatteras, lay Roanoke Island, the site of Raleigh's "Lost Colony" and birthplace of the first English child born in the Western Hemisphere. Just now, however, this boggy tract had an importance beyond the historic. Pamlico, the lower and larger sound, had fallen to Stringham's gunboats back in August; Albemarle could be taken, too, once the narrows flanking the island had been forced. Loss of the lower sound had given the Federals a year-round anchorage and access to New Bern, principal eastern depot on the vital railroad supply line to Richmond and the armies in Virginia. That was bad enough, though the invaders had not yet exploited it, but loss of the upper sound would expose Norfolk and Gosport Navy Yard to attack from the rear. This would be worse than bad; it would be tragic, for the Confederates had things going on in the navy yard that would not bear interruption. The focal point for its defense, as anyone could see, was Roanoke Island. Situated north of all four barrier inlets, it was like a loose-fitting cork plugging the neck of a bottle called Albemarle Sound.

★

Nothing that went by water could get in there without going past the cork.

One who saw this clearly was Henry Wise. Still seething from his defeat in West Virginia at the hands of his fellow ex-governor Floyd, he arrived and took command of the island forces in late December. He entered upon his duties with his usual enthusiasm. By the time he was halfway through his first inspection, however, he saw that the cork was not only loose, but also apt to crumble under pressure. Little had been done to block the passes, either by driving pilings or by sinking obstructions in the channel. What was worse, the water batteries were badly sited, clustered up at the northern end of the island as if in expectation of attack from that direction after Norfolk fell, while the southern end, giving down upon Pamlico Sound—which the enemy fleet had held for four months now—was left open to amphibious assault. In the face of this threat Wise had a garrison of about 2500 men, fewer than he believed were necessary to slow, let alone halt, such an attack once the Federals got ashore. Yet he was no defeatist. He got to work, driving pilings and sinking hulks in the channel, and called on the district commander at Norfolk, Major General Benjamin Huger, for additional artillery and ammunition, pile drivers, supplies of every kind, and especially more soldiers. A fifty-six-year-old South Carolina aristocrat, West Pointer and Chief of Ordnance under Scott in Mexico, Huger was placid in manner and deliberate in judgment. He had never inspected the island defenses, but he replied to Wise's requisitions by recommending "hard work and coolness among the troops you have, instead of more men."

Being told to keep cool only lowered Wise's boiling point, which was reached when Flag Officer William F. Lynch, of the Confederate navy, commandeered all his work boats except a single tug, converting them to one-gun gunboats. A "mosquito fleet," Wise dubbed the result in derision, and left for Norfolk to protest in person. When Huger still gave him no satisfaction, he set out for Richmond, where he had influential friends bound to him during years of politics. He would appeal directly to the Secretary of War. This was contrary to Army Regulations, he knew; to go was to risk court martial. But he believed the situation justified irregularity. "Damn the execution, sir!" he had cried in West Virginia; "it's the *sound* that we want." As tactics, this could be applied to more than field artillery.

Arriving January 19 he stayed three days; but he got nowhere with the Secretary. Already Benjamin had replied to his urgent demands for cannon powder by informing him that the Confederacy's "very limited" reserve was being saved for use at more closely threatened points. "At the first indication, however, of an attack on Roanoke Island," he wrote, "a supply will be sent you." Wise replied that there *was* no more closely threatened point and that once the assault had begun it would be too late, but the Secretary had considered the matter closed. Now, face to face with Benjamin in Richmond, the Virginian fared no better in his plea for powder. Nor did he get reinforcements. When he pointed out that Huger had 13,000 men lying idle around Norfolk, the Secretary, obviously preferring the military judgment of the professionally trained senior to that of the politically appointed subordinate, shrugged and said that he supposed the district commander knew best. He would not interfere.

Wise remained in town, complaining vociferously to his high-placed friends until the 22d, when a dispatch arrived from Commander Lynch announcing symptoms of an enemy build-up and attack: whereupon Benjamin, doubtless glad to be rid of him, issued a peremptory order for the general to go back to his island post. Bad weather and transportation difficulties delayed his return till the end of the month. On the 31st —while Stonewall Jackson was composing his resignation out in the Valley—the distraught Wise, his condition aggravated by the frustration of trying to get someone to realize the weakness of his tactical position, took to his bed with a severe attack of pleurisy.

He was still there a week later when the all-out Federal amphibious assault was launched, just as he had said it would be, against the undefended south end of the island.

★ ★ ★ 　*I*n his search for someone who understood the difficulties and dangers of his assignment Wise was cut off from the one person who, next to himself, appreciated them best. The trouble was, the man wore blue and exercised his authority on the other side of the line.

Ambrose Burnside had not gone home with his Rhode Islanders when they were mustered out in early August, two weeks after crossing Bull Run as the fist of the roundhouse right McDowell had swung at Beauregard in an effort to end the war on the plains of Manassas. He had tried civilian life as a businessman a few years back and, failing, hadn't liked it. Now, at thirty-seven, an Indiana-born West Pointer and a veteran of the Mexican War, he accepted promotion to brigadier and stayed on in the service. A tall, rather stout, energetic man with large features and dark-socketed eyes, he made up for his premature baldness with a fantastic set of whiskers describing a double parabola from in front of his ears, down over his chops, and up across his mouth. This was his trademark, a half-ruff of facial hair standing out in dark-brown contrast to his shaven jowls and chin. Affecting the casual in his dress—low-slung holster, loose-fitting knee-length double-breasted jacket, and wide-brimmed bell-crowned soft felt hat—he was something of a pistol-slapper, but likable all the same for his hearty manner and open nature, his forthright, outgoing friendliness. McClellan liked him, at any rate, and called him "Dear Burn" in letters. So that when Burnside approached him in the fall with a plan for the seizure of coastal North Carolina, completing what had been begun at Hatteras Inlet and opening thereby a second front in the Confederate rear, the general-in-chief was

★

attentive and said he would like to see it submitted in writing. Burnside did so, expanding his original plan, and McClellan liked it even more. He indorsed it, got the Secretary of War to give it top priority, and told the Hoosier general to go ahead, the quicker the better.

The Burnside Expedition, as it was designated, was assembled and ready for action by early January, Annapolis being the staging area for its 13,000 troops and 80 vessels. Grouped into three divisions under brigadiers who had been cadets with their commander at West Point — J. G. Foster, Jesse L. Reno, John G. Park; "three of my most trusted friends," he called them — the men were mostly rock-ribbed New Englanders, "many of whom would be familiar with the coasting trade, and among whom would be found a goodly number of mechanics." The naval components of this task force, under Rear Admiral Louis M. Goldsborough, a big, slack-bodied regular of the type called "barnacles," had no such homogeneity. In addition to twenty light-draft gunboats armed with cannon salvaged from the armories of various navy yards, there was a rick-

---

Seafaring men among the soldiers took one look at the shallow-draft transports and shook their heads. At the worst, they had volunteered for getting shot at, not drowned . . .

---

ety lot of sixty-odd transports and supply ships, including tugs, ferries, converted barges, and flat-bottomed river steamers: a conglomeration, in short, of whatever could be scraped together by purchasing agents combing northern rivers and harbors for vessels rejected by agents who had come and gone before them. The only characteristic they shared was that they all drew less than eight feet of water, the reported high-tide depth across the bar at Hatteras Inlet.

This was the cause of much grumbling at the outset. Seafaring men among the soldiers took one look at the shallow-draft transports and shook their heads. At the worst, they had volunteered for getting shot at, not drowned — which was what they believed would happen, once those tubs reached open water. Burnside answered the grumbling by taking the smallest, least seaworthy craft of the lot for his headquarters boat. Thus reassured, or anyhow reproached, the troops filed onto the transports, and on the morning of the 9th the flotilla steamed out of the harbor to rendezvous next day off Fort Monroe. On the 11th, clearing Hampton Roads, the skippers broke open their sealed orders and steered south.

The near-mutiny among his sea-going soldiers at the outset was only the first of Burnside's troubles. In fact, the method by which he had quelled the

★

grumbling almost cost him his life the following night, when the fleet ran into a gale off Hatteras. The dinky little headquarters boat got into the trough of the sea and nearly foundered. As he remembered it years later, still somewhat queasy from the experience, everything not securely lashed above-decks was swept overboard, while "men, furniture, and crockery below decks were thrown about in a most promiscuous manner." Eventually, her steersman brought her head-to and she rode the storm out, staggering up and down the mast-high waves to arrive next morning off Hatteras Inlet, the entrance to Pamlico Sound, where an even worse shock awaited him.

The water through there was not eight feet deep, as he had been told, but six: which barred many of his vessels from a share in the expedition as effectively as if they had been sunk by enemy action. Here was where the "goodly number of mechanics, . . . familiar with the coasting trade," stood their commander in good stead. The tide running swift above the swash, they sent several of the larger ships full-speed-ahead to ground on the bar, and held them there with tugs and anchors while the racing current washed the sand from under their bottoms. It was a slow process, bumping them forward length by length; but it worked. By early February a broad eight-foot channel had been cut and the fleet assembled safely in the sound. On the 4th, after a conference with the flag officer, Burnside gave his brigadiers detailed instructions for the landing on Roanoke Island. Another two-day blow delayed it, but on the morning of the 7th, a fine, clear day with sunshine bright on the placid, sapphire water, the fleet steamed forward in attack formation.

Still suffering from the multiple pangs of pleurisy and frustration, Wise had been confined all this time at Nags Head, the Confederate command post on the sandy rim of Albemarle Sound, just opposite the north end of the island. He knew what was coming, and even how, though until now he had not realized the strength of the blow the Federals were aiming. Goldsborough's warships were out in front, mounting a total of 64 guns, eager to take on the seven makeshift rebel vessels, each mounting a single 32-pounder rifle. Behind the Yankee gunboats came the transports, crowded with 13,000 assault troops ready to swarm ashore and try their strength against the island's fewer than 3000 defenders. The mosquito fleet took station in front of the uncompleted line of pilings Wise had started driving across the channel, but when the Federals roared and bore down on them belching smoke and flame from 9-inch guns and 100-pounder rifles, they scurried back through the gap and out of range, leaving the water batteries to take up the defense.

There were two of these, both up toward the northern end of the island, and while the warships took them under fire the transports dropped anchor three miles astern and began unloading troops for the landing at Ashby's Harbor, midway up the island's ten-mile length. The first boats hit the beach at

4 o'clock. All this time the duel between the gunboats and the batteries continued, with more noise than damage on either side. At sundown the mosquito fleet attempted a darting attack that was repulsed about as soon as it began. By midnight all the troops were ashore. The undefended southern half of the island had been secured without the infantry firing a shot. Drenched by a chill rain, they tried to get what sleep they could before the dawn advance, knowing that tomorrow would be tougher.

Down the boggy center of the island, a little more than a mile from the opposite beaches, ran a causeway. Astride this backbone of defense the Confederates had placed a three-gun battery supported by infantry and flanked by quicksand marshes judged impenetrable. To advance along the causeway toward those guns would be like walking up a hardwood alley toward a bowler whose only worry was running out of balls before the advancer ran out of legs. Yet there was no other way, and the men of both armies knew it: Burnside as well as anyone, for he had been briefed for the landing by a twenty-year-old contraband who had run away from his island master the week before and was thoroughly familiar with the dispositions for defense. Instructing Foster to charge straight up the causeway while Reno and Park were probing the boggy flanks, Burnside put

Union Zouaves charge across a causeway to help secure and hold a Confederate battery on Roanoke Island.

all three brigades into line and sent them forward as soon as the light was full.

Right off, the center brigade ran into murderous head-on fire. Bowled over and pinned down, they were hugging the sandy embankment and wondering what came next, when off to the right and left fronts they heard simultaneous whoops of exultation. The flank brigades had made it through the knee-deep ooze and slush of the "impenetrable" marsh. While the rebel cannoneers tried frantically to turn their guns to meet these attacks from opposite and unexpected directions, the men along the causeway jumped up, whooping too, and joined the charge. The battery was quickly overrun.

With the fall of the three-gun battery the island's defenses collapsed of a broken backbone. Burnside's infantry broke into the clear, taking the water batteries in reverse while the fleet continued its bombardment from the channel. By midafternoon the Confederates had retreated as far as they could go. Corralled on the northern tip of the island, their ammunition exhausted, they laid down their arms. Casualties had been relatively light on both sides: 264 for the attackers, 143 for the defenders. The difference came in the fruits of victory; 2675 soldiers and 32 cannon were surrendered, losses which the South could ill afford. Best of all, from the northern point of view, Burnside had won control of North Carolina's inland sea, thereby tightening the blockade one hard twist more, opening a second front in the Virginia army's rear, gaining access to the back door to Norfolk, and arousing the immediate apprehension of every rebel posted within gunshot of salt water. No beach was safe. This newly bred amphibious beast, like some monster out of mythology — half Army, half Navy: an improbable, unholy combination if ever there was one — might come splashing and roaring ashore at any point from here on down.

★ ★ ★ *N*orth and south the news went out and men reacted. In New York, Horace Greeley swung immediately to the manic, celebrating the double conquest of Roanoke Island and Fort Henry even as Grant was knocking at the gates of Donelson: "The cause of the Union now marches on in every section of the country. Every blow tells fearfully against the rebellion. The rebels themselves are panic-stricken, or despondent. It now requires no very far-reaching prophet to predict the end of this struggle."

In Richmond, as elsewhere throughout the Confederacy and among her representatives overseas, the spirits of men were correspondingly grim. As if in confirmation of Greeley's paean in the *Tribune,* letters came from Mason and Slidell. The former wrote from London that "the late reverses ... have had an unfortunate effect upon the minds of our friends here." The latter wrote from Paris: "I need not say how unfavorable an influence these defeats, following in such quick succession, have produced in public sentiment. If not soon counterbalanced by some decisive success of our arms, we may not only bid adieu to all hopes of seasonable recognition, but must expect that the declaration of the in-efficiency of the blockade, to which I had looked forward with great confidence at no distant day, will be indefinitely postponed."

These were hard lines for Davis on the eve of his inaugural, but he had other reactions to deal with, nearer and far more violent. Norfolk was in turmoil — with good cause. Lynch's mosquito fleet, attempting to make a stand against Goldsborough's gunboats at the mouth of the Pasquotank River, was wrecked in short order, six of the seven vessels being captured, rammed, blown up, or otherwise sunk. Only one made its escape up the river and through the Dismal Swamp Canal to Norfolk, barely forty miles away, bringing wild stories of the destruction it had run from and predicting that Norfolk was next on the monster's list. The consternation which followed this report was hardly calmed by the arrival of Wise, who, convalescent from pleurisy, had made his escape by marching up the breakwater from Nags Head. "Nothing! Nothing!! Noth-ing!!!" he proclaimed. "That was the disease which brought disaster at Roanoke Island." Thus he shook whatever confidence the citizens had managed to retain in Huger, who was charged with their defense.

The city seethed with rumors of doom, and the panic spread quickly up the James to Richmond. Davis met it as he had met the East Tennessee crisis early that winter. Five days after the inaugural in which he had excoriated Lin-coln for doing the same thing, and scorned the northern populace for putting up with it, he suspended the privilege of habeas corpus in the Norfolk area, placing the city under martial law. Two days later, March 1, Richmond itself was gripped by the iron hand.

This action added fuel to the fire already raging in certain breasts. Taking their cue from Wise, who was vociferous in accusation, the people put the blame where he pointed: squarely at the Secretary of War. Benjamin took it as he took everything, blandly. "To do the Secretary justice," one observer wrote, "he bore the universal attack with admirable good nature and sang froid." More than that, "to all appearances, equally secure in his own views and indifferent to public odium, he passed from reverse to reverse with perfectly bland manner and unwearying courtesy."

The principal charge against him was that he had failed, despite re-peated pleas, to supply the island defenders with powder for their cannon. He had the best possible answer to this: that there was and had been none to send. But to admit as much would have been to encourage his country's enemies and alienate the Europeans considering recognition and support. The Louisianian kept silent under attack and abuse, and Davis was given further proof of his loyalty and devotion to the cause. However, his very urbanity was more infuriating to his foes than any defense or counterattack he might have made. The Richmond *Examiner* was irked into commenting acidly, "The Administration has now an opportunity of making some reputation; for, nothing being expected of it, of course every success will be clear gain." Plainly, the ultimate sacrifice was called for. Benjamin had to go.

He had to go, but not from the cabinet entirely. That would be a loss which Davis believed the nation could not afford. At any rate *he* could not. And though, as always, he would not attempt to justify or even explain his action — would not say to the hostile editors and fuming politicians, "Let me keep this man; I need him" — he found a way to keep him: a way, however, that infuriated his critics even more.

The post of Secretary of State had been vacant since Hunter left in a huff the month before. Davis had kept it so, with this in mind. Now in mid-March the Permanent Congress, which had convened four days before his inauguration, received for confirmation the name of the man he wanted appointed to fill the vacancy: Judah P. Benjamin of Louisiana, former Attorney General and present Secretary of War. Some in that body called the move audacious. Others called it impudent. Whatever it was, Davis had the devotion of the people and the personal support of a majority of the legislators, and he was willing to risk them both,

George Wythe Randolph, the grandson of Thomas Jefferson, served for eight months as the Confederate Secretary of War.

here and now, to get what he believed both he and the Confederacy needed to win the war and establish independence. And he got it. Despite the gasps of outrage and cries of indignation, Benjamin was quickly confirmed as head of the State Department and thus assured a voice in the nation's councils, a seat at the right hand of Jefferson Davis.

Having angered many congressmen by requiring them to promote the Secretary of War as a reward for what they termed his inefficiency, the President now proceeded to make them happy and proud by placing before them, for confirmation, the name of George Wythe Randolph as Benjamin's successor.

Appointment of this forty-four-year-old Richmond lawyer, scion of the proud clan of Randolph, would make amends for the snub given Hunter and restore to the Old Dominion a rightful place among those closest to the head of government. What was more, Randolph had had varied military experience as a youthful midshipman in the U.S. Navy, as a gentleman ranker in a prewar Richmond militia company, and as artillery commander under Magruder on the peninsula, where in eight months he had risen from captain to colonel, with a promotion to brigadier moving up through channels even now. All this was much, and augured well. But best of all, from the point of view of those who had the privilege of voting his confirmation, he was the grandson of Thomas Jefferson, born at the hilltop shrine of Monticello and dandled on the great Virginian's knee. Blood would tell, as all Southerners knew, and this was the finest blood of all, serving to reëmphasize the ties between the Second American Revolution and the First. The appointment was confirmed at once, enthusiastically and with considerable mutual congratulation among the senators.

Whether the highborn Randolph would bear up better than Hunter had done as a "clerk of Mr Davis" remained to be seen. For the present, at least, the Chief Executive had placated the rising anger of his friends by nominating Randolph, and had foiled his critics by tossing his personal popularity into the balance alongside the hated Benjamin, causing the opposite pan to kick the beam. How long he could continue to win by such methods, standing thus between his favorites and abuse, was another question. Certainly every such victory subtracted from the weight he would exert in any weighing match that followed. What he lost, each time, his critics gained: particularly those who railed against his static defensive policy and his failure to share with the public the grim statistics of the lengthening odds. Down in Georgia, even now, an editor was writing for all to read: "President Davis does not enjoy the confidence of the Southern people.... With a cold, icy, iron grasp, [he] has fettered our people, stilled their beating pulses of patriotism, cooled their fiery ardor, imprisoned them in camps and behind entrenchments. He has not told the people what he needed. As a faithful sentinel, he has not told them what of the night."

So far, the Georgian was one among a small minority; but such men were vociferous in their bitterness, and when they stung they stung to hurt. The people read or heard their complaints, printed in columns alongside the news of such reverses as Fort Donelson and Roanoke Island, and they wondered. They did not enjoy being told that they were not trusted by the man in whom their own trust was placed. A South Carolina matron, friendly to Davis and all he stood for, confided scornfully in her diary: "In Columbia I do not know a half-dozen men who would not gaily step into Jeff Davis's shoes with a firm conviction that they would do better in every respect than he does."

★

★ ★ ★   *T*here was one glimmer in the military gloom — indeed, a brightness — though it was based not on accomplishment, but on continuing confidence despite the lengthening odds and the late reverses. The gleam in fact proceeded from the region where the gloom was deepest: off in the panic-stricken West, where the left wing of the Confederacy had been crippled. What his wife represented in private life, what Benjamin meant to him in helping to meet the cares of office, Albert Sidney Johnston was to Davis in military matters. He was in plain fact his notion of a hero. They had not been together since mid-September, when the tall, handsome Kentucky-born Texan came to Richmond to receive from Davis his commission and his assignment to command of the Western Department. That had been a happy time, the plaudits of the entire nation ringing in his ears. They had kept on ringing, too, until Grant called his game of bluff on the Tennessee and the Cumberland, and the whole western house of cards went crash.

At the outset the newspapers had expected "results at once brilliant, scientific, and satisfactory" (the diminution of the adjectives was prophetic) but not this: not defeat, with the loss of half his army, all of Kentucky, and a goodly portion of Tennessee including its capital. The uproar outdid anything the nation had known since the defection of Benedict Arnold. Johnston was accused of stupidity and incompetence or worse, for there were the usual post-defeat cries of treason and corruption. Those who had sung his praises loudest such a short while back were loudest now in abuse. The army was demoralized, they shrilled; Johnston must be removed or the cause would fail. New troops being sworn in made it a condition of their enlistment oath that they would not be required to serve under his command.

He took the blame as he had taken the praise. Calm at the storm center, he displayed still the nobility of mind and strength of character which had drawn men to him all his life. Urged by friends to make a public defense, he replied: "I cannot correspond with the people. What the people want is a battle and a victory. That is the best explanation I can make." Retreating again — from Murfreesboro now, all the way to Decatur, Alabama, where he would be south of the Tennessee River and on the Memphis & Charleston Railroad, in a position to coöperate with the forces under Beauregard, retreating south along the Mississippi — he wrote to Davis more explicitly of his reason for keeping his temper: "I observed silence, as it seemed to me the best way to serve the cause and the country." He offered then to yield the command, saying: "The test of merit in my profession is success. It is a hard rule, but I think it right." To concentrate and strike was his present aim, in which case "those who are now declaiming against me will be without an argument."

It was a letter to warm the heart of any superior in distress — which Davis certainly was. He replied: "My confidence in you has never wavered, and I hope the public will soon give me credit for judgment rather than continue to arraign me for obstinacy."

The public might, in time; but for the present the clamor did not die; it grew. Davis stood under an avalanche of letters, protests, and demands for his friend's dismissal. Yet all this time, as he said, he never wavered. When a delegation of Tennessee congressmen called at his office to insist en masse that Johnston be relieved — he was no general, they said scornfully — Davis stood at his desk and heard their demand with an icy silence. When they had spoken, he told them: "If Sidney Johnston is not a general, we had better give up the war, for we have no general," and bowed them out.

★ ★ ★ The other Johnston, back in Virginia, was another matter. There would never be any such letter from him, and Davis knew it: not only because it was not in Joe Johnston's nature to be selfless in a crisis — he had small belief in the efficacy of silence — but also because his problems were quite different. He had no quarrel with the public; the public, like his soldiers, now and always, showed the greatest affection for him. His difficulties were rather with his superiors, the Commander in Chief and the Secretary of War, and with the laws and regulations which Congress passed in an attempt to be what it called helpful, but which Johnston himself considered meddlesome and harmful.

A case in point was the so-called Furlough and Bounty Act, which had been passed in December in an effort to meet the crisis that would arise when the enlistments of the twelve-month volunteers expired in late winter and early spring. Obviously something would have to be done to encourage reënlistments; few men were likely to expose themselves voluntarily to a continuance of the dull life they had been leading all through the Virginia fall and winter. Under the act, all who would sign on for three years — or the duration, in case the end came first — would receive a sixty-day furlough and a fifty-dollar bounty. Further, on their return they would be allowed to transfer to whatever outfit they chose, even into another arm of service, and elect their own field- and company-grade officers once the reorganization was effected. Johnston realized the necessity for some such encouragement, but the only part of this particular act that he approved of was the bounty. The transfer and election privileges he considered ruinous, and the furloughs, if granted in numbers large enough to be effective, would expose the remainder of his army to slaughter at the hands of the Federals, already twice his strength around Manassas and likely to attack at any time. Besides, when he wrote to the War Department, asking how the act was to be applied and what numbers were to be furloughed at any one time, the Secretary replied that he was to go to the "extreme verge of prudence." Now Johnston was a very prudent man; entirely too much so, his critics said. The extreme verge of his prudence was still very prudent indeed. As a result, the act accomplished little except to vex the general charged with its application.

Another, more serious vexation was the loss of experienced officers of rank. He had lost the embittered Beauregard and he had nearly lost Stonewall Jackson as a result of Benjamin's out-of-channels interference. Kirby Smith had returned to duty, healed of his Manassas wound, only to be assigned to deal with the powder-keg East Tennessee situation. Earl Van Dorn, whose dash and brilliance promised much, had been sent to the Transmississippi. These were hard losses, and there were more, in addition to some who were so disgruntled that they threatened to resign. "The Army is crippled and its discipline greatly impaired by a want of general officers," Johnston reported plaintively to Richmond.

These were causes enough for disturbance in any commander, let alone one as irascible and gloomy as Joe Johnston; but coming as they did, at a time when the odds were what he knew them to be in northern Virginia, they

These Confederate huts at Centreville, built as winter quarters in 1861, were dank and crowded, spreading misery and disease.

filled him with forebodings of disaster. His loss of respect for McClellan's character as a man of war—in letters he now referred to him as "George" or "the re-
doubtable McC" or even " 'George,' " employing the pointed sarcasm of inverted
commas—did not preclude a respect for McClellan's numbers or his ability to
forge them into an effective striking force. And not only were the numerical odds
forbidding; the situation itself was bad from the southern point of view. Operating
behind the screen of the Potomac, the northern host could concentrate and strike
at any point from the Blue Ridge Mountains down to Aquia Creek, and thus be
on the flank or in the rear of the army around Manassas and Occoquan. All that
was holding them back, so far as Johnston could see, was rainy weather and the
mud that it produced. Spring was coming, the sudden vernal loveliness of blue
skies, new grass, and solid roads. A week of sunshine would remove all the obstacles that stood between McClellan and success, or between Johnston and ruin.

It was at this point, aggravated further by a shortage of arms and powder, that the general was summoned to ride down to Richmond, two days before
the inauguration, for a conference on the military situation. Reporting to the President at 10 o'clock that morning, he found the cabinet in session and the discussion already begun. After an exchange of greetings, in which there was no evidence of the lately strained relations, he was asked to state his views as to the
disposition of his army. He replied that from its present position along Bull Run
and the Potomac it could not block the multiple routes by which McClellan could
march against the capital. Unequivocally, he stated that his army must fall back to
a position farther south before the roads were dry. Somewhat taken aback, Davis
asked to just what line the retreat would be conducted. When Johnston replied
that he did not know, being unfamiliar with the country between Richmond and
Manassas, Davis was even more alarmed. As he said later, "That a general should
have selected a line which he himself considered untenable, and should not have
ascertained the typography of the country in his rear was inexplicable on any other
theory than that he had neglected the primary duty of a commander."

For the present, however, he let this pass. If Johnston advised retreat, retreat it had to be, so long as he was in command. Davis had to content
himself with trying to get assurances from the general that the army's supplies
and equipment, particularly the large-caliber guns along the Potomac and the
mountains of subsistence goods now stored in forward depots, would not be
abandoned. He did not get it. Johnston merely said that he would do what he
could to delay the retreat until the last possible moment, so that the roads
would be firm enough to bear the heavy guns and the high-piled wagons. Further than that he would not go. The meeting broke up without any specific date
being set for the withdrawal. All that was determined was that the army would
move southward to take up a securer line whenever practicable.

Back at his hotel, it was Johnston's turn to be alarmed. He found the

★

lobby buzzing with rumors that the Manassas intrenchments were about to be abandoned. The news had moved swiftly before him, though he had come directly from the conference: with the result that his reluctance to discuss military secrets with civilians, no matter how highly placed, was confirmed. No tactical maneuver was more difficult than a withdrawal from the presence of a superior enemy. Everything depended on secrecy; for to be caught in motion, strung out on the roads, was to invite destruction. Yet here in the lobby of a Richmond hotel, where every pillar might hide a spy, was a flurry of gossip predicting the very movement he was about to undertake. Next day, riding back to Manassas on the cars, his reluctance was reconfirmed and his anger heightened when a friend approached and asked if it was true that the Bull Run line was about to be abandoned. There could be no chance that the man had overheard the news by accident, for he was deaf. Nor did it improve the general's humor when he arrived that afternoon to find his headquarters already abuzz with talk of the impending evacuation.

No tactical maneuver was more difficult than a withdrawal from the presence of a superior enemy. Everything depended on secrecy; for to be caught in motion, strung out on the roads, was to invite destruction.

Two things he determined to do in reaction: 1) to get his army out of there as quickly as he could — if possible, before McClellan had time to act on the leaked information — and 2) to confide no more in civilians, which as far as he was concerned included the Chief Executive. The first was easier said than done, however. Rain fell all the following day, drenching alike the inaugural throng on Capitol Square and the roads of northern Virginia. The army was stalled in a sea of mud, just when Johnston was most anxious to get it moving. Well-mounted cavalry, riding light, could not average two miles an hour along the roads. Four-horse teams could not haul the field artillery guns, and nothing at all could budge the heavier pieces. The general's determination to share none of his plans with the Government did not prevent his expressing his ire and apprehension in dispatches which repeated his former complaints and advanced new ones. "A division of five brigades is without generals," he wrote on the 25th, "and at least half the field officers are absent — generally sick. The accumulation of subsistence stores at Manassas is now a great evil. The Commissary General was requested more than once to suspend these supplies. A very extensive meat-packing establishment at Thoroughfare is also a great incumbrance.

★

A photo of the Manassas Junction rail yard shows destruction wrought by Confederates before they evacuated in March 1862.

The great quantities of personal property in our camps is a still greater one."

He did what he could to hasten his army's departure, but with horses and wagons foundered and mired on the roads, he had to depend solely on the single-track Orange & Alexandria Railroad. Overcrowded, it quickly snarled to a standstill and pitched the general's anguished cries an octave higher. In truth, there was much to vex him, here where ruin stared him in the face. The amount of personal baggage piled along the railroad "was appalling to behold," one witness said. A "trunk had come with every volunteer," Johnston later declared, reporting now that the army, over his protest, "had accumulated a supply of baggage like that of Xerxes' myriads." All this time, while he was struggling to save what he could with so little success, there had been reports of enemy advances, each a confirmation of his fears. Soon after his return from the capital, a Union force had appeared at Harpers Ferry, from which position it could move forward and outflank him on the left. Two weeks later, March 5, he was warned of "unusual activity" on the Maryland shore opposite Dumfries, indicating preparations for attack. This was the movement he feared most, considering it not only the most dangerous, but also the most likely. An advance from there would turn his right and bring the Federals between his army and Richmond.

That did it. He did not intend to let himself get caught like that other Johnston in the West, who lost half his army through delay in pulling back when enemy pressure increased the strain beyond the breaking point. To retreat now meant the loss of much equipment. The heavy guns were still in place along the Potomac; supplies and personal baggage were still piled high along the railroad. But equipment was nothing, compared to the probable loss of men and possible loss of the war itself. Nor was terrain, not even the "sacred soil" of his native state. That same day he issued orders for all his forces east of the Blue Ridge to fall back to the line of the Rappahannock.

Davis in Richmond knew nothing of this. Ever since Johnston's departure he had been urging a delay in the retrograde movement. In fact, when Virginia officials came to him with a plan for mass recruitment to turn back the invaders, Davis took heart and urged the general to hold his ground while the army was brought up to strength for an offensive, which he now referred to as "first policy." March 10, believing that Johnston and his army still held the Manassas intrenchments, he wired: "Further assurance given to me this day that you shall be promptly and adequately reënforced, so as to enable you to maintain your position and resume first policy when the roads will permit."

Johnston was not there to receive it, nor were any of his men. The cavalry rear guard had pulled out that morning, following the southward trail of the army on its way to the Rappahannock, accompanied by its general—who was already contemplating another retreat, from there back to the Rapidan. The one in progress had not gone well. One division, in an advance position, had not been informed of the movement at all, but was left to find its way out as best it could. The heavy guns were left in their emplacements, some of them not even thrown from their carriages. Supplies and equipment, including the trunks the volunteers had brought, went up in smoke. The packing plant at Thoroughfare Gap was put to the torch, along with one million pounds of meat remaining after farmers in the neighborhood had been given all they could haul away. For twenty miles around, all down the greening slopes of Bull Run Mountain, there was a smell of burning bacon, an aroma which the natives would remember through the hungry months ahead.

★ ★ ★

Shelby Foote

The ironclads U.S.S. Monitor (center) and C.S.S. Virginia (left) exchange shots at close range during their duel at Hampton Roads on March 9, 1862.

McClellan Moves to the Peninsula

1862 ★ ★ ★ ★ ★

Lincoln's efforts all this time as **Commander in Chief,** though on the face of it they were exerted in quite the opposite direction and for an entirely different purpose, were much like those of his southern counterpart; for while Davis had been trying to get Johnston to hold his ground, Lincoln had been doing his best to nudge McClellan forward. All through the fall and winter, as far as these two tasks were concerned, Lincoln had failed and Davis had succeeded. Both generals stayed exactly where they were. Yet in the end it was the northern leader who was successful: Johnston fell back and McClellan at last went forward. In both cases, however, on that final day, March 9, the civilian heads were shown to have urged good counsel to generals who now were exposed before the public in a cold unflattering light. Johnston fled where no man pursued, and McClellan encountered none of the bloody opposition he had predicted.

For both civil leaders the time had been long and harrowing, a season of waste and unhappiness for Lincoln no less than for Davis. The burden of action was on the North; the South had only to keep the status quo, which was exactly what she had been doing here in Virginia. If on the northern side the gloom had been relieved by victories East and West — Roanoke Island and Fort Donelson — it had no bright, original, face-to-face East-West triumph such as

Manassas or Wilson's Creek to hark back to. Also, for Lincoln, the period of inaction around Washington had been darkened by personal tragedy, including the death of one of his sons and signs that his wife was losing her mind. For him the year had opened, not with a glimmer as of dawn, but rather with gathering shadows, as of dusk. The army head was down with typhoid; the bottom was out of the tub; "What shall I do?" he groaned in his melancholy.

It was January 10; Quartermaster General M. C. Meigs replied that if the typhoid diagnosis was correct it meant a six-weeks' illness for McClellan, during which time the nation's armies would be leaderless and vulnerable. He suggested that the President call a conference of the ranking officers of the Army of the Potomac, one of whom might have to take over in a crisis. Lincoln liked the advice and called the meeting for that evening. Two generals attended, McDowell and William B. Franklin, along with several cabinet members. Lincoln told

Lincoln told them the situation and expressed his desire for an early offensive. If McClellan did not want to use the army, he said, he would like to borrow it for a while.

them the situation and expressed his desire for an early offensive. If McClellan did not want to use the army, he said, he would like to borrow it for a while.

McDowell replied that he would be willing to try his hand at another advance on Richmond by way of Manassas, while Franklin, who had taken part in that first debacle under McDowell and was moreover in the confidence of McClellan, favored the roundabout salt-water route, approaching the southern capital from the east. On this divided note the conference adjourned. Next night, when they met again, the generals were agreed that the overland method was best, despite the previous failure, because it would require less time for preparation. Pleased with this decision, Lincoln adjourned the second meeting, instructing the generals to go back to their headquarters, work on the plan, and return tomorrow night. They did return, having worked on it all through the day, but the third White House session was brief, since they still had much to do.

The fourth such conference, on the 13th, was the last. McClellan was there—pale and shaky, but very much there. He had gotten wind of what was going on: perhaps from Stanton, who had been visiting him and murmuring, "They are counting on your death": Stanton was adept at this kind of thing, having served in Buchanan's cabinet as an informer for the opposition. Anyhow, Mc-

Clellan had learned of the meetings and had risen from his sickbed to confront these men who met behind his back. As a result, the atmosphere was strained. According to McClellan, "my unexpected appearance caused very much the effect of a shell in a powder magazine." When Lincoln asked McDowell to outline the plan he had been working on, McDowell gave it nervously and wound up with an apology for offering his opinion in the presence of his chief. "You are entitled to have any opinion you please!" McClellan said, obviously miffed.

During the discussion which followed, while Lincoln kept asking where and when an offensive could be launched, McClellan remained silent. Seward drawled that he didn't much care whether the army whipped the rebels at Manassas or in Richmond itself, so long as it whipped them *some*where. McClellan kept silent. Finally Chase questioned him directly, asking what he intended to do with the army and when he intended to do it. The general replied that he had a perfectly good plan, with a perfectly good schedule of execution, but he would not discuss it in front of civilians unless the President ordered him to do so. He would say, however, that Buell was about to move forward in Kentucky, after which he himself would move. Another awkward silence followed. Presently Lincoln asked him if he "counted upon any particular time." He was not asking him to divulge it, he added hastily; he just wanted to know if he had it in mind. McClellan said he did. "Then I will adjourn this meeting," Lincoln said.

McClellan did not go back to his sickbed. Now that he was up, he stayed up, his youth and stout constitution — he had reached thirty-five in December — permitting him to convalesce on horseback, so to speak. Once more he spent "long days in the saddle and . . . nights in the office," riding to inspect the camps and returning with a jaunty salute the worshipful cheers of his soldiers. There was something other than cheering in the air, however. For one thing, there was suspicion: which meant that the Joint Committee on the Conduct of the War was interested. Now that he was up where they could get at him, the committeemen summoned the general to appear and be examined.

Ben Wade and Zachariah Chandler — who, along with Andrew Johnson, were the members from the Senate — did most of the questioning. Chandler began it by asking why the army, after five long months of training, was not marching out to meet the enemy. McClellan began explaining that there were only two bridges across to Alexandria, which did not satisfy the requirement that a commander must safeguard his lines of retreat in event that his men were repulsed.

"General McClellan," Chandler interrupted. He spoke with the forthright tone of a man translating complicated matters into simpler terms for laymen. "If I understand you correctly, before you strike at the rebels you want to be sure of plenty of room so you can run in case they strike back."

"Or in case you get scared," Wade put in.

McClellan then went into a rather drawn-out explanation of how wars were fought. Lines of retirement were sometimes as necessary to an army's survival, he said, as lines of communication and supply. The committeemen listened scornfully. It was not this they had called him in to tell them.

"General," Wade said, "you have all the troops you have called for, and if you haven't enough, you shall have more. They are well organized and equipped, and the loyal people of this country expect that you will make a short and decisive campaign. Is it really necessary for you to have more bridges over the Potomac before you move?"

"Not that. Not that exactly," McClellan told him. "But we must bear in mind the necessity of having everything ready in case of a defeat, and keep our lines of retreat open."

After this, they let him go in disgust. When he had gone, Chandler turned to Wade and sneered. "I don't know much about war," he

The Albany Contractors who have "influence" at Washington, a

said, "but it seems to me that this is infernal, unmitigated cowardice."

Wade thought so, too, and as chairman he went to see Lincoln about it. McClellan must be discarded, he cried. When the President asked who should be put in his place, Wade snorted: "Anybody!"

"Wade," Lincoln replied sadly, "anybody will do for you, but I must have somebody."

★ ★ ★ **A**lready that week he had made one replacement in a high place. For months now there had been growing reports of waste and graft in the War Department; of contracts strangely let; of shoddy cloth, tainted pork, spavined horses, and guns that would not shoot; of the Vermont jobber who boasted at Willard's, grinning, "You can sell anything to the government at almost any price you've got the guts to ask."

Simon Cameron was responsible, though there was no evidence that the Secretary had profited personally except in the use of his office to pay off his political debts and strengthen his political position. Lincoln could understand this last, having himself done likewise —in point of fact, that was how Cameron got the job—and he knew, too, that much of the waste and bungling, much of the greed and dishonesty, even, was incident to the enormous task of preparing the unprepared nation for war and increasing the army from 16,000 to better than half a million men in the process. All the same, the Pennsylvanian was unquestionably lax in his conduct of business affairs, and when Lincoln warned him of this, resisting the general outcry for his removal, Cameron

Their Victim.

HW
1861

A wartime cartoon shows the sale of shoddy goods to Federal agents and, at right, the victim of their greed.

made his first really serious mistake. He made it, however, not through any ordinary brand of stupidity — Cameron was a very canny man — but rather through his canniness in trying to safeguard his position in the cabinet by strengthening his position in the public eye and in the minds of the increasingly powerful radicals in Congress. He fell because he did what many men had done before and what others would do in the future, after he himself was off the scene. He underestimated Lincoln.

Despite the example of Frémont, or perhaps because he thought that the furor which had followed Frémont's dismissal would have taught Lincoln a lesson, Cameron reasoned that by ingratiating himself with the Jacobins he would insure himself against any action by the President, who would not dare to antagonize them further by molesting another man who had won their favor. Any attack on slavery was the answer. Emancipation was the issue on which Lincoln was treading softest, since it was the one that cut sharpest along the line dividing the Administration's supporters and opponents. Accordingly, with the help of his legal adviser Stanton, Cameron drafted and included in his annual Department report a long passage advocating immediate freedom for southern slaves and their induction into the Union army, thereby adding muscle to the arm of the republic and weakening the enemy, who as "rebellious traitors" had forfeited their rights to any property at all, let alone the ownership of fellow human beings. Without consulting the President — though it was usual for such documents to be submitted for approval — the Secretary had the report printed and sent out to the postmasters of all the principal cities for distribution to the press as soon as it was being read to Congress.

So far all was well. Even when Lincoln discovered what had been done and recalled the pamphlet by telegraphic order, for reprinting without the offensive passage, things still went as Cameron had expected. Critics of the President's tread-easy policy, comparing the original with the expurgated report — some copies of course escaped destruction, so that both versions appeared in the papers — were harsh in their attacks, charging Lincoln simultaneously with dictatorship and timidity. The Jacobins reacted as expected by taking the Secretary to their bosoms and pronouncing him "one of us." Other praises came his way, less vigorous perhaps, but no less pleasant. "You have touched the national heart," a friend declared, while another, in a punning mood, wrote that he much preferred the "Simon pure" article in the *Tribune* to the "bogus" report in the *World*. From Paris a member of the consulate, hearing of the dissension in the President's official family, wrote home asking: "Are Cameron and Frémont to be canonized as martyrs?"

Cameron might be canonized, at any rate by the antislavery radicals, but it did not appear that he would be martyred by anyone, least of all by Lincoln, who seemed to have learned a dearly bought lesson in martyring Frémont. The report had been published in mid-December, and now in January he still had made no further reference to the matter. Outwardly the relationship between the two men remained cordial, though Cameron still felt some inward qualms, perhaps because he sensed that Lincoln's measure was not so easily taken. The thing had gone *too* well.

Then on January 11, a Saturday—the date of the second of the three conferences with McDowell and Franklin, none of which Cameron had been urged to attend, despite his position as Secretary of War—he learned that he had been right to feel qualms. He received a brief note in which Lincoln informed him curtly, out of the blue: "I... propose nominating you to the Senate next Monday as Minister to Russia." Almost literally, he was being banished to Siberia for his sins.

Cameron was on his way to St Petersburg, having earned not martyrdom and canonization, as some had hoped or feared, but banishment and damage to a reputation already considered shaky.

The sins were political, and as a politician he could appreciate the justice of his punishment. He suffered anguish, though, at the manner in which it was inflicted. To be rebuked thus in a brief note, he complained, "meant personal as well as political destruction." So Lincoln, who cared little for the manner of his going, just so he went, agreed that Cameron might antedate a letter of resignation, to which he would reply with a letter of acceptance expressing his "affectionate esteem" and "undiminished confidence" in the Secretary's "ability, patriotism, and fidelity to the public trust." It was done accordingly and Cameron's name was sent to Congress for confirmation as Minister to Russia. There, however, he encountered opposition, not only from members of his own party, the Democrats, but also from some of the radical Republicans who so lately had clustered round him and proclaimed him "one of us." At last the nomination was put through; Cameron was on his way to St Petersburg, having earned not martyrdom and canonization, as some had hoped or feared, but banishment and damage to a reputation already considered shaky. One senator, a

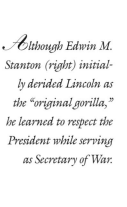

Although Edwin M. Stanton (right) initially derided Lincoln as the "original gorilla," he learned to respect the President while serving as Secretary of War.

former colleague, remarked on his departure: "Ugh! ugh! Send word to the Czar to bring in his things of nights."

In this case Lincoln engaged in no fruitless search for "somebody" to replace him. The somebody was ready and very much at hand: Edwin McMasters Stanton, who as his predecessor's legal adviser had helped to charge and fuse the bomb that blew him out of the War Department and the Cabinet, while Stanton himself was sucked into the resultant vacuum and sat ensconced as successor before all the bits of wreckage had hit the ground. Whether he had proceeded with malice aforethought in this instance was not known; but it was not unthinkable. Stanton had done devious things in his time. A corporation lawyer, he delighted also in taking criminal cases when these were challenging and profitable enough. His fees were large and when one prospective client protested, Stanton asked: "Do you think I would argue the wrong side for less?" For a murder defense he once took as his fee the accused man's only possession, the house he lived in. When he had won the case and was about to convert the mortgage into cash, the man tried to persuade him to hold off, saying that he would be ruined by the foreclosure. "You deserve to be ruined," Stanton told him, "for you were guilty."

And yet there was another side to him, too, offsetting the savagery, the joy he took in fixing a frightened general or petitioner with the baleful glare of his black little near-sighted eyes behind small, thick-lensed, oval spectacles. He was a bundle of contradictions, his father a New Englander, his mother a Virginian. In private, the forty-seven-year-old lawyer sometimes put his face in his hands and wept from the strain, and if his secretary happened in at such a time he would say, "Not now, please. Not now." He was asthmatic, something of a hysteric as well, and he had more than a touch of morbidity in his nature. His bushy hair was thinning at the front, but he made up for this by letting it grow long at the back and sides. His upper lip he kept clean-shaven to expose a surprisingly sensitive mouth — a reminder that he had been considered hand- some in his youth — while below his lower lip a broad streak of iron-gray ran down the center of his wide black beard. His body was thick-set, bouncy on short but energetic legs. His voice, which was deep in times of calm, rose to piercing shrillness in excitement. One petitioner, badly shaken by the experience, described a Stanton interview by saying, "He came at me like a tiger."

He came at many people like a tiger, especially at those in his De- partment who showed less devotion to work than he himself did. Soon after he took office he received from Harpers Ferry an urgent call for heavy guns. He or- dered them sent at once. Going by the locked arsenal after hours, he learned that the guns were still there: whereupon he ordered the gates broken open, helped the watchmen drag the guns out, and saw them loaded onto a north- bound train. Next morning the arsenal officer reported that he had not found it convenient to ship the guns the day before; he would get them off this morn- ing, he said. "The guns are now at Harpers Ferry!" Stanton barked. "And you, sir, are no longer in the service of the United States Government."

He would engage in no secret deals. Whoever came to him on busi- ness, as for instance seeking a contract, was required to make his request in the sight and hearing of all. Stanton would snap out a Yes or No, then wave him on to make way for the next petitioner. He did not care whose toes he stepped on; "Individuals are nothing," he declared. To a man who came demanding release for a friend locked up on suspicion of treason, Stanton roared: "If I tap that lit- tle bell, I can send *you* to a place where you will never hear the dogs bark. And by heaven I'll do it if you say another word!" He brought to the War Depart- ment a boundless and bounding energy. "As soon as I can get the machinery of the office working, the rats cleared out, and the rat holes stopped," he told an assistant, "we shall *move*." Lincoln himself was by no means exempt from Stan- ton's scorn. Asked when he took office, "What will you do?": "Do? ..." he replied. "I will make Abe Lincoln President of the United States."

The government could use such a man, despite his idiosyncrasies, his sudden judgments and hostile attitude. So could Lincoln use him in his official family, despite the abuse he knew that Stanton had been heaping on him since they first met in Cincinnati, when the big-time lawyer referred to the country one as "that long-armed creature." More recently he had been employing circus epithets; "the original gorilla," he called him, "a low, cunning clown," and "that giraffe." Lincoln knew of some of this, but he still thought he could use him—provided he could handle him. And he believed he could. Stanton's prancing and bouncing, he said, put him in mind of a Methodist preacher out West who got so wrought up in his prayers and exhortations that his congregation was obliged to put bricks in his pockets to hold him down. "We may have to serve Stanton the same way," Lincoln drawled. "But I guess we'll let him jump a while first."

The bricks were applied much sooner than anyone expected. One day the President was busy with a roomful of people and Stanton came hurrying through the doorway, clutching a sheet of paper in his hand. "Mr President," he cried, "this order cannot be signed. I refuse to sign it!" Lincoln told him calmly, "Mr Secretary, I guess that order will have to be signed." In the

---

"This army has got to fight or run away. And while men are striving nobly in the West, the champagne and oysters on the Potomac must be stopped."

— Edwin M. Stanton

---

hush that followed, the two men's eyes met. Then Stanton turned, still with the order in his hand, and went back to his office and signed it.

Whether or not McClellan could handle him, too, was one of the things that remained to be seen. At the outset, the general had good cause to believe that the change in War Department heads would work to his advantage. For on the evening of January 13—the one on which he rose from his sickbed to confront the men who had been conferring behind his back—Stanton came by his quarters and informed him that his nomination as Secretary of War had gone to the Senate that afternoon. Personally, he went on to say, he considered the job a hardship, but the chance of working in close harness with his friend McClellan persuaded him to undergo the sacrifice involved. If the general would approve he would accept. McClellan did approve; he urged acceptance on those grounds. Two days later the nomination was confirmed. Stanton took the post the following day. And almost immediately, from that January 16 on, McClellan found the doors of the War Department barred to him. The Secretary, suddenly hostile, became at once the Young Napoleon's most outspoken critic. McClellan had been given another lesson in the perfidy of the human animal. One more had been added, at the top, to that "set of men . . . unscrupulous and false."

What he did not know was that, all this time, Stanton had been working both sides of the street. While his name was up for approval in the Senate, Charles Sumner was saying: "Mr Stanton, within my knowledge, is one of us." Ben Wade thought so, too. And on the day the new Secretary moved into office their opinion was confirmed. After saying that he was going to "make Abe Lincoln President," Stanton added that as the next order of business, "I will force this man McClellan to fight or throw up." Later that same day he said baldly, "This army has got to fight or run away. And while men are striving nobly in the West, the champagne and oysters on the Potomac must be stopped."

Formerly he had run with the fox and hunted with the hounds. Now he was altogether with the latter. On January 20, at his own request, he appeared before the Joint Committee, and after the hearing its members were loud in his praise. "We are delighted with him," Julian of Indiana exclaimed. In the Senate, Fessenden of Maine announced: "He is just the man we want! We agree on every point: the duties of the Secretary of War, the conduct of the war, the Negro question and everything." In the *Tribune* Horace Greeley hailed him as the man who would know how to deal with "the greatest danger now facing the country — treason in Washington, treason in the army itself, especially the treason which wears the garb of Unionism."

★ ★ ★ **T**reason was a much-used word these days. For Greeley to use it three times within a dependent clause was nothing rare. In fact it was indicative. The syllables had a sound that caught men's ears, overtones of enormity that went beyond such scarehead words as rape or arson or incest. Observing this, the radicals had made it their watchword, their cry in the night, expanding its definition in the process.

Many acts were treasonous now which had never been considered so before. Even a lack of action might be treason, according to these critics in long-skirted broadcloth coats. Delay, for instance: all who counseled delay were their special targets, along with those who favored something less than extermination for rebels. Obviously, the way to administer sudden death was to march out within musket range and bang away until the serpent Rebellion squirmed no more. And as a rallying cry this forthright logic was effective. Up till now the Administration's opposition had been no more than an incidental irritant. By mid-January of this second calendar year of the war, however, so many congressmen had discovered the popular value of pointing a trembling finger at "treason" in high places that their conglomerate, harping voice had grown into a force which had to be reckoned with as surely as the Confederates still intrenched around Manassas.

★

Lincoln the politician understood this perfectly. They were men with power, who knew how to use it ruthlessly, and as such they would have to be dealt with. McClellan the soldier could never see it at all, partly because he operated under the disadvantage of considering himself a gentleman. For him they were willful, evil men, "unscrupulous and false," and as such they should be ignored as beneath contempt, at least by him. He counted on Lincoln to keep them off his back: which Lincoln in fact had promised to do. "I intend to be careful and do as well as possible," McClellan had said. "Don't let them

Although he initially planned to invade Virginia through Urbanna on the Rappahannock, circumstances led McClellan to Fortress Monroe on the York-James peninsula instead.

★

hurry me, is all I ask." And Lincoln had told him, "You shall have your own way in the matter, I assure you." Yet now he seemed to be breaking his promise to McClellan, just as he had broken his word to Frémont, whom he had told: "I have given you carte-blanche. You must use your own judgment, and do the best you can." Frémont had used his judgment, such as it was, and been flung aside. McClellan was discouraged.

That was something else he never understood: Lincoln himself. Some might praise him for being flexible, while others called him slippery, when in truth they were both two words for just one thing. To argue the point was to insist on a distinction that did not exist. Lincoln was out to win the war; and that was all he was out to do, for the present. Unfettered by any need for being or not being a gentleman, he would keep his word to any man only so long as keeping it would help to win the war. If keeping it meant otherwise, he broke it. He kept no promise, anyhow, any longer than the conditions under which it was given obtained. And if any one thing was clear in this time when treason had become a household word, it was that the conditions of three months ago no longer obtained. McClellan would have to go forward or go down.

On January 27, without consulting anyone — least of all McClellan — Lincoln himself composed and issued over his signature, as Commander in Chief of the nation's military forces, General War Order Number 1, in which he announced that a forward movement by all land and naval units would be launched on February 22, to celebrate Washington's Birthday and also, presumably, to disrupt the Confederate inaugural in Richmond. It was not a suggestion, or even a directive. It was a peremptory order, and as such it stated that all commanders afield or afloat would "severally be held to their strict and full responsibilities" for its "prompt execution." Lest there be any misunderstanding as to whether this applied to the general-in-chief and his army around Washington, Lincoln supplemented this with a Special Order four days later, directing that on or before the date announced an expedition would move out from the capital, leaving whatever force would insure the city's safety, and seize a point on the railroad "southwestward of... Manassas Junction."

McClellan was aghast. He had counted on the President to keep the hot-eyed amateurs off his back: yet here, by a sudden and seemingly gleeful leap, Lincoln had landed there himself, joining the others in an all-out game of pile-on. Besides, committed as he was to the Urbanna Plan for loading his army on transports, taking it down the Potomac and up the Rappahannock for a landing in Johnston's rear, the last thing he wanted now was any movement that might alarm the enemy at Manassas into scurrying back to safety. So he went to Lincoln and outlined for the first time in some detail the plan which would be spoiled by any immediate "forward" movement. Lincoln did not like it. It would endanger Washington, he said, in case the rebels tried a quick pounce

while the Federal army was making its roundabout boat-trip to Urbanna. Mc-
Clellan then asked if he could submit in writing his objections to the President's
plan and his reasons for favoring his own. Lincoln said all right, go ahead. While
the general was preparing his brief he received from Lincoln a set of questions,
dated February 3: "Does not your plan involve a larger expenditure of time and
money than mine? Wherein is a victory more certain by your plan than mine?
Would it not be less valuable in that yours would not break a great line of the
enemy's communications, while mine would? In case of disaster, would it not be
more difficult to retreat by your plan than mine?"

In asking these questions Lincoln was meeting McClellan on his own
ground, and McClellan answered him accordingly, professionally ticking off the
flaws in Lincoln's plan and pointing up the strong points of his own. At best, he
declared, the former would result in nothing more than a barren and costly victory which would leave still harder battles to be fought all the way to Richmond,
each time against an enemy who would have retired to a prepared defensive position, while the Federal supply lines stretched longer and more vulnerable with
every doubtful success: whereas the latter, striking at the vitals of the Confederacy, would maneuver Johnston out of his formidable Bull Run intrenchments by
requiring him to turn in defense of his capital and give battle wherever McClellan
chose to fight him, with control of all Virginia in the balance. Supply lines would
run by water, which meant that they would be secure, and in event of the disaster
which Lincoln seemed to fear, the army could retreat down the York-James
peninsula, an area which afforded plenty of opportunity for maneuver because,
"the soil [being] sandy," the roads were "passable at all seasons of the year." Nor
was this all. Besides its other advantages, he wrote, his plan had a flexibility which
the other lacked entirely. If for some reason Urbanna proved undesirable, the
landing could be made at Mobjack Bay or Fortress Monroe, though admittedly
this last would be "less brilliant." As for the question as to whether victory was
more certain by the roundabout route, the general reminded his chief that
"nothing is certain in war." However, he added, "all the chances are in favor of
this project." If Lincoln would give him the go-ahead, along with a little more
time to get ready, "I regard success as certain by all the chances of war."

There Lincoln had it. In submitting the questions he had said, "If you
will give me satisfactory answers . . . I shall gladly yield my plan to yours." Now that
the Young Napoleon had given them, Lincoln yielded; but not gladly. Though he
liked McClellan's plan better now that the general had taken him into his confidence and explained it in detail, he was still worried about what Johnston's army
—better than 100,000 men, according to the Pinkerton reports—might do while
McClellan's was in transit. Confederates in Washington might win foreign recognition for their government, and with it independence. However, since McClellan
had come out so flatly in favor of his own plan and in rejection of the other, Lin-

coln had no choice except to fire him or sustain him. And that in fact was no choice at all. To fire Little Mac would be to risk demoralizing the Army of the Potomac on the eve of great exertions. All the same, Lincoln did not rescind the order for an advance on the 22d. He merely agreed not to require its execution.

Whereupon the radicals returned to the charge, furious that their demands had gone unheeded. Lincoln held them off as best he could, but they were strident and insistent. "For God's sake, at least push back the defiant traitors!" Wade still cried. Lincoln saw that something had to be done to appease them — perhaps by clearing the lower Potomac of enemy batteries, or else by reopening the B & O supply line west of Harpers Ferry. Either would be at least a sop to throw the growlers. So he went again to McClellan; who explained once more that the rebels along the lower Potomac were just where he wanted them to be when he made his Urbanna landing in their rear, forcing them thus to choose between flight and capture. It would be much better to have them there, he said, than back on the Rappahannock contesting his debarkation. Lincoln was obliged to admit that as logic this had force.

As for the reopening of the B & O, McClellan remarked that he had it in mind already. What he wanted to avoid was another Ball's Bluff or anything resembling the fiasco which had resulted from making a river crossing without a way to get back in event of repulse. He was bringing up from downriver a fleet of canal boats which could be lashed together to bridge the upper Potomac. Across this newfangled but highly practical device he would throw a force for repairing and protecting the railroad, a force that would be exempt from disaster because its line of retreat would be secure. Lincoln liked the notion and was delighted that something at last was about to be done. Then came word from McClellan that the project had had to be abandoned because the boats turned out to be six inches too wide for the lift-locks at Harpers Ferry. Once more Lincoln was cast down, his expectations dashed, and Secretary Chase, a solemn, indeed a pompous man, got off his one joke of the war. The campaign had died, he said, of lockjaw.

Washington's Birthday came and went, and the Army of the Potomac remained in its training camps, still awaiting the day when its commander decided that the time had come for it to throw the roundhouse left designed to knock Virginia out of the war. In the West, meanwhile, Thomas had counterpunched Crittenden clean out of East Kentucky, and Grant had delivered to Sidney Johnston's solar plexus the one-two combination that sent him reeling, all the way from Bowling Green to northern Alabama. Burnside, down in North Carolina, had rabbit-punched Huger and Wise, and even now was following up with a series of successes. Everywhere, boldness had been crowned with success: everywhere, that was, except in Virginia, where boldness was unknown.

Stanton could see the moral plainly enough, and when Greeley came out with an editorial praising the new Secretary and giving him chief credit for the victories—he had been in office exactly a month on the day Fort Donelson fell—Stanton replied with a letter that was printed in the *Tribune*, declining the praise and making a quick backthrust at McClellan in the process: "Much has been said recently of military combinations and 'organizing victory.' I hear such phrases with apprehension. They commenced in infidel France with the Italian campaign, and resulted in Waterloo. Who can organize victory? We owe our recent victories to the spirit of the Lord, that moved our soldiers to rush into battle and filled the hearts of our enemies with terror and dismay. . . . We may well rejoice at the recent victories, for they teach that battles are to be won now, and by us, in the same and only manner that they were ever won by any people, since the days of Joshua—by boldly pursuing and striking the foe. What, under the blessing of Providence, I conceive to be the true organization of victory and military combinations to win this war was declared in a few words by General Grant's message to General Buckner: 'I propose to move immediately upon your works.'"

Lincoln, too, could praise Grant and the Lord for victories in the West, but the news came at a time when there was sickness in the house and, presently, sorrow. Robert was at Harvard; "one of those rare-ripe sort," his father called him once, "that are smarter at about five than ever after." It was Willie, the middle son and his mother's favorite, who was the studious member of the family; Tad, the youngest, could still neither read nor write at the age of nine. Now Willie lay sick with what the doctor said was "bilious fever." He got better, then worse, then suddenly much worse, until one afternoon Lincoln came into the room where one of his secretaries lay half-asleep on a couch. "Well, Nicolay," he said, "my boy is gone. He is actually gone!" And then, as if having spoken the words aloud had brought their reality home to him, he broke into tears and left.

Hard as it was for Lincoln to absorb the shock in this time of strain, the blow was even harder on his wife. All her life she had been ambitious, but in her ambition she had looked forward more to the pleasures than to the trials of being First Lady—only to discover, once the place was hers, that the tribulations far outnumbered the joys. In Richmond, Varina Davis could overlook, or anyhow seem to overlook, being referred to as "a coarse Western woman," which was false. Mary Lincoln could not weather half so well being criticized for "putting on airs," which was true. A fading Kentucky belle, she clung to her gentility, already sorely tried by two decades of marriage with a man who, whatever his political attainments, liked to sit around the house in slippers and shirtsleeves. She punctuated her conversation with "sir" and spent a great deal of money on dresses and bonnets and new furnishings for the antiquated White House. Washington was not what she had expected, its former social grace having largely departed with the southern-mannered hostesses whose positions had been taken over by Republican ladies whose chief virtues were not social.

Yet these disappointments were by no means the worst she had to bear. Her loyalty was undivided, but the same could not be said of her family, which had split badly over the issues that split Kentucky and the nation. A brother and a half-sister stayed with the Union; another brother and three half-brothers went with the South, while three half-sisters were married to Confederates. This division of her family, together with her Bluegrass manner, caused critics to say that she was "two-thirds slavery and the other third secesh." The rumors were enlarged as the war continued. The President's enemies sought to make political

While the death of their son Willie (right) devastated President Lincoln, the loss was an even bigger blow to the boy's already disturbed mother, Mary Todd Lincoln (below).

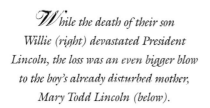

capital with a whispering campaign, accusing Mrs Lincoln of specific acts of treason, which at last reached such proportions that the matter was taken up by a
congressional investigating committee. One morning her husband came unexpectedly into one of its secret sessions to announce in a sad voice: "I, Abraham
Lincoln, President of the United States, appear of my own volition before this
committee of the Senate to say that I, of my own knowledge, know that it is un-
true that any of my family hold treasonable communication with the enemy."

That removed her from the reach of the committee, but it did not
spare her the ridicule being heaped upon her almost daily in the opposition papers, which struck at the husband through the wife. And now, with all this burden on her, to lose her favorite child was altogether more than she could bear.
She wept grievously and was often in hysterics. She could neither accept nor reject her sorrow, and between the two she lost her mental balance. Lincoln had
Tad, whom he took more and more for his own and even slept with. He had,
too, the day-long, sometimes night-long occupation of running the country. She
had nothing, not even Lincoln: who did not help matters by leading her one day
to a window and pointing to the lunatic asylum as he said, "Mother, do you see
that large white building on the hill yonder? Try and control your grief, or it
will drive you mad and we may have to send you there."

★ ★ ★ A distracted wife was one among the many problems
Lincoln faced. His main problem was still McClellan.
During the weeks since the general first outlined the Ur-
banna plan, much of what he called its brilliance had worn off, at least for Lincoln, who still had fears that it would expose the capital to capture. Again he
told McClellan his doubts, and once more McClellan sought to allay them, this
time by proposing to submit the plan to his twelve division commanders for a
professional decision. They assembled March 8, many of them hearing details of
the plan for the first time. When the vote was taken they favored it, eight to
four, and repaired in a body to the White House to announce the result to the
President, whose objections thus were effectively spiked again. As he told Stanton, who shared his mistrust, "We can do nothing else than accept their plan
and discard all others. . . . We can't reject it and adopt another without assuming
all the responsibility in the case of the failure of the one we adopt."

One thing he could do, and did, that same day. The members of the
Joint Committee had called on him the week before with a plan for reorganizing
the Army of the Potomac into corps. This, they saw, would not only gain prestige
for certain generals who had their favor—McDowell, for example—but would
weaken McClellan's authority as general-in-chief, since, as the committeemen
saw it, corps commanders would take orders directly from Stanton. Lincoln saw
other merits in the plan. For one thing it would simplify the transmission of or-

★

ders and lessen the burden on the Young Napoleon. Besides, he was anxious to placate Wade and the others wherever he could. When he went to McClellan, however, to urge that it be effected and to get the general's recommendations for the appointments, McClellan told him that he had already thought it over and had decided that it would be best to wait until all the division commanders had been tested in combat before making his recommendations. Once more Lincoln had been shown that he would lose in any face-to-face encounter with the general over military logic. So the following week, when he decided to act on the matter, he did so without consulting McClellan. Later that day, after having reported their vote on the Urbanna plan, the division commanders learned that four of their number had been appointed to corps command: McDowell, E. V. Sumner, S. P. Heintzelman, and E. D. Keyes. Notification came in the form of a paper headed "President's General War Order Number 2."

Whatever elation this document produced in the breasts of the men thus elevated, it came as a terrible shock to McClellan, even though the earlier General War Order's being numbered had indicated that there might well be others. The shock was mainly due to the fact that among the four who were raised to corps command — and would therefore have the principal responsibility, under McClellan himself, for executing the Urbanna plan — three had voted against it in the balloting that morning. The officers he wanted had been held back. Franklin, for instance, who had spoken in favor of the sea route at the conference held while McClellan was in bed with fever, was not appointed, nor were any of the others among his protégés; "gentlemen and Democrats," he called them, who thought of war and politics as he did. He felt himself hobbled at the outset, held in check by a high council of Republicans friendly toward the enemies who were working for his ruin.

If he had ever doubted that they were out to wreck him, any such doubts had been dispelled during the early morning hours of that same busy March 8. He learned of whispered charges, touching his honor as a soldier, and he learned of them from Lincoln himself, who had sent for him to come over to the White House after breakfast. As McClellan told it later, he found the President looking worried; there was "a very ugly matter," Lincoln said, which needed airing. Again he hesitated, and McClellan, seated opposite, suggested that perhaps it would be best to come right out with it. Well, Lincoln said, choosing his words cautiously at first, there was an ugly rumor going round, to the effect that the Urbanna plan "was conceived with the traitorous intent of removing its defenders from Washington, and thus giving over to the enemy the capital and the government, thus left defenseless." He added that the whole thing had a sound and look of treason.

The word was out, and it brought McClellan straight up out of his chair, declaring that he would "permit no one to couple the word treason with my name," and demanding an immediate retraction. No, no, Lincoln said hastily; he did not believe a word of it; he was only repeating what had been told him. Somewhat calmer, McClellan suggested "caution in the use of language," and reëmphasized that he could "permit no doubt to be thrown upon my intentions." Lincoln again apologized, and let the matter go at that. McClellan left to round up his division commanders for a vote that would prove that the proposed campaign was militarily sound, then brought them back to announce their eight-to-four support in Lincoln's presence.

As far as McClellan was concerned, that settled it. He had shown him, once and for all. But then, as soon as he turned his back, War Order 2 came dropping onto his desk, and he was upset all over again. The day had opened with charges of treason and closed with the appointment of unsympathetic officers to head the corps of the army he was about to take into battle. As he saw it, Lincoln had gone over to the scoundrels, bag and baggage; or, in McClellan's words, "the effects of the intrigues by which he had been surrounded became apparent."

He did not see, then or ever, that he had helped to bring all this trouble on himself by not taking Lincoln into his confidence sooner. And if he had seen it, the seeing would not have made the end result any easier to abide; McClellan was never one to find ease in admission of blame. Nor did he see that Lincoln had not called him to the White House merely to insult him by repeating ugly rumors, that what he was really trying to tell him was that Wade and the others were powerful and vindictive men who would hurt him all they could, and with him the cause, if they were not dealt with in some manner that would take some of the pressure off their anger: whereas the Young Napoleon, who had been before them and heard them accuse him of cowardice, was determined to yield them not a single military inch of the solid ground he stood on. Whatever they took from him they must take by force, with Lincoln's help. Already they had taken much, including his trust of Lincoln, and he could see that they were after more, with an excellent chance of getting it.

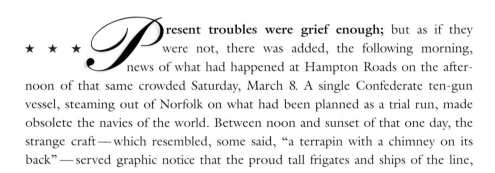

★ ★ ★ *P*resent troubles were grief enough; but as if they were not, there was added, the following morning, news of what had happened at Hampton Roads on the afternoon of that same crowded Saturday, March 8. A single Confederate ten-gun vessel, steaming out of Norfolk on what had been planned as a trial run, made obsolete the navies of the world. Between noon and sunset of that one day, the strange craft — which resembled, some said, "a terrapin with a chimney on its back" — served graphic notice that the proud tall frigates and ships of the line, with their billowing sails and high wooden sides that could flash out hundred-gun salvos, would soon be gone in all their beauty and obsolescence.

She herself had been one of them, once: the 350-ton, forty-gun U.S. steam frigate *Merrimac*, burned and scuttled in her berth when the Union forces abandoned Gosport Navy Yard the previous spring. She sank so quickly her hull and engines were saved from the fire, and Lieutenant John M. Brooke, C.S.N., went to Secretary Mallory with a plan for converting her into a seagoing ironclad, wherewith the tightening Federal blockade might be lifted. Mallory approving, she was plugged, pumped out, and raised, the salt mud swabbed out of her engines and her hull cut down to the water's edge. While some workers were attaching a four-foot iron ram-beak to her prow, others were building amidships a slope-walled structure, 130 feet long and seven feet tall, in which to house her guns, two 6- and two 7-inch rifles and six 9-inch smoothbores, the

A single Confederate ten-gun vessel, steaming out of Norfolk on what had been planned as a trial run, made obsolete the navies of the world.

two lightest pieces being bound at the breech with iron hoops, shrunk on like the tires on wagon wheels, to strengthen them for firing extra-heavy powder charges: another Brooke innovation. Finally, they covered her all over, down to two feet below the waterline, with overlapping plates of two-inch armor rolled from railroad iron at the Tredegar Works in Richmond. She was finished. What she lacked in looks, and she was totally lacking there, she made up for in her ability to give and take a pounding.

However, she had faults more serious than her ugliness: faults which caused head-shakings and predictions that she would be "an enormous metallic burial-case" for her crew. For one, the weight of all that iron made her squat so low in the water, 22 feet, that she had to confine her movements to deep-water channels. Not that she was much at maneuvering in the first place; "unwieldy as Noah's ark," one of her officers called her. Her top speed was five knots, and what with her great length and awkward steering, it took half an hour to turn her in calm water. This was mainly because of her wheezy, antiquated engines, which had been condemned on the *Merrimac*'s last cruise and had scarcely been improved by the fire and the months of immersion. Nevertheless, Mallory and her builders expected great things of her: nothing less, in fact, than the raising of the blockade by the destruction of whatever attempted to enforce it. They renamed her the *Virginia*, recruited a large part of her 300-man crew from the army, and placed her in the charge of Commodore Franklin Buchanan, the sixty-two-year-old "Father of Annapolis," so called because, under the old flag, he had been instrumental in founding the Naval Academy and had served as its first superintendent. Some measure of Mallory's expectations of the *Virginia* was shown by the fact that he had given command of her to the ranking man in the whole Confederate navy.

When she steamed down Elizabeth River on her trial run at noon that Saturday, her inherent faults—low speed, deep draft, and sluggish handling—were immediately apparent. Her guns had not yet been fired, and workmen still swarmed over her superstructure, making last-minute adjustments. But as she came in sight of open water, Buchanan saw across the Roads five warships of the blockade squadron lying at anchor, three off Fort Monroe and two off Newport News. The three were the *Minnesota* and the *Roanoke*, sister ships of the *Merrimac*, and the fifty-gun frigate *St Lawrence*. The two were the *Congress*, another

Pierced by the C.S.S. Virginia's ram and listing badly, the U.S.S. Cumberland fights on in Hampton Roads, March 8, 1862.

fifty-gun frigate, and the thirty-gun sloop *Cumberland*. It was more than the commodore could resist. He hove-to off Craney Island, sent the workmen ashore, cleared the *Virginia*'s decks for action, and set out north across the Roads with his crew at battle stations. The "trial run" would be just that—all-out.

On the southern shore, from Willoughby Spit to Ragged Island, gray-clad infantry and artillerymen lined the beaches. They saw his intention and tossed their caps, cheering and singing "Dixie." Across the water, from Old Point Comfort westward, men in blue observed it too, but with mixed emotions. They had heard that this strange new thing was being built, and now they saw her coming slowly toward them. To an Indiana volunteer, watching her across five miles of water, she "looked very much like a house submerged to the eaves, borne onward by a flood."

It was washday aboard the Federal warships, sailor clothes drying in the rigging. Yet there was plenty of time in which to get ready for what was coming so slowly at them. The *Congress* and the *Cumberland* cleared for action, and when the *Virginia* came within range, the former gave her a well-aimed broadside: which broke against the sloping iron with no apparent effect at all. Ports closed tight, she came on, biding her time as she closed the range, unperturbed and inexorable. Another salvo struck her, together with shots from the coastal batteries: with no more effect than before. Then her ports came open, swinging deliberately upward on their hinges to expose the muzzles of her guns. Turning, she raked the *Congress* with a starboard broadside and rammed the *Cumberland* at near right-angles just under her fore rigging, punching a hole which one of her officers said would admit "a horse and cart"—except for the iron beak which broke off in her when the Confederate swung clear. The *Cumberland* began to fill, firing as long as a gun remained above water. Called on to surrender, her captain shouted, "Never! I'll sink alongside!"

Presently he did just that, his flag still flying from the mainmast, defiant above the waves after the ship herself struck bottom. Horrified, the captain of the *Congress* slipped his cable and tried to get away before the ironclad could complete its ponderous turn, but ran aground in the attempt. The *Virginia*, held at 200-yard range by her deeper draft, raked the helpless ship from end to end until, her captain dead and her scuppers running red with blood, a lieutenant ran up the white flag of surrender.

Buchanan ceased firing and stood by to take on prisoners, but the coastal batteries redoubled their fire under command of Brigadier General Joseph K. Mansfield, West Point '22. When one of his own officers protested that the enemy had the right to take possession unmolested once the *Congress* struck her flag, the crusty old regular replied, "I know the damned ship has surrendered, but *we* haven't!" Two Confederate lieutenants were killed in this unexpected burst of artillery and musketry, and Buchanan himself was wounded.

★

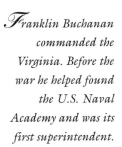

Franklin Buchanan commanded the Virginia. Before the war he helped found the U.S. Naval Academy and was its first superintendent.

So were many of the Union sailors on the decks of the surrendered ship—including Buchanan's brother, a lieutenant who had stayed with the old flag and who presently died in the flames on the quarterdeck when the *Virginia* dropped back and retaliated by setting the *Congress* afire with red-hot cannonballs that started fires wherever they struck wood.

By now the three frigates off Old Point Comfort had started west to join the fight. Hugging the northern shore to avoid the rebel guns on Sewell's Point, however, the *Roanoke* and the *St Lawrence* ran aground, and presently the *Minnesota*, left alone to deal with the iron monster, did likewise. It was well for her that it happened so, for the *Virginia*, having finished with the *Congress*, turned to deal with her erstwhile sister ship and found that, the tide being on the ebb, she could not come within effective range. So she drew off across the Roads to unload her wounded, survey her damage, and wait for the flooding of the tide tomorrow morning, when she intended to complete this first day's work by sinking the three grounded frigates.

Her 21 killed and wounded, including Buchanan, were removed, after which the officers surveyed the effects of the fight on the ship herself. The damage, though considerable, was not vital. In spite of having been exposed to the concentrated fire of at least one hundred guns, her armor showed only dents, no cracks, and nothing inside the shell was hurt. Outside was another matter. She had lost her iron beak, and two of her guns had had their muzzles blown off; besides which, one of her crew later wrote, "one anchor,

★

the smoke-stack, and the steam pipes were shot away. Railings, stanchions, boat-davits, everything was swept clean."

All this seemed a small enough price to pay for the victory they had won that afternoon and the one they had prepared for completion tomorrow. Officers and men stayed up on deck, too elated to sleep, and watched the *Congress* burn. She lit up the Roads from across the way and paled the second-quarter moon, which came up early. From time to time, another of her loaded guns went off with a deep reverberant boom, but the big effect did not come until 1 o'clock in the morning, when her magazine blew up. After that, the Confederate crew turned in to get some sleep. Ashore, a Georgia private, writing home of the sea battle he had watched, exulted that the *Virginia* had "invented a new way of destroying the blockade. Instead of raising it, she sinks it. Or I believe she is good at both," he added, "for the one she burned was raised to a pretty considerable height when the magazine exploded."

★ ★ ★ *A* telegram reached Washington from Fort Monroe within two hours of the explosion of the *Congress*, informing the War Department that the Confederates' indestructible "floating battery" had sunk two frigates and would sink three more tomorrow before moving against the fortress itself—after which there was no telling what might happen.

Lincoln had his cabinet in session by 6.30, the prevailing gloom being broken only by the Secretary of War, who put on for his colleagues a remarkable display of jangled nerves. The jaunty Seward was glum for once; Chase was petulant; the President himself seemed quite unstrung; but Stanton was unquestionably the star of the piece. According to Welles, who did not like him, he was "inexpressibly ludicrous" with his "wild, frantic talk, action, and rage" as he "sat down and jumped up . . . swung his arms, scolded and raved." The *Virginia* would "change the whole character of the war," the lawyer-statesman cried. "She will destroy, *seriatim*, every naval vessel; she will lay all the cities on the seaboard under contribution." He would recall Burnside, abandon Port Royal, and "notify the governors and municipal authorities in the North to take instant measures to protect their harbors." Then, crossing to a window which commanded a long view of the Potomac, he looked out and, trembling visibly, exclaimed: "Not unlikely, we shall have a shell or a cannonball from one of her guns in the White House before we leave this room."

Welles, who recorded with pride that his own "composure was not disturbed," replied that Stanton's fear for his personal safety was unfounded, since the heavily armored vessel would surely draw too much water to permit her passage of Kettle Bottom Shoals; he doubted, in fact, that she would venture outside the Capes. This afforded at least a measure of relief for the assem-

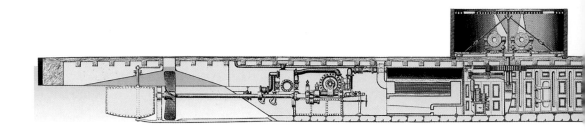

bly. Besides, Welles said, the navy already had an answer to the rebel threat: a seagoing ironclad of its own. *Monitor* was her name. She had left New York on Thursday, and should have reached Hampton Roads last night. "How many guns does she carry?" Stanton asked. Two, the Naval Secretary told him, and Stanton responded with a look which, according to Welles, combined "amazement, contempt, and distress."

The gray-bearded brown-wigged Welles spoke truly. The *Monitor* had arrived the night before. She had not only arrived; she was engaged this Sunday morning, before the cabinet adjourned to pray in church for the miracle which Stanton said was all that could save the eastern seaboard. And in truth it was something like a miracle that she was there at all. Coming south she had run into a storm that broke waves over her, down her blower-pipes and stacks, flooding her hold; pumps were rigged to fight a losing battle — and the wind went down, just as the ship was about to do the same. The fact was, she had not been built to stand much weather. She was built almost exclusively for what she was about to do: engage the former *Merrimac*, rumors of which had been coming north ever since work on the rebel craft began in mid-July.

There was a New York Swede, John Ericsson, who thought he had the answer, but when he went before the naval board with his plan for "an impregnable steam-battery of light draft," the members told him that calculations of her displacement proved the proposed *Monitor* would not float. He persisted, however; "The sea shall ride over her, and she will live in it like a duck," he said; until at last they offered him a contract with a clause providing for refund of all the money if she was not as invulnerable as he claimed. Ericsson took them up on that and got to work. Her keel was laid in October, three months behind the beginning of work on her rival, and she was launched within one hundred days.

As Welles had said, she had only two guns; but they were hard-hitting 11-inch rifles, housed in a revolving turret (another Ericsson invention) which gave them the utility of many times that number, though it caused the vessel to be sneered at as "a tin can on a shingle" or "a cheese-box on a raft."

★

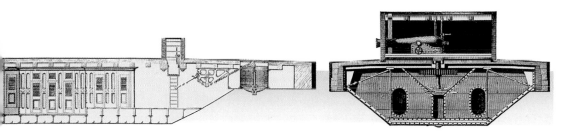

*Ericsson's plan gave the Monitor
a low profile, with a revolving gun turret
amidships and a pilot house at the bow.*

Her armor was nine inches thick in critical locations, and nowhere less than five, which would give her an advantage over her thinner-skinned opponent. The factors that made her truly the David to meet Goliath, however, were her 12-foot draft and her high maneuverability, which would combine her heavy punch with light fast footwork. Her sixty-man crew, men-of-war's men all, had volunteered directly from the fleet, and "a better one no naval commander ever had the honor to command," her captain said. His name was John L. Worden, a forty-four-year-old lieutenant with twenty-eight years in the service. He had been given the assignment — admittedly no plum — after seven months in a rebel prison, the result of having been captured back in April while trying to return from delivering secret messages to the Pensacola squadron. Obviously he was a man for desperate ventures, and perhaps the Department heads believed his months in durance would make him extra-anxious to hit back at the people who had held him. If they thought so, they were right. Nine days after the *Monitor* was commissioned he took her south for Hampton Roads.

Having weathered the storm, Worden rounded Cape Henry near sundown Saturday and heard guns booming twenty miles away. He guessed the cause and cleared for battle. But when he passed the Rip Raps, just before moonrise, and proceeded up the brightly lighted roadstead — each wave-crest a-sparkle with reflections of the flame-wrapped *Congress* — all he saw of the *Virginia* was the damage she had done: one ship sunk, another burning, and three more run ingloriously aground. An account of what had happened quickly told him what to do. Believing the *Virginia* would head first for her next morning, he put the *Monitor* alongside the *Minnesota*, kept his steam up, and waited.

Dawn came and at 7.30 he saw the big rebel ironclad coming straight for his stranded charge: whereupon he lifted anchor, darted out from behind the screening bulk of the frigate, and steamed forward to the attack. The *Monitor's*

★

sudden appearance was as unexpected as if she had dropped from the sky or floated up from the harbor bottom, squarely between the *Virginia* and her intended prize. "I guess she took us for some kind of a water tank," one of the *Monitor* crewmen later said. "You can see surprise in a ship just as you can see it in a man, and there was surprise all over the *Merrimac*."

He was right, or almost right. Instead of a water tank, however, "We thought at first it was a raft on which one of the *Minnesota*'s boilers was being taken to shore for repairs," a *Virginia* midshipman testified, "and when suddenly a shot was fired from her turret we imagined an accidental explosion of some kind had taken place on the raft."

This mistake was not for long. Rumors of work-in-progress had been trickling south as well as north, and the *Monitor* was recognized and saluted in her own right with a salvo which broke against her turret with as little effect as the ones that had shattered against the armored flanks of the *Virginia* yesterday, when the superiority of iron over wood was first established. Now it was iron against iron. The *Monitor* promptly returned the fire, swinging her two guns to bear in rapid succession. The fight was on.

It lasted four hours, not including a half-hour midway intermission, and what it mainly showed — in addition to its reinforcement of what one of them had proved the day before: that wooden navies were obsolete — was that neither could sink the other. The *Monitor* took full advantage of her higher speed and maneuverability, of her heavier, more flexible guns, and particularly of her lighter draft, which enabled her to draw off into the shallows for a breather where the other could not pursue. The *Virginia*'s supposed advantages, so impressive to the eye, were in fact highly doubtful. Her bigness, for example — the "Colossus of Roads," one northern correspondent dubbed her — only made her more sluggish and easier to hit, and her eight guns were limited in traverse. The effectiveness of her knockout punch, demonstrated yesterday when she rammed the *Cumberland*, was considerably reduced by the loss of her iron beak. Also, she had come out armed for the destruction of the frigates; her explosive shell shattered easily against an armored target, and she had brought only a few solid rounds to be used as hot shot. Worden's task, on the other hand, was complicated by the need for protecting the grounded *Minnesota*, which the *Virginia* would take under fire if he allowed her to get within range. Then too, his gun crews were disconcerted by whizzing screwheads that flew off the inner ends of the armor bolts and rattled about inside the turret whenever the enemy scored a direct hit.

Buchanan gone, command of the *Virginia* had passed to her executive, Lieutenant Catesby ap R. Jones. He gave the *Monitor* everything he had given the wooden warships yesterday, and more: to no avail. When he tried to ram her, she drew aside like a skillful boxer and pounded him hard as he passed.

John Worden was appointed captain of the Monitor because of his reputation for aggressiveness and expert seamanship

After a few such exchanges, the crews of his after-guns, deafened by the concussion of 180-pound balls against the cracking railroad iron, were bleeding from their noses and ears. Descending once to the gundeck and observing that some of the pieces were not engaged, Jones shouted: "Why are you not firing, Mr Eggleston?" The gun captain shrugged. "Why, our powder is very precious," he replied, "and after two hours' incessant firing I find that I can do her about as much damage by snapping my thumb at her every two minutes and a half."

At this point the *Monitor* hauled off into shallow water, where she spent fifteen minutes hoisting a new supply of shot and powder to her turret. Left alone, the *Virginia* made one of her drawn-out turns to come as near as possible to the grounded *Minnesota*, whose captain received her with what he called "a broadside which would have blown out of the water any timber-built ship in the world." Unwincing, the ironclad put a rifled bow-gun shell into her and was about to swing broadside, bringing all her guns to bear, when the *Monitor* came steaming out of the shallows and intervened again, Worden having refreshed himself with a stroll on the deck and a general look-round while the fresh supply of ammunition was being made handy for his guns. The two ironclads reëngaged.

Jones by now had decided that if he was going to destroy his foe, it would have to be with something other than his guns. First he tried ramming, despite the absence of his iron beak. But the *Monitor* was too spry for him. The best he could manage was a blunt-prowed, glancing blow that shivered her timbers — "a tremendous thump," one of her officers called it — but did her no real damage. The smaller ship kept circling her opponent, pounding away, one crewman said, "like a cooper with his hammer going round a cask." Doubly frustrated, Jones then determined to try an even more desperate venture, one that would bring his crew's five-to-one numerical advantage to bear. Having taken naval warfare a long stride forward yesterday, today he would take it an even longer one — back to the pistol-and-cutlass days of John Paul Jones. He would board his adversary. Equipping his men with tarpaulins for blinding the *Monitor*'s gun-slits and iron crows for jamming her turret and prying open her hatch, he had them stand by the sally ports while he maneuvered to get within grappling distance. It was a risky plan at best (far riskier than he knew; the Federal gunners were supplied with hand grenades for just such an emergency) yet it might have worked, if he could only have managed to bring the *Virginia* alongside. He could not. Nimble as a skittish horse, the smaller vessel danced away from contact every time.

For two more hours this second act of the long fight continued, and all this time the *Monitor* was pounding her opponent like an anvil, cracking and breaking her armor plate, though not enough to penetrate its two-foot oak and pitch-pine backing. Soon after noon, in a last attempt at boarding — though by now the *Virginia*'s stack was so riddled that her fires could get almost no draft and her speed, already slow, was cut in half — Jones brought his ship within ten yards of the enemy and delivered at that point-blank range a 9-inch shell which exploded against the pilot house, squarely in front of the sight-slit where Worden had taken station to direct the helm and relay fire commands. The concussion cracked the crossbeam and partly lifted the iron lid, exposing the dark interior. Worden was stunned and blinded, ears ringing, beard singed, eyes filled with burning powder; but not too stunned to feel dismay, and not so blind that he did not see the sudden glare of the noonday sky through the break in the overhead armor. "Sheer off!" he cried, and the helmsman put her hard to starboard, running for the shallows.

While the *Monitor* retired to shoal water, and remained there to assess the damage she and her captain had suffered, the *Virginia* steamed ponderously across the deep-water battle scene with the proud air of a wrestler who has just thrown his opponent out of the ring. Presently, however — the ebb tide was running, keeping her out of range of the *Minnesota*, and she had settled considerably as a result of taking water through her seams — she drew off south across the Roads for Norfolk, claiming victory. As she withdrew, the *Monitor* came forward and took her turn at dominating the scene, basing her victory counterclaim on the fact that the *Virginia* did not turn back to continue the fight. This would result in much argument all around, though privately both antagonists admitted the obvious truth: that, tactically, the fight had been a draw. In a stricter sense,

★

the laurels went to the *Monitor* for preventing the *Virginia* from completing her mission of destruction. Yet in the largest sense of all, and equally obvious, both had been victorious—over the wooden navies of the world.

Stretched out on the sofa in his cabin, Worden was "a ghastly sight," according to the executive who went to receive instructions from him upon assuming command. When the captain could speak, lying there with his beard singed, his face bloody, and his eyes tight shut as if to hold the pain in, his first words were a question: "Have I saved the *Minnesota?*"

"Yes," he was told, "and whipped the *Merrimac.*"

"Then I don't care what happens to me," he said.

★ ★ ★ As it had a perverse tendency to do in times of crisis, the telegraph line to Washington from Fort Monroe had gone out that Sabbath morning, and it stayed dead till just past 4 that afternoon. During all this long, exasperating time, among all the officials waiting fidgety behind the sound-proof curtain which sealed them off from news of the fight at Hampton Roads, none awaited the outcome with a deeper concern than George McClellan. The campaign he was about to launch depended on the Federal navy's maintaining domination of the bays and coastal rivers north of the James. It required very little imagination—far less, at any rate, than McClellan was blessed or cursed with—to picture what would happen if enemy gunboats—even wooden ones, let alone the frigate-killing *Merrimac-Virginia*—got among his loaded transports on their way down Chesapeake Bay or up the Rappahannock River.

Before news of the ironclad duel reached Washington, however, he received outpost dispatches which shipwrecked the Urbanna plan as completely as the sinking of the *Monitor* would have done: Joe Johnston was gone from the Manassas line. Most of his army was already back on the banks of the Rappahannock, intrenching itself near the very spot McClellan had picked for a beachhead. To land at Urbanna now, he saw, would be to land not in Johnston's rear, but with Johnston in his own.

Despite this abrupt and, so to speak, ill-mannered joggling of the military chessboard after all the pains he had taken to dispose the pieces to his liking, he was none the less relieved when, immediately following the news of Johnston's retrograde maneuver, the wire from Fort Monroe came suddenly alive with jubilant chatter of a victory by stalemate. The rebel ironclad had gone limping back to Norfolk, neutralized. He could breathe. What was more, he saw in this new turn of events an opportunity to put the finishing touch to his army's rigorous eight-month course of training: a practice march, deep into enemy territory — under combat conditions, with full field equipment and carefully worked-out logistics — and then another march right back again, since there was nothing there that he would not gain, automatically and bloodlessly, by going ahead with his roundabout plan for a landing down the coast. Warning orders went out that night, alerting the commanders. Next day the troops were slogging south, well-ordered dark-blue columns probing the muddy North Virginia landscape.

Excellent as this was as a graduation exercise to cap the army's basic training program, it had a bad effect on the public's opinion of Little Mac as the man to whip the rebels. Armchair strategists found in it the answer to the taunting refrain of a current popular song, "What are you waiting for, tardy George?" What he had been waiting for, apparently, was the departure of Johnston's army, which he had not ventured to risk encountering face-to-face. There was truth in this, though it omitted the balancing truth that, however frightened he might have been of Johnston, the thing he had least wanted was for Johnston to be frightened of him — frightened, that was, into pulling back and thus eluding the trap McClellan had spent all these months contriving. Lacking this restricted information, all the public could see was that Tardy George had delayed going forward until he knew there was nothing out there on the southern horizon for him to fear.

The outrage was screwed to a higher pitch when reports came back from newspapermen who had marched with the army through the supposedly impregnable fortifications along the Centreville ridge, where Quaker guns had been left in the embrasures to mock the Yankees. It was Munson's Hill all over again, the correspondents cried; "Our enemies, like the Chinese, have frightened us by the sound of gongs and the wearing of devils' masks." What was more, the smoldering wreckage of the Confederate camps showed conclusively that Johnston's army had been no more than half the size McClellan estimated. "Utterly dispirited, ashamed and humiliated," one reporter wrote, "I return from this visit to the rebel stronghold, feeling that their retreat is *our defeat*." The feeling was general. "It was a contest of inertia," another declared; "our side outsat the other."

These were nonprofessional opinions, which in general the army did not share. Civilians liked their victories bloody: the bloodier the better, so long as the casualty lists did not touch home. Soldiers — except perhaps in retrospect, when they had become civilians, too — preferred them bloodless, as in this case. The Centreville fortifications looked formidable enough to the men who would have had to assault them, peeled log guns or no. Besides, some of them — old-timers now — could contrast this march with the berry-picking jaunt which had ended so disastrously in July.

It went smoothly, with a minimum of stop-and-go. There was no need to fall out of column when everything a man could want was right there in the supply train. They were an army now, and they looked it, in their manner and their dress. There were still a few outlandish Zouave outfits to lend the column sudden garish bursts of color, like mismatched beads on a string, but for the most part they wore the uniform which had lately become standard: light-blue trousers and a tunic of dark blue, with a crisp white edge of collar showing just under the jowls of the men in regiments whose colonels, being dudes or incurable old-army martinets, preferred it so.

Whatever truth there might once have been in the Confederate claim that Southerners made better soldiers, or anyhow started from a better scratch because they came directly from life in the open and were familiar with the use of firearms, applied no longer. After six months of army drill, a factory hand was indistinguishable from a farmer. Individually, the Northerners knew, they were at least as tough as any men the South could bring against them, and probably as a whole they were better drilled — except of course the cavalry, since admittedly it took longer to learn to fork a horse in style. McClellan's men were

This so-called Quaker gun was left in abandoned Confederate fortifications near Centreville to delay the Federal pursuit.

*Federal troops occupy a former
Confederate camp near Manassas after it
was evacuated by rebels on March 7, 1862.*

aware of the changes he had wrought and they were proud of them; but the thing that made them proudest of all was the sight of Little Mac himself. He was up and down the column all that day, glad to be out from under the shadow of the Capitol dome and the sneers of the politicians, not answering ignorant questions or countering even more ignorant proposals, but returning the cheers of his marching men with a jaunty horseback salute.

Presently, crossing Bull Run by Blackburn's Ford, they came onto the scene of last year's smoky, flame-stabbed panorama. It was a sobering sight, for those who had been there then and those who hadn't: the corpse of a battlefield, silent and deserted except perhaps for the ghosts of the fallen. Shell-blasted, the treetops were twisted "in a hundred directions, as though struck by lightning," one correspondent wrote. Manassas Junction lay dead ahead, the embers of it anyhow, at the base of a column of bluish-yellow smoke, and off to the right were the tumbled bricks of Judith Henry's chimney, on the hill where the Stonewall Brigade had met the jubilant attackers, freezing the cheers in their throats, and flung them back; Jeb Stuart's horsemen had come with a thunder of hoofs, hacking away at the heads of the New York Fire Zouaves. All that was left now was wreckage, the charred remains of a locomotive and four freight cars, five hundred staved-in barrels of flour, and fifty-odd barrels of pork and beef "scattered around in the mud." McDowell was there, at the head of his corps, and one of his soldiers wrote that he saw him weeping over the sun-bleached bones of the light-hearted berry-picking men he had led southward under the full moon of July.

McClellan was not weeping. This field held no memories for him, sad or otherwise, except that what had happened here had prompted Lincoln to

★

send for him to head the army he found "cowering on the banks of the Potomac" and later to replace Scott as chief of all the nation's armies. He went to bed that night, proud to have taken without loss the position McDowell had been thrown back from after spilling on it the blood of 1500 men. Next day he was happy still, riding among the bivouacs. But the day that followed was another matter. He woke to find his time had come to weep.

Once more he had turned his back on Lincoln, and once more Lincoln had struck with a War Order. This one, numbered 3, relieved McClellan as general-in-chief and left him commanding only the Department of the Potomac, one of seven in the eastern theater. The worst of it, in damage to his pride, was that he learned of the order, not through military channels, but by a telegram from friends in Washington who read it in the papers: Stanton's office had leaked the order to the press before forwarding it to McClellan in the field. Within one week of learning that his Commander in Chief had listened to charges of treason against him, of being forced to reorganize his army on the eve of committing it to action under corps commanders who had gone on record as being opposed to his military thinking, he was toppled unceremoniously from the highest rung of the professional ladder.

This was hard. Indeed, it might have been the crowning blow, except that later that same day, March 12, he was comforted by a mutual friend whom the President sent with the full text and an explanation of the order. He was relieved of the chief command "until otherwise ordered," it read: which implied that the demotion was temporary. Furthermore, the envoy explained, the order had been issued primarily to allow him to concentrate, without distractions, on the big campaign ahead. McClellan took heart at this and wrote to Lincoln at once, informing him that "I shall work just as cheerfully as before, and that no consideration of self will in any manner interfere with the discharge of my public duties."

So he said, and doubtless believed. He would have been considerably less cheerful, though, if he had known of other things that were happening be-hind his back, this same week in Washington; "that sink of iniquity," he called it.

Ethan Allen Hitchcock, a sixty-four-year-old Vermonter, West Point graduate and veteran of the Seminole and Mexican Wars, was surprised to re-ceive from the War Department in mid-March a telegram summoning him to Washington. He had been retired from the army since 1855, and never would have entered it in the first place if his parents had not insisted that the grand-son and namesake of the Hero of Ticonderoga was obliged to take up arms as a profession. Hitchcock's principal interests were philosophy and mysticism; he considered himself "a scholar rather than a warrior," and had written books on Swedenborg and alchemy and Jesus. His first reaction to the summons that plucked him from retirement was a violent nosebleed. He got aboard a train, however, suffering a second hemorrhage on the way and a third on arrival,

---

"I shall demand of you great, heroic exertions, rapid and long marches, desperate combats, privations perhaps. We will share all these together."

— George B. McClellan

---

each more violent than the one before. Checking into a Washington hotel, he took to the bed in a dazed, unhappy condition.

Presently the Secretary of War was at his bedside. While the old soldier lay too weak to rise and greet him, Stanton told him why he had been sent for. He and Lincoln needed him as a military adviser. The air was thick with treason! . . . Be-fore Hitchcock could recover from his alarm at this, the Secretary put a question to him: Would he consider taking McClellan's place as commander of the Army of the Potomac? Hitchcock scarcely knew what to make of this. Next thing he knew, Stan-ton had him out of bed and on the way to the White House, where Lincoln repeat-ed the Secretary's request. Badly confused, Hitchcock wrote in his diary when he got back to his room that night: "I want no command. I want no department. . . . I am uncomfortable." Finally he agreed to accept an appointment as head of the Army Board, made up of War Department bureau chiefs. In effect, this amounted to being the right-hand man of Stanton, who terrified him daily by alternately bul-lying and cajoling him. He was perhaps the unhappiest man in Washington.

Unsuspecting that the President and the Secretary of War were even now casting about for a replacement for him, McClellan completed his army's graduation exercise by marching it back to its starting point, Fairfax Court House, to deliver the baccalaureate address. After congratulating his soldiers on their progress, he announced that their long months of study were behind them; he was about to take them "where you all long to be — the decisive battlefield." In solicitude, he added, "I am to watch over you as a parent over his children; and you know that your general loves you from the depths of his heart. It shall be my care, as it ever has been, to gain success with the least possible loss; but I know that, if necessary, you will willingly follow me to our graves for our righteous cause. . . . I shall demand of you great, heroic exertions, rapid and long marches, desperate combats, privations perhaps. We will share all these together; and when this sad war is over we will return to our homes, and feel that we can ask no higher honor than the proud consciousness that we belonged to the Army of the Potomac."

With their cheers ringing in his ears, he turned at once to perfect his plans for a landing down the coast. Urbanna was out, but Mobjack Bay and Fort Monroe were still available. In fact, though he had pronounced these alternatives "less brilliant" — by which he meant that they would not outflank the enemy, neither Johnston to the north nor Magruder to the south — now that he came to examine it intently, Fort Monroe had definite advantages Urbanna had not afforded. For one thing, the beachhead was already established, Old Point Comfort having been held throughout the secession furor despite the loss of Norfolk across the way. For another, during his advance up the York-James peninsula toward Richmond, his flanks would be protected by the navy, which could also assist in the reduction of any strongpoints he encountered within range of its big guns. The more he studied the scheme the better he liked it.

By now, however, he had learned to look back over his shoulder. Lincoln had to be considered: not only considered, but outmaneuvered. Once before, he had accomplished this by calling a conference of his generals and confronting the President with their concerted opinions as to the soundness of a military plan. In that case Lincoln had not dared to override him; nor would he now. So McClellan called his corps commanders together, there at Fairfax, and presented them with his proposal for a landing at Fort Monroe. Having heard him out, the four generals expressed unanimous approval — provided four conditions could be met. These were that the *Merrimac* could be kept out of action, that there were sufficient transportation facilities to take the army down the coast, that the navy could silence certain fortifications on York River, and that enough troops were left behind to give the capital "an entire feeling of security for its safety from menace." They were not in full agreement as to how many men would be needed to accomplish this last condition, but their estimates ran generally to 40,000.

McClellan had them put their approval in writing, that same March 13, then sent McDowell to Washington to present it to Stanton and Lincoln. As soon as McDowell had had time to get there, McClellan received a wire from Stanton. McDowell had shown up with a paper signed by the corps commanders; did McClellan intend for the plan it approved to be taken as his own? McClellan replied that it did. After another interval, allowing time for the Secretary and Lincoln to confer, a second Stanton telegram arrived. Lincoln did not exactly approve; rather, as Stanton phrased it, he "[made] no objection," so long as enough of McClellan's men were left behind to keep Washington and Manassas safe while the army was down the coast. The final paragraph, which made consent explicit, was petulant and sneering: "Move the remainder of the force down the Potomac, choosing a new base at Fortress Monroe, or anywhere between here and there, or, at all events, move such remainder of the army at once in pursuit of the enemy by some route."

Perhaps by now McClellan had learned to abide the tantrums and exasperations of his former friend and sympathizer. At any rate, having won the consent he sought, he could overlook the tone in which it was given. However, that Manassas, too, was to be afforded what the generals called "an entire feeling of security" imposed an additional manpower drain on which he had not counted. He was tempted to give Lincoln another tactics-strategy lecture, proving that the place would be in no danger, and in fact of small importance, once his landing on the Peninsula had drawn Johnston's army farther south to oppose his swoop on Richmond. But there was too much else to do just now; he had no time for arguments and lectures. The transports were being assembled at Alexandria — 113 steamers, 188 schooners, and 88 barges: by far the largest amphibious expedition the hemisphere had ever seen — to take his army down the Virginia coast, with all its equipment and supplies, guns and wagons, food and ammunition, horses and beef cattle, tents and records, all the impedimenta required to feed, clothe, and arm 146,000 men. They were to move in echelons of 10,000, on a schedule designed to complete the shuttle within three weeks. McClellan worked hard and long, giving the loading his personal attention. Within four days of receiving Lincoln's approval, or anyhow what amounted to approval, he stood on an Alexandria wharf and saw the first contingent off on its journey south.

"The worst is over," he wired Stanton. "Rely upon it that I will carry this thing through handsomely."

★ ★ ★ *S*uch optimistic expressions by the **Young Napoleon** were usually precursors of disappointment or disaster. Not only was this one no exception, it had in fact a double repercussion, set off in his rear by two men who opposed McClellan as well as each other: Stonewall Jackson, who had done so much to wreck McDowell on

Henry Hill, and John Charles Frémont, who had done so much — though with less success — to damage Lincoln in Missouri. The two blows landed in that order, both before the Army of the Potomac had completed its roundabout journey down Chesapeake Bay. The first echelon left Alexandria on March 17, a Monday. Before the week was up, Jackson stabbed hard at the troops McClellan had left behind (in accordance with Lincoln's concern) to block any Confederate drive on Washington through the Shenandoah Valley, that corridor pointed shotgun-like at the Union solar plexus.

When Johnston fell back to the Rappahannock he instructed Jackson to conform by retreating southward up the Valley in event of a Federal push, taking care meanwhile to protect the main army's western flank by guarding the eastern passes of the Blue Ridge. Jackson of course obeyed, but not without a plea that he be allowed at least a chance to hurt the man who pushed him. As he put it, "If we cannot be successful in defeating the enemy should he advance, a kind Providence may enable us to inflict a terrible wound and effect a safe retreat in the event of having to fall back."

Old Blue Light, his soldiers called him; they had seen the fire of battle in his eyes. He read the New Testament in his off-hours, but did his military thinking in accordance with the Old, which advised smiting the enemy, hip and thigh, and assured the assistance of Providence in the infliction of terrible wounds.

At any rate, he soon had the chance he prayed for. When Johnston fell back the Federals came forward, two divisions of them marching up the Valley in coöperation with McClellan's excursion east of the mountains. Jackson, with 4600 men, retreated watchfully before the Federal 17,000, awaiting the answer to his prayers. Then it came. As he fell back through Winchester, spies reported the enemy regiments scattered. A quick slash at the head might confuse the whole column into exposing one or two of its segments to destruction. When he called a meeting of his officers to plan the attack, however, he learned that his wagon train was already miles to the south. Without food or reserve ammunition, his hungry men would have to continue their retreat. Jackson was furious, somehow placing the blame on the assembly of officers. "That is the last council of war I will ever hold!" he vowed. And it was.

The retreat continued through Kernstown, four miles to the south, then another forty miles up the Valley pike, past the slopes of Massanutton Mountain. All through the retreat Jackson watched and prayed, but for ten days Providence did not smile on him again. Then suddenly it did. On Friday the 21st his cavalry commander reported the enemy pulling back; one division had turned off eastward toward Manassas, and the other was retiring north toward Winchester. Next morning Jackson had his infantry on the road. Twenty-five miles they marched that day and fifteen the next, retracing their steps to reach Kernstown at 2 p.m. Sunday and find the horse artillery already skirmishing with what the cavalry commander said was the Federal rear guard, four regiments left to protect the tail of the column slogging north for Harpers Ferry. Jackson's blue eyes lighted. Here was the chance to inflict that terrible wound.

Certain considerations urged postponement. He had made no detailed personal reconnaissance. His ranks were thinned by 1500 stragglers he had left along the pike in the past two days. Last but not least, this was the Lord's day; Jackson would not even write a letter on a Sunday, or post one that would be in transit then, fearing that Providence might punish the profanation. These were all set aside, however, when weighed against the chances for success. There must be no delay; the sun was already down the sky. Without taking time to brief his commanders, he put his men into attack formation, the Stonewall Brigade in the center, and threw them forward. This was his first full-scale battle on his own, and he intended to make the victory sudden and complete.

It was sudden enough, but it was so far from complete that it was not even a victory. It was a repulse, and a bloody one at that. When the men in gray went forward, the Federals absorbed the shock and held their ground, returning the fire. Quickly it swelled to crescendo as Jackson sent in his reserves. Presently, to his amazement, men began to stumble out of the roar and flash of battle, making for the rear. He rode forward to block the way. "Where are you going, man?" he shouted at one retreater. The soldier explained that he had fired all his cartridges. "Then go back and give them the bayonet!" Jackson cried. But the man ran on, unheeding, one among many. Even the Stonewall Brigade, with its hard core of veterans who had stood fast on Henry Hill, was wavering. Just as it was about to break, its commander Brigadier General Richard Garnett gave the order to retreat. Amazed at what appeared to be his army's disintegration, Jackson seized a drummer boy by the shoulder and dragged him onto a knoll, shouting as he held him: "Beat the rally!" The roll of the drum did nothing to slow the rout; Jackson fell back in the demoralized wake of his soldiers. Fortunately for him, the Federals did not pursue. The Battle of Kernstown, such as it was, was over.

Suffering 700 casualties to the enemy's 590, Jackson's men had done a better job than Jackson himself when it came to estimating Federal strength. That was no mere rear guard they had charged, but a whole 9000-man division. When he learned that he had thus unknowingly reversed the dictum that the attacker must outnumber the defender three-to-one, Jackson did not allow it to temper the sternness of his discipline. Garnett had retreated without orders; peremptorily Jackson relieved him of command and put him in arrest to await court martial for neglect of duty. It did not matter that he had graduated from West Point the year before Jackson came there as a plebe, that he was a member of the proud Tidewater family which had given the Confederacy the first general officer lost in battle, or that his men loved him and resented the harshness that took him from them.

★

Richard Garnett remained a great admirer of Jackson even after Stonewall had him arrested for retreating at Kernstown.

It did not even matter that his brigade might have been cut to pieces if he had held it there, outnumbered, outflanked, and out of ammunition, while he went fumbling along the chain of command in search of permission to withdraw. What mattered was that the next officer who found himself in a tight spot would stay there, awaiting higher sanction, before ordering a retreat.

As for accepting any personal blame for this loss of nearly one-fourth of his little army because of ragged marching, faulty reconnaissance, poor intelligence, ill-prepared assault, or disorganized retreat, Jackson could not see it. In fact, he did not seem to understand that he had been defeated. "The Yankees don't seem willing to quit Winchester, General," a young cavalryman said in bivouac that night. Jackson replied, "Winchester is a very pleasant place to stay in, sir." The trooper attempted a further pleasantry: "It was reported that they were retreating, but I guess they were retreating after us." Jackson, who had a limited sense of humor, kept looking into the campfire. "I think I may say I am satisfied, sir," he said.

How far he saw into the future as he said this would remain a question to be pondered down the years, but most likely Old Blue Light would have been still more "satisfied" if he had known the reaction his repulse was producing that night in the enemy camp, even as he warmed his hands at the bivouac fire and refused to admit that what he had suffered was a defeat. His adversary, while congratulating himself on a hard-fought victory, could not believe that Jackson would have dared to attack without expecting reinforcements. Orders went out, recalling to the Valley the division that had left for Manassas two days ago: which meant, in effect, a loss of 8000 men for McClellan, who was charged with leaving a covering force to protect the Junction when the balance of his army sailed. Equally important, if not more so, was the effect on Lincoln, who quarter-faced at the news of the battle, victory or no, and found himself looking once more down the muzzle of the Shenandoah shotgun. The Kernstown explosion seemed to prove that it was loaded.

Whatever it was for Lincoln, news of the battle, coupled with the recall of the division headed eastward, was a thorn in McClellan's side —a hurt which in time might fester and hurt worse. As such, however, it was no sharper than the thorn that stuck him one week later, on the eve of his own departure for Fort Monroe. He had in his army, in Sumner's corps, a division commanded by Louis Blenker, a man of considerable flamboyance. Blenker was a soldier of fortune, a German, and his men were known as Germans too, this being the current generic term — along with "Dutchmen" and "Hessians" — for immigrants of all origins except Ireland. But the fact was, they were almost everything: Algerians, Cossacks,

Sepoys, Turks, Croats, Swiss, French Foreign Legionnaires, and a Garibaldi regiment with a Hungarian colonel, one d'Utassy, who had begun his career as a circus rider and was to end it as an inmate of Sing Sing. Blenker affected a red-lined cape and a headquarters tent made of "double folds of bluish material, restful to the eye," where the shout, "*Ordinans numero eins!*" was the signal for the serving of champagne. His soldiers got lager beer and there was a prevailing aroma of sauerkraut around the company messes. All this — the glitter of fire-gilt buttons,

*Preparing to advance to the York-James
peninsula, Federals manhandle a limber
and a fieldpiece on board a transport at
Alexandria in March 1862.*

the babble of polyglot commands, and the smell of German cooking—was reminiscent of one of Frémont's old Transmississippi outfits. And the fact was, Frémont was doing all he could to get hold of the division even now.

The Pathfinder was back on the road to glory, though it led now, not through Missouri or down the winding course of the Mississippi, but along the western border of Virginia and across the rolling peaks of the Alleghenies. Under pressure from the Jacobins, who had never stopped protesting their favorite's dismissal and urging that he be returned to duty, Lincoln, in the same War Order which removed McClellan from over-all command, plucked Frémont out of retirement and gave him what was called the Mountain Department, specially created for this purpose, along with 25,000 men. Having learned that the former explorer was a poor administrator, he now presented him with this chance to prove himself a fighter. Frémont at once came up with a plan he knew would delight the President. Give him 10,000 additional soldiers, he said, and he would capture Knoxville. What was more, he had a particular 10,000 in mind: Blenker's Germans.

Lincoln pricked up his ears at this offer to accomplish one of his pet war aims, then went down to Alexandria to see if McClellan was willing to give up the division. Far from willing, McClellan urged the Commander in Chief not to weaken the Army of the Potomac at the moment when it was half-embarked on its trip to the gates of Richmond. Lincoln agreed on second thought that it would not do, and returned to Washington. Once more he had gotten nowhere with McClellan face-to-face. Within the week, however, on the final day of March, the general received a presidential note: "This morning I felt constrained to order Blenker's division to Frémont; and I write this to assure you that I did so with great pain, understanding that you would wish it otherwise. If you could know the full pressure of the case I am confident that you would justify it, even beyond a mere acknowledgment that the Commander in Chief may order what he pleases. Yours very truly, A. Lincoln."

The closing phrase had a Stantonian ring, administering a backhand cut that stung; but what alarmed McClellan most was the undeniable evidence that, under political pressure, the nation's leader would swerve into paths which he knew were militarily unwise. How much grief this might hold for the army remained to be seen. For the present, McClellan could only repeat what he had written to his wife three weeks ago, when he learned of War Order 3: "The rascals are after me again. I had been foolish enough to hope that when I went into the field they would give me some rest, but it seems otherwise. Perhaps I should have expected it. If I can get out of this scrape you will never catch me in the power of such a set again."

Now as then, however, he was too busy to protest. Just before embarking next afternoon—All Fools' Day—he sent Lincoln a roster of the troops he was leaving for the protection of the capital. His generals had advised

★

a covering force of 40,000. McClellan listed 77,465, thus: 10,859 at Manassas, 7780 at Warrenton, 35,476 in the Shenandoah Valley, 1350 along the lower Potomac, and 22,000 around Washington proper. This done, he went aboard a steamer, worked in his cabin on last-minute paperwork details till after midnight, then set out for Fort Monroe. McDowell's corps and what was left of Sumner's were to come along behind within the week. Looking back on the journey after landing at Old Point Comfort, he informed his wife, "I did not feel safe until I could see Alexandria behind us."

What was called for now, he saw, was action. He kept busy all that day and the next. "The great battle," he wrote his wife, "will be (I think) near Richmond, as I have always hoped and thought. I see my way very clearly, and, with my trains once ready, will move rapidly." The following morning, April 4, he put two columns in motion for Yorktown, where the Confederate left was anchored on York River, behind fortifications whose reduction his corps commanders had said would depend on naval coöperation. All went well on the approach march. The day was clear, the sky bright blue, the trees new-green and shiny. Near sundown, exultant, he wired Stanton: "I expect to fight tomorrow."

His spirits were much improved at the prospect, and also perhaps from having observed what he called "a wonderfully cool performance" by three of his soldiers that afternoon. The trio of foragers had chased a sheep within range of the rebel intrenchments, where, ignoring the fire of sharpshooters — but not the fact that they were being watched by McClellan and their comrades while they demonstrated their contempt for the enemy's marksmanship — they calmly killed and skinned the animal before heading back for their own lines. The Confederates then brought a 12-pounder to bear, scoring a near miss. Undaunted, the soldiers halted, picked up the shot, and lugged it along, still warm, for presentation to Little Mac.

"I never saw so cool and gallant a set of men," he declared, seeing in this bright cameo of action a reflection of the spirit of his whole army. "They did not seem to know what fear is."

This gap in their education was about to be filled, however.

★ ★ ★

Shelby Foote

*In April 1862, Federals
swarm ashore to take one of five
Confederate batteries outlying
Island Ten on the Tennessee side of
the Mississippi at Madrid Bend.*

F O U R

Pea Ridge; Glorieta; Island Ten

1862 ★ ★ ★ ★ ★ **E**arl Van Dorn came west with great
expectations. He knew what oppor-
tunities awaited a bold commander
there, and his professional boldness had been tested and applauded. Approaching his prime at forty-one, he was dark skinned and thin-faced, with a shaggy
mustache, an imperial, and a quick, decisive manner; "Buck," his fellow Confederates called him. Except for his size (he was five feet five: two inches taller than
Napoleon) he was in fact the very beau sabreur of Southern fable, the Bayard-
Lochinvar of maiden dreams. Not that his distinction was based solely on his
looks. He was a man of action, too — one who knew how to grasp the nettle,
danger, and had done so many times. Appointed to West Point by his great-uncle
Andrew Jackson, he had gone on to collect two brevets and five wounds as a
lieutenant in the Mexican War and in skirmishes with Comanches on the
warpath. In the end, he had been rewarded with a captaincy in Sidney Johnston's
2d Cavalry, adding his own particular glitter to that spangled company.

He was a Mississippian, which simplified his decision when the South
seceded; for him there was little or none of the "agony" of the border state pro-
fessionals. Furthermore, as it did for others blessed or cursed with an ache for
adventure, the conflict promised deferment of middle age and boredom. He
came home and was made a brigadier, second only to Jefferson Davis in com-

★

mand of Mississippi troops, and then received the command itself, with the rank
of major general, when Davis left for Montgomery. This was much, but not
enough. Wanting action even more than rank, and what he called "immortal
renown" more than either, Van Dorn resigned to accept a colonel's commission
in the Confederate army and assignment to service in Texas. Here he found at
least a part of what he was seeking. At Galveston he assembled a scratch brigade
of volunteers and captured three Federal steamships in the harbor — including
the famous *Star of the West*, which had been fired on, back in January, for attempting relief of Sumter — then marched on Indianola, where he forced the
surrender of the only body of U.S. regulars in the state.

For these exploits, characterized by incisiveness and daring, he was
tendered a banquet and ball in San Antonio and had his praises sung in all the
southern papers, though perhaps the finest compliment paid him was by a
northern editor who put a price of $5000 on his head, this being nearly twice
the standing offer for the head of Beauregard. In acknowledgment of his services and fame, the government gave him a double promotion and summoned
him to Richmond; he was a major general again, this time in command of all the
cavalry in Virginia. Even this did not seem commensurate with his abilities,
however. Presently, when Davis was in need of a commander for what was to be
called Transmississippi Department Number 2, he had to look no farther than
his fellow-Mississippian Earl Van Dorn, right there at hand. It was another case,
apparently, of History attending to her own.

Within nine days of his mid-January assignment to the West, despite the fact that he was convalescing from a bad fall suffered while attempting
a risky ditch jump — he was an excellent horseman; his aide, required by custom to try it too, was injured even worse — Van Dorn established headquarters
at Pocahontas, Arkansas, and began a first-hand estimate of the situation. This
in itself was quite a task, since the command included all of Missouri and
Arkansas, Indian Territory, and Louisiana down to the Red River. But one
thing he had determined at the outset: he would go forward, north along the
line of the Mississippi, taking cities and whipping Yankee armies as he went. In
short, as Van Dorn saw it, the campaign was to be a sort of grand reversal of
Frémont's proposed descent of the big river. On the day of his appointment,
already packing for the long ride west from Richmond, he had written his wife:
"I must have St Louis — then huzza!"

So much he intended; but first, he knew, he must concentrate his scattered troops for striking. Ben McCulloch's army of 8000 was camped in the
Boston Mountains south of Fayetteville, the position it had taken after the victory
over Lyon at Wilson's Creek. Off in the Territory, moving to join him, was a band
of about 2000 pro-Confederate Indians, Creeks and Seminoles, Cherokees, Chick-
asaws and Choctaws, won over by the persuasions of the lawyer-poet, scholar-

★

Earl Van Dorn (left), an experienced, dashing, and incisive fighter, was given command of the Transmississippi Department Number 2 in January 1862.

duelist, orator-soldier Albert Pike, who led them. Sterling Price's 7000 Missourians, under pressure from a superior Federal army after their late fall and early winter successes in their home state, had fallen back to a position near the scene of their August triumph. Combined, these three totaled something under half the striking force the new commander had envisioned; but 17,000 should be enough to crush the Federals threatening Springfield—after which would come St Louis, "then huzza!" Van Dorn planned to unite at Ironton, fight, and then swing north, augmented by the enthusiasts a victory would bring trooping to the colors. Deep in the bleak western woods, he hailed his army with Napoleonic phrases: "Soldiers! Behold your leader! He comes to show you the way to glory and immortal renown. . . . Awake, young men of Arkansas, and arm! Beautiful maidens of Louisiana, smile not on the craven youth who may linger by your hearth when the rude blast of war is sounding in your ears! Texas chivalry, to arms!"

This might have brought in volunteers, a host bristling with bayonets much as the address itself bristled with exclamation points, though as events turned out there was no time for knowing. By now it was late February, and the pressure of the 12,000-man northern army against Springfield was too great. Price gave way, retreating while his rear guard skirmished to delay the Federals: first across the Arkansas line, then down through Fayetteville, until presently he was with McCulloch in the Boston Mountains, the southernmost reach of the Ozarks. By that time, Pike had come up too; Van Dorn's command was concentrated — not where he had wanted it, however, and not so much by his own efforts as by the enemy's. Then too, except in the actual heat of battle, Price and McCulloch had never really got along, and they did no better now. Both appealed to their leader at Pocahontas to come and resolve their differences in person.

Van Dorn was more than willing. In four days, after sending word for them to stand firm and prepare to attack, he rode two hundred horseback miles through the wintry wilds of Arkansas. Arriving March 3, he was given a salute of forty guns, as befitted his rank, and that night orders went out for the men to prepare three days' cooked ra-

The Five Nations Indians followed their leader Albert Pike, a big man bearded like Santa Claus except that the beard was not white but a vigorous gray. He rode in a carriage and was dressed in Sioux regalia, buckskin shirt, fringed leggins, and beaded moccasins . . .

tions and gird themselves for a forced march, with combat at its end. The Federals, widely separated in pursuit of Price, were about to be destroyed in detail.

Early next morning the Southerners set out, 17,000 men and sixty guns moving north to retake what had been lost by retrograde: as conglomerate, as motley an army as the sun ever shone on, East or West — though as a matter of fact the sun was not shining now. Snow fell out of an overcast sky and the wind whipped the underbrush and keened in the branches of the winter trees. Price's Missourians led the way, marching homeward again, proud of the campaign they had staged and proud, too, of their 290-pound ex-governor commander, who could be at once so genial and majestic. McCulloch, the dead-shot former Ranger, wearing a dove-gray corduroy jacket, sky-blue trousers, Wellington boots, and a highly polished Maynard rifle slung across one shoulder, rode among his Texans and Arkansans; "Texicans" and "Rackansackers," they were

★

called — hard-bitten men accustomed to life in the open, who boasted that they would storm hell itself if McCulloch gave the order. Off on the flank, in a long thin file, the Five Nations Indians followed their leader Albert Pike, a big man bearded like Santa Claus except that the beard was not white but a vigorous gray. He rode in a carriage and was dressed in Sioux regalia, buckskin shirt, fringed leggins, and beaded moccasins, while his braves, harking back to their warpath days, wore feathers stuck in their hats and scalping knives in their waistbands, some marching with a musket in one hand and a tomahawk in the other. The knives were for more than show; they intended to use them, having promised their squaws the accustomed trophies of battle.

Van Dorn also rode horse-drawn. He rode, in fact, supine in an ambulance, still feeling the effects of the ditch-jump back in Virginia and down as well with chills and fever as a result of swimming his mare across an icy river two days ago in his haste to join the army and get it moving. The mare was hitched alongside now, available in emergencies, and Price rode alongside too, identifying passing units and ready to relay orders when the time came. The new commander was nothing if not a man of action, bold and forward, sick or well, and the troops he led had caught something of his spirit. Trudging up the road down which they had retreated just the week before, they were in a high good humor despite the norther blowing wet snow in their faces.

★ ★ ★ *T*he previous afternoon, some dozen miles away on a grassy knoll near Cross Hollows, Arkansas, where his headquarters tent was pitched, the commander of the army that had just cleared southwest Missouri of organized Confederates sat writing a letter home. At fifty-seven, having put on weight, he found that long hours in the saddle wearied him now a good deal more than they had done fifteen years before, when he had abandoned army life for civil engineering. A dish-faced man with a tall forehead and thinning, wavy hair, hazel eyes and a wide, slack-lipped mouth, he drew solace from such periods of relaxation as this, sitting in full uniform, polished boots, epaulets and spurs, enjoying the sounds of camp life in the background and the singing of the birds, while he inscribed to the wife of his bosom letters which he signed, rather ponderously, "yours Saml R. Curtis." A West Pointer like the opponent he did not yet know he was facing, he had commanded an Ohio regiment in the Mexican War, had been chief engineer for the city of St Louis, and had served for the past three years as Republican congressman from Iowa. Of all his accomplishments, however, he was proudest of the current one, performed as a brigadier general of volunteers. Chasing the rebels out of Missouri might not sound like much, compared to Grant's recent unconditional capture of two forts and one whole army in Tennessee, but Curtis felt that it was a substantial achievement. He was saying so in the letter when his writing was interrupted by the sudden far-off rumble of cannon. It came from the south, and he counted forty well-spaced booms: the salute for a major general.

This gave him pause, and with the pause came doubts. His four divisions were rather scattered, two of them twelve miles in his rear and two thrown forward under Franz Sigel, the immigrant mathematics instructor who had shown a talent for retreat at Wilson's Creek. Curtis was a cautious or at any rate a highly methodical person; he liked to allow for contingencies, an engineer's margin for stress and strain, and he could never feel comfortable until he knew he had done so. Back in the fall, inspecting Frémont's pinwheel dispositions, he had reported that the Pathfinder "lacked the intelligence, the experience, and the sagacity necessary to his command." Placing as he did the highest value on all three of these qualities — especially the last, which he himself personified — that was about the worst he could say of a man. Accordingly, when Frémont was removed and Curtis was given the task of driving the rebels out of Missouri — which Frémont had considered more or less incidental to the grand design — he went about it differently. He gave it his full attention, and it went well: too well, in fact, or anyhow too easy. Price fell back and the Federals followed through a deserted region, cabins empty though food was still bubbling in pots on ranges, laundry soaking in lukewarm sudsy water, clocks ticking ominously on mantels, and now this: forty booms from across the wintry landscape, signifying for all to hear that an over-all enemy chieftain had arrived. Curtis thought perhaps he had better consolidate to meet developments that threatened stress and strain.

Next day his fears were reinforced, and indeed confirmed, when scouts — including young Wild Bill Hickok, addicted to gaudy shirts and a mustache whose ends could be knotted behind his head — came riding in with reports that the Confederates were marching north in strength. Convinced and alarmed, Curtis sent word for Sigel to exercise his talent by falling back on Sugar Creek, up near the Missouri line, where he himself would be waiting with the other two divisions. There they would combine and, in turn, await the enemy. It was a good defensive position, with a boggy stream across the front and a high ridge to protect the rear, as both men knew from having come through it the week before, in pursuit of Price. Also, if they hurried, there would be time to fortify. Curtis fell back, as planned, and presently received word that Sigel was coming, skirmishing as he came. Near sundown, March 6, he got there with the grayback cavalry close behind him, hacking at his rear. He strode into the commander's tent, a small, quick-gestured, red-haired man in gold-frame spectacles, each lens scarcely bigger around than a quarter, and announced in broken English that he was hungry. He had lost two regiments, pinched off in the chase as had been feared; otherwise he was whole and hearty, eager for more fighting. Just now, though, he was hungry.

Curtis hardly knew what to make of such a man, but he fed him and took him out for an inspection of the lines. Sigel's two divisions were on the right, the other two having side-stepped to make room for them on the two mile-long shelf of land overlooking the hollow of Sugar Creek. A mile to their rear was the hamlet of Leetown, a dozen cabins clustered around a store and blacksmith shop, which in turn lay about halfway between the line of battle and the sudden rise of Pea Ridge, rearing abruptly against the northern sky like a backdrop for a theatrical production. Outcropped with granite and feathered with trees along its crest, the ridge extended east-ward for two miles, then gave down upon a narrow north-south valley. Through this defile ran the Springfield-Fayetteville road, known locally as the wire road because the telegraph had its southern terminus here in a two-story frame building where the telegrapher lived and took in lodgers overnight; Elkhorn Tav-ern, it was called, acquiring its name from the giant skull and antlers nailed to the rooftree. The tavern lay to the left rear of the position Curtis had chosen, and the road led down past it, through the intrenchments his troops had been digging all that day, and on across the creek to where the rebel army, filing in, was settling down and kindling campfires in the dusk. They had brought their weather with them. It was snowing, and their fires twinkled in the gathering moonless dark-ness, more and more of them as

Shown here as a major general, Samuel Cur-tis was a Mexican War veteran, an engineer, and a Republican congressman from Iowa.

more soldiers filed in from the south to extend the line. Down to 10,500 as a re-sult of Sigel's losses, the Federals were outnumbered and they knew it, watching the long, strung-out necklace of enemy campfires growing longer every hour. Still, they felt reasonably secure behind their new-turned mounds of dirt and logs, white-blanketed under the sift of snow falling softly out of the darkness. They built their own fires higher against the cold, then bedded down for a good night's sleep before the dawn which they believed would light the way for an all-out Confederate lunge across the creek and against their works.

★

March 7 came in bleak and gray, overcast but somewhat warmer. The snow had stopped; the wind had fallen in the night. As Curtis' men turned out of their bedrolls, peering south through the fog that rose out of the hollow, they saw something they had not expected to see. The plain was empty over there. Last night's rebel campfires were cold ashes, and the men who had kindled and fed them were nowhere in sight.

★ ★ ★   *I*n the past three days the Confederates had marched better than fifty miles, the wind driving wet snow in their faces all the way. Their rations were gone, consumed on the march, and they were tired and hungry. There had to be a battle now, if only for the sake of capturing enemy supplies.

However, Van Dorn had no intention of sending his weary men against breastworks prepared for their reception. Impetuous though he was, that was not his way. Conferring with his generals, who knew the country well, he decided to send half his troops on a night march, clean around the north side of Pea Ridge, then down the road past Elkhorn Tavern for a dawn attack on the Union left rear. Once this was launched, the other half of his army, having made a coincidental, shorter march to the west end of the ridge, would come down through Leetown to strike the enemy right rear, which by then should be in motion to support the hard-pressed left. In short, it was to be a double envelopment much like the one Nathaniel Lyon had attempted at Wilson's Creek, except that this time the attackers would outnumber the defenders, 17,000 men with sixty guns opposing 10,500 with fifty.

Price's Missourians drew the longer march, beyond the screening ridge. McCulloch and Pike, with their Texans, Arkansans, Louisianians, and Indians, would make the secondary attack. Van Dorn himself, still in his ambulance — the three-day ride through wind and snow had not reduced his fever — would go with the roundabout column, to be on hand for the charge that would open the conflict. Soon after dark the army filed off to the left, leaving its long line of campfires burning to deceive the Federals, and moved northward in column beyond the enemy right flank. In this hare-and-tortoise contest — the youthful, impetuous cavalryman Earl Van Dorn against the aging, methodical engineer Sam Curtis — the hare was off and running.

Puzzled by the disappearance of the rebels from across the creek next morning, Curtis was in the worse-than-tortoise position of not even knowing that a race was being run, let alone that the goal was his own rear. Through the early morning hours, while the sun climbed higher up the sky to melt away the fog and fallen snow, he was left wondering where and why Van Dorn had gone. Then suddenly he knew. Just as they had confirmed his fears about the forty-gun salute he had heard on Monday, so now on Friday his scouts came rid-

ing in to solve the mystery of the rebels' disappearance. They were behind Pea
Ridge, about to enter the north-south valley that gave down upon his unprotected rear. They had been delayed by obstructions along the road, the scouts
reported, but they were coming fast now and in strength. Curtis would have to
do one of two things. He could wheel about and meet them here, fighting with
his back to his own intrenchments, or he could try to make a run for it. In the
latter case, the choice lay between possible and probable destruction. If he tried
to get away northward, up the wire road through the defile, the Confederate
spearhead would be plunged into the flank of his moving column. If on the other hand he ran southward, through enemy country — retreating *forward*, so to
speak — Van Dorn would be across his lines of supply and communication; the
rebels would have him bottled in a wintry vacuum.

He chose to meet them. His four divisions were in line, facing
south: Sigel's two on the right, led by Peter Osterhaus and Alexander Asboth,
the former a German, the latter a Hungarian: then his own two, under Eugene
Carr, a vigorous, hard-mannered regular, and an Indiana-born colonel with the
improbable name of Jefferson Davis. Curtis ordered them to about-face, the
rear thus becoming the front, the left the right, the right the left. Carr was sent
at once to meet the threat beyond Elkhorn Tavern. Osterhaus moved up past
Leetown to protect the western flank, and presently on second thought Curtis
sent Davis to support him, while Asboth remained under Sigel, in reserve. Curtis had confidence in his commanders. Colonels Osterhaus, Carr, and Davis had
had considerable combat experience, the first two at Wilson's Creek and the
third from as far back as Fort Sumter, where he had been an artillery lieutenant;
Asboth, a brigadier, had been Frémont's chief of staff and a fighter under Kos-
suth back in Europe. How far beyond the claims of past performance they de
served their leader's confidence was about to be determined. And this was especially true of Carr, who stood where the first blow was about to fall.

At 10.30 it fell, and it fell hard. Tired and hungry after their stumbling all-night march, but keyed up by the order to charge at last, Price's men
came crashing through the brush along both sides of the wire road, guns bark-
ing aggressively on the flanks and from the rear. Carr had prepared a defense in
depth, batteries staggered along the road and a strong line of infantry posted to
support the foremost while the other three fired over their heads. Presently,
though, they had nothing to support. A well-directed salvo knocked out three
of the four guns and blew up two caissons, killing all the cannoneers. Un-
nerved, the infantry fell back on the second battery, just north of the tavern,
where they managed to repulse the first attack, then the second, both of which
were piecemeal. Bearded like a Cossack, Carr rode among his soldiers, shouting
encouragement. Out front, the brush was boiling with butternut veterans form-
ing for a third assault. This one would come in strength, he knew, and he

doubted if his thin line could resist it. He sent a courier galloping back to Curtis with an urgent request for reinforcements.

Curtis had his headquarters on a little knoll just south of a farm road leading from Elkhorn Tavern to Leetown; here the courier found him surrounded by his staff, mounted and resplendent, wearing their best clothes for battle. They were looking toward the left front, their attention drawn by a sudden rattle of musketry and a caterwaul of unearthly, high-pitched yelling. Carr's message had scarcely been delivered when a horseman came riding fast from that direction. Osterhaus had been swamped by a horde of befeathered, screaming men who bore down on him brandishing scalping knives and hatchets. Taken aback — they had bargained for nothing in all the world like this — his troops had broken, abandoning guns and equipment. Davis had moved up; he was holding as best he could, but he needed reinforcements. Appealed to thus by the commanders of both wings at once, Curtis chose to wait before committing his reserve. He sent word for both to hold with what they had. At this point the battle racket swelled to new and separate climaxes, right and left.

★ ★ ★ In contrast to the gloom that had descended on him — first as a result of his failure to gobble up the scattered Federal units on the march, and then because of the delay of his flanking column as it moved around Pea Ridge in the night, which had thrown him three hours behind schedule and cost him the rich fruits of full surprise — Van Dorn was exultant. Price's men were surging ahead, knocking back whatever stood in their way, and off to the west the rolling crackle of McCulloch's attack told him of success in that quarter as well. The fighting still raged furiously at the near end of the ridge; Carr's second line was thrown back by the all-out third assault, so that presently the Missourians were whooping around the tavern itself and drinking from the horse trough in the yard.

All this took time, however. As the sun slid down the sky, Van Dorn's exultation began to be tempered by concern. His men had had no sleep all night and nothing to eat since the day before, whereas the Federals had had a good night's rest and a hot breakfast. The Confederates still fought grimly, battering now at Carr's third line, drawn south and west of the tavern, but weariness and hunger were sapping their strength; much of the steam had gone out of their attacks. Worse still, there was no longer any sound of serious fighting on the far side of the field, where McCulloch's earlier gains had been announced by the clatter moving south and east to mark his progress. Van Dorn was left wondering until near sundown, when a messenger arrived to explain the silence across the way.

There, as here, the battle had opened on a note of victory. Pike's Indians, delighted at having frightened Osterhaus into hurried retreat, pranced

*This battle flag of the Confederate 1st Chero-
kee Mounted Rifles was carried into battle at
Pea Ridge, Arkansas, in March 1862.*

around the cannon the white men had abandoned; "wagon guns," they called them, and took the horse collars from the slaughtered animals to wear about their own necks; "me big Injun, big as horse!" they chanted, dancing so that the trace-chains jingled against the frozen ground. It was a different matter, though, when Pike tried to get them back into line to help McCulloch, who had run into stiffer resistance on the left. They had had enough of that. They wanted to fight from behind rocks or up in trees, not lined up like tenpins, white-man-style, to be struck by the iron bowling balls the wagon guns threw with a terrifying boom and a sudden, choking cloud of smoke. Some stood firm—a dismounted cavalry battalion of mixbloods, for example, under Colonel Stand Watie, a Georgia-born Cherokee—but, in the main, whatever was to be accomplished from now on would have to be done without the help of anything more than a scattering of red men.

Not that McCulloch particularly minded. He was not given to calling on others for help, either back in his Texas Ranger days or now. When his advance was held up by an Illinois outfit which had rallied behind a snake-rail fence at the far end of a field, he brought up an Arkansas regiment, shook out a skirmish line, and took them forward, sunlight glinting on the sharpshooter's rifle he carried for emergencies and sport. The Illinois troops delivered a volley that sent the butternuts scampering back across the field. They re-formed and charged again. Sixty yards short of the tree-lined fence, they came upon a body in sky-blue trousers and a dove-gray corduroy jacket, sprawled in the grass: McCulloch. His rifle was gone, along with a gold pocket watch he had prized, but he still wore the expensive boots he had died in when the bullet found his heart.

Quickly then word spread among the men who had sworn that they would storm hell itself at his command: "McCulloch's dead. They killed McCulloch!" Their reaction to the news was much the same, in effect, as the Indians' reaction to artillery. Whatever they had sworn they would do with McCulloch to lead them, it soon became clear that they would do little without him. To complete the confusion, his successor was killed within the hour, and the third commander was captured while attempting to rally some soldiers who, as it turned out, were Federals. By the time Pike was found and notified — he had been trying vainly, all the while, to reorganize his frightened or jubilant Indians — the sun was near the landline and there were considerably fewer troops for him to head. Dazed with grief for their lost leader, many had simply wandered off the field, following him in death as they had in life; Osterhaus and Davis, having themselves had enough fighting for one day, had been content to watch them go, unmolested. At sundown Pike assembled what men he could find and set out on a march around the north side of Pea Ridge to join Van Dorn and Price, whose battle still raged near Elkhorn Tavern.

News of his right wing's disintegration reached Van Dorn as one more in a series of disappointments and vexations. Repeated checks and delays, here on the left where Price's men were being held up by less than half their number, had brought him to the verge of desperation. There was another problem, no less grave and quite as vexing. Having left his wagon train on the far side of the battleground, the diminutive commander had discovered an unwelcome military axiom: namely, that when you gain the enemy's rear you also place him in your own, unless you bring it with you. Consequently, in addition to a numbing lack of sleep and food, just as he was doing all he could to launch a final charge that would crush Carr at last and sweep the field before nightfall ended the fighting and gave the Federals a chance to realign their now superior forces, his men were experiencing an ammunition shortage. Desperately he ordered them forward, putting all he had into what he knew would use up the last of daylight, as well as the last of their strength and ammunition. Price was there to help him. Nicked by a bullet, but refusing to retire for medical treatment, he wore his wounded arm in a sling as he rode from point to point to bolster his men's spirits for an all-out climax to the night-long march and day-long battle. At last, between the two of them, they got the Missourians into assault formation and sent them forward, streaming around the tavern and down both sides of the wire road, across which Carr had drawn his third stubborn line of resistance.

The red ball of the sun had come to rest on the horizon; Carr's men could see it over their left shoulders — the direction in which they had been watching all these hours for reinforcements that did not come. Now as before, their batteries were distributed in depth along the road, and now as then the Confederates wrecked them, gun by gun, with a preliminary bombardment. After an ominous lull they saw the rebels coming, yelling and firing as they came, hundreds of them bearing down to complete the wreckage their artillery had begun. As the Federals fell back from their shattered pieces an Iowa cannoneer paused to toss a smoldering quilt across a caisson, then ran hard to catch up with his friends. Still running, he heard a tremendous explosion and looked back in time to see a column of fire and smoke standing tall above the place where he had fuzed the vanished caisson. Stark against the twilight sky, it silhouetted the lazy-seeming rise and fall of blown-off arms and legs and heads and mangled trunks of men who just now had been whooping victoriously around the captured battery position.

Over on his headquarters knoll, Curtis heard and saw it too, and finally—as if that violent column of smoke and flame standing lurid against the twilight on the right, followed after an interval by the boom and rumble as the sound of the explosion echoed off the ridge to the north, had at last brought home to him, like the ultimate shout of despair from a drowning man, at least some measure of the desperation Carr had been trying to communicate ever since Price first

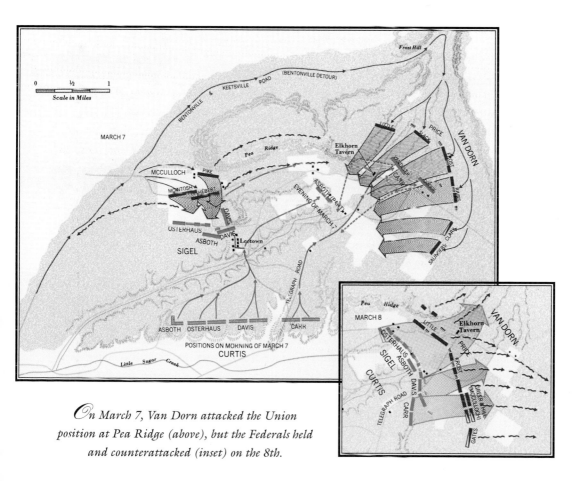

On March 7, Van Dorn attacked the Union position at Pea Ridge (above), but the Federals held and counterattacked (inset) on the 8th.

struck him, eight hours back—responded. By then the sporadic firing on the left had died away; Osterhaus and Davis reported the rebels gone or going. Van Dorn was tricky, but Curtis felt the danger from that direction had been removed; he could look to the right, where by now the column of fire had turned into a mushrooming pillar of smoke. Asboth, who had remained all this time in reserve to meet disaster in either direction, was sent up the wire road in relief of Carr.

Arriving at 7 he found the firing reduced to a sputter here as well. Torn and weary, Carr's regiments moved back from their fourth position of the day, retiring through the ranks of the division that relieved them. Forward of there, extending right and left of the tavern, half a mile each way, the Confederates were bedding down for the rest they sorely needed, their campfires in the tavern yard illuminating the building up to the bleached skull and antlers on the rooftree. The long day's fight was over.

★ ★ ★ **C**urtis rode out for a night inspection of his lines, which at some points were so near the enemy's that the opposing soldiers could overhear each other's groans and laughter. Despite their bone-deep weariness, the men were still too keyed up for sleep. They amused themselves by taunting the rebs across the way, hooting at the replies provoked, and recounting, for mutual admiration, exploits they had performed on the field today. Several could even substantiate their claims. One, for example—an Illinois private, Peter Pelican by name—displayed a gold watch he had taken as a trophy off a rebel he had shot: an officer, he said, in "sky-blue britches" and a dove-colored jacket. Some other quick-thinking scavenger had got the Maynard rifle, much to Pelican's regret, and the Johnnies had come swarming back too soon for him to have time to strip the dead man of his fancy boots.

The Federal commander might have heard this as he made the rounds, along with much else like it; but the truth was, he took little pleasure in small talk, and especially not now. He had too much on his mind. For one thing, he was irked at Sigel, who he considered had undertaken considerably less than his share of the work today, sparing Osterhaus and Asboth while Davis and Carr were doing most of the bleeding. Consequently, when he discovered that the German planned a temporary withdrawal to feed his troops, his temper snapped. "Let Sigel's men hold their lines. Send supper out, not the men in," he said gruffly. And having thus relieved his spleen he returned to his headquarters tent. It was time to decide what to do about tomorrow. Still fully dressed, he lay down on some blankets spread on a pile of straw and sent for his division commanders to join him for a council of war.

It was midnight when they assembled. Sigel spoke first, and he spoke from desperation, proposing his specialty: slashing retreat. The army, he said, must select an escape route and cut its way out in the morning. Osterhaus agreed, and so did Carr, whose command had been fought to a frazzle. He was nursing a wound, as was Asboth, who had been winged by a stray bullet in the dark and also saw no answer but retreat. Davis was silent, but that was his manner — a gloomy man with a long nose and lonesome-looking eyes. Reclined on the blanketed pile of straw, Curtis weighed their counsel. No less deliberate in conference than he had been in combat, he was not going to be stampeded by his own commanders, any more than he had been stampeded by Van Dorn. In his opinion the Confederates had most likely shot their bolt. The threat to his left having been abolished, he could reinforce his right. Thus bolstered, the army could hold its own, he believed, and even perhaps go forward. On this note the council adjourned, and its members, their advice declined, went out into the darkness to consolidate their commands and await the dawn.

The night was cold and windless, so that when dawn came through at last, smoke from yesterday's battle still hung in long folds and tendrils about the fields, draping the hillsides and filling the hollows level-full. The sun rose red, then shone wanly through the haze, like tarnished brass; Van Dorn's dispositions were at once apparent across the way. South and west of Elkhorn Tavern, between the Federals and the sunrise, Price's Missourians held the ground they had won when nightfall closed the fighting. Pike having arrived in the night with his and McCulloch's remnants, the Confederate commander had stationed the Indians along the crest of Pea Ridge, supporting several batteries — stark up there against the sky they looked like stick-men guarding toy guns — while the Texans and Arkansans occupied the fields along its base.

It was a long, concave line, obviously drawn with defense in mind: Curtis had been right. Also right, as it turned out, were the dispositions he had made to meet what dawn revealed. Davis was posted opposite the tavern, with Carr's division in support, still binding up its wounds. The left belonged to Sigel, who had strung out Osterhaus and Asboth to overlap the enemy in the shadow of the ridge. After a drawn-out silence, during which the Unionists enjoyed a hot breakfast and the rebels ate what they could find in the knapsacks of the fallen, Van Dorn opened with his batteries, stirring the smoke that wreathed the Federal line.

The cannonade was perfunctory and had no real aggressive drive behind it. Low as he was on ammunition — his unprotected train had gone off southward, fearing capture — Van Dorn fired his guns, not as a prelude to attack, nor even to signify his readiness to receive one, but merely to see what the Yankees would do. In fact, that was why he had remained in position overnight. It had seemed wrong to retreat after the gains he had made, and for all he knew the dawn might show the Federals gone or ready to surrender. Dawn had shown no such thing. It showed them, rather, in what seemed greater strength than ever: a long, compact line, with batteries glinting dangerously through the cop-

Franz Sigel, graduate of the German Military Academy and a leader of the U.S. German community, led the counterattack at Pea Ridge.

pery haze. Hungry, weary, down to their last rounds of ammunition, Van Dorn's men had done their worst and he knew it. Yet, for all he knew, after yesterday's hard knocks Curtis too might be reduced to his last ounce of powder and resistance, needing no more than a prod to send him scampering. At any rate the Mississippian thought it worth a try.

It soon became apparent that the Federals could take a good deal more prodding than the Southerners could exert. Sensing the weakness behind the cannonade, Curtis sent word to Sigel on the left. Yesterday the German had held back: now let him seize the initiative and go forward if he could. Sigel could and did. With a precision befitting a mathematician, he ordered his infantry to lie down in the muddy fields while he advanced his batteries 250 yards

out front and opened fire. He rode among the roaring guns, erect as on parade
except when he dismounted to sight an occasional piece himself, then patted the
breech and stepped back, as if for applause, to observe the effects of his gunnery. It was accurate. Battery after Confederate battery was shattered along the
ridge and on the flat, and when others came up to take their places, they were
shattered too. Sigel's soldiers, many of them German like himself, cheered him
wildly as they watched the rebel cannoneers fan backward from the wreckage of
their guns. Over on the right, the men of Carr and Davis, watching too, began
to understand the pride that lay behind the boast: "I fights mit Sigel."

Van Dorn's artillerymen were not the only ones disconcerted by the
deadliness of the Yankee gunnery. His infantry showed signs of wavering too.
Sigel rode back to where his cheering soldiers lay obedient in the mud. Gestur-
ing with his saber, he ordered them to stand up and go forward. They did so,
still cheering, in a long, undulating line, like a huge snake moving sideways, the
head coiling over the lower slope of the ridge, the center thrusting forward with
a lunging, sidewinder motion, the tail following in turn. On it moved, with a series of curious sidewise thrusts, preceded by a scattering of graybacks as it slith-
ered over whatever stood in its broad path. The reserve Union regiments, waiting in ranks, tossed their hats and contorted their faces with screams of pride
and pleasure at the sight. Exhilarated, Sigel stood in his stirrups, saber lifted,
eyes aglow. "Oh — dot was lofely!" he exclaimed.

Over near the tavern, watching the great snake glide sideways up
the ridge, the men with Davis began shouting for a charge on this front too,
lest Sigel's troops get all the loot and glory. Curtis was with them. Indeed, he
was everywhere this morning; already two of his orderlies had been killed riding with him as he galloped amid shellbursts to inspect his line and strengthen
weak spots. All the same, active as he was, he had not put aside his meticulous
insistence on precision. Sending for reinforcements, he remained to check
their prompt arrival by the second hand on his watch, then was off again
through the smoke and whistling fragments of exploding shells. When the
men in front of the tavern began yelling for a chance to match the tableau
Sigel was staging on the left, Curtis nodded quick assent and rode forward
onto a low knoll — he had a fondness for such little elevations, in battle or
bivouac — to watch as they advanced.

Close-ranked and determined, they surged past him, cheering.
Abruptly then, beyond their charging front, he saw the Confederates give way,
retreating before contact, and heard his soldiers whooping as they swarmed
around and past Elkhorn Tavern, where the telegrapher's family huddled in the
cellar and rebel dead were stacked like cordwood on the porch. The Union right
and left wings came together with a shout, driving the gray confusion of scampering men, careening guns, and wild-eyed horses pell-mell up the wire road

through the defile, past the position Carr's men had abandoned under pressure from the opening guns, twenty-four hours back.

As quickly as that, almost too sudden for realization, the battle was over—won. Curtis rode down off the knoll, then cantered back and forth along his lines. His aging engineer's brown eyes were shining; all his former stiff restraint was gone. Boyishly he swung his hat and shouted, performing a little horseback dance of triumph as he rode up and down the lines of cheering men. "Victory!" he cried. He kept swinging his hat and shouting. "Victory! Victory!" he cried.

Thus Curtis. But Van Dorn was somewhat in the predicament of having prodded a shot bear, thinking it dead, only to have the creature rear up and come charging at him, snarling. Consequently, his main and in fact his exclusive concern, in the face of this sudden show of teeth and claws, was how to get away unmangled. Horrendous as it was, however, the problem was not with him long. His soldiers solved it for him. Emerging from the north end of the defile, they scattered in every direction except due south, where the prodded bear still roared. All through what was left of the day and into the night (while, a thousand miles to the east, the *Merrimac-Virginia* steamed back from her first sortie, leaving the burning *Congress* to light the scene of wreckage she had left in Hampton Roads) various fragments of his army retreated north and east and west, swinging wide to avoid their late opponents when they turned back south to reach the Boston Mountains. Though unpursued, they took a week to reassemble near Van Buren.

★ ★ ★ **B**ack at his starting point in the foothills of the Ozarks, Van Dorn counted noses and reported his losses as 1000 killed and wounded, 300 captured. He was by no means willing to admit that the battle had been anything more than a temporary setback. Least of all could it be considered a defeat; "I was not defeated, but only foiled in my intentions," he told Richmond. Still with his main goal in mind, he was ready to try again, this time by marching "boldly and rapidly toward St Louis, between Ironton and the enemy's grand depot at Rolla."

Within another week, March 23, he was heading north with 16,000 effectives when he received a peremptory order to turn east, crossing the river by "the best and most expeditious route," and join the concentration being effected in North Mississippi by Johnston and Beauregard after their long retreat from Kentucky. "Your order received," Van Dorn replied, pleased no doubt at the prospect of exchanging the wilds of Arkansas for the comparative comforts of his native state.

Unlike his opponent, who was as dashing, or as slapdash, on a retreat as in an advance, Curtis had not been satisfied to report his casualties in round figures. That would have been neither respectful to the dead nor indicative of sound administration. Consolidating subordinate reports, which showed that Carr's division had suffered more than the other three combined, he prepared a careful table — killed, 203; wounded, 980; captured or otherwise missing, 201; total, 1384 — and forwarded it to Halleck, declaring that he had "completely routed the whole rebel force, which retired in great confusion, but rather safely, through the deep, impassable defiles."

He did not speculate, as others would surely have done in his place — especially Van Dorn — on what the future might reveal as to the importance of the victory he had won at Elkhorn Tavern, in the shadow of Pea Ridge. That was not his way. Besides, he had no means of knowing that Van Dorn would be called east, beyond the Mississippi, and would not be coming back. He did not claim, as in truth he could have done, that he had secured Missouri to the Union for all time; that guerilla bands might rip and tear her, that raider columns of various strengths might cut swaths of destruction up and down her, but that her star in the Confederate flag, placed there like Kentucky's by a fleeing secessionist legislature, represented nothing more from now on than the exiles who bore arms beneath that banner.

Though he did not deal in military imponderables, other imponderables were another matter: those of nature, for example. Spring had come to upland Arkansas at last, and it put him in mind of the ones he had known in his Ohio boyhood. The day after the battle a warm rain fell, washing away the bloodstains, but as the burial squads went about their work the air was tainted with decay. Curtis moved his headquarters off a ways, once more to enjoy the singing birds as he sat at a camp table, writing home. "Silent and sad" were words he used to describe the present scene of recent conflict. "The vulture and the wolf have now communion, and the dead, friends and foes, sleep in the same lonely grave." So he wrote, this highly practical and methodical engineer. Looking up at the tree-fledged ridge with its gray outcroppings of granite, he added that he hoped it would serve hereafter as a monument to perpetuate the memory of those who had fallen at its base.

*   *   *   **S**outh and west of Pea Ridge lay Texas, where Van Dorn had first shown dash and won success. North and west of Texas — twice the size of that vast Lone Star expanse — the Territories of Utah and New Mexico stretched on beyond the sunset to the California gold fields and the shores of the Pacific. In the minds of most, this sun-baked half-million-square-mile wasteland with its brackish lakes and its few, thirsty rivers was of less than doubtful value, fit only as a breeding ground of

lizards and Apaches. Others knew better: Jefferson Davis, for one. Believing in his Union days that the nation's destiny pointed south and west, he had engineered the Gadsden Purchase and even imported camels in an attempt to solve the sandy transportation problem.

Now in his Confederate days, the nebulous future being translated into terms of the urgent present, his belief was reinforced. Out there beyond the sunset lay the gold fields and the ocean. Control of the former would establish sound financial credit on which the South could draw for securing war supplies abroad, while the opening of Confederate ports along the Pacific Coast would insure their delivery by stretching the tenuous Federal blockade past the snapping point. Satisfying as all this was as a solution to present problems, an even more dazzling prospect still remained. Having forged its independence in the crucible of war, the new nation could then return to the old southern nationalist dream of expansion, acquiring by purchase or conquest the adjoining Mexican states of Chihuahua, Sonora, and Baja California. After these would come others, less near but no less valuable: Cuba, for instance, then Central America, and all that lay between. Van Dorn seizing St Louis as a base for a march through Illinois to subdue the Middle West, Beauregard dictating peace terms in the White House after the Battle of Cleveland or Lake Erie — glorious as these scenes were to contemplate in the mind's eye, they were pale indeed in contrast to the glittering light of victory by way of California.

None of this could be accomplished, however, until safe passage west had been assured at the start by clearing Federal troops from the Territory of New Mexico. The answer to this, as Davis knew, lay in control of the Rio Grande. It was therefore with considerable pleasure, two months after Sumter, that he welcomed to Richmond a forty-four-year-old Louisiana-born West Pointer, Henry H. Sibley, lately Major, U.S. Army. Indeed, from Davis's point of view the caller might have tumbled straight out of heaven into the arms of the Confederacy. He had come to offer his services — preferably for duty in the region where he had been stationed for years, commanding various forts throughout the Southwest and along the Rio Grande. An enterprising officer, he had invented a conical tent modeled after the wigwams of the Sioux, and he had kept busy in other ways out there. What was more, he had a plan. And as he told it — a stocky, wind-burnt man with a big-featured face and a heavy mustache that grew down past the corners of his mouth so that his aggressive chin looked naked as a heel — Davis might have been listening to the echo of his own thoughts on the dazzling possibilities of victory by way of California. Granted the authority, Sibley said, he would raise a force in Texas and set out northward from El Paso, capturing forts along the river all the way to Santa Fe. This done, he would consolidate and turn west, his ranks swollen with volunteers whose watchword would be "On to San Francisco."

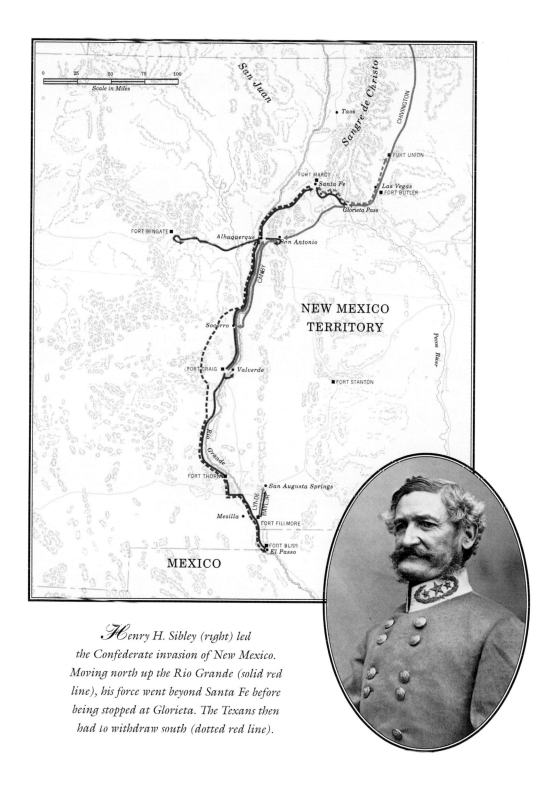

*H*enry H. Sibley (right) led
the Confederate invasion of New Mexico.
Moving north up the Rio Grande (solid red
line), his force went beyond Santa Fe before
being stopped at Glorieta. The Texans then
had to withdraw south (dotted red line).

Davis liked the sound of it and was more than willing to grant him the authority he asked. Unfortunately, however, that was all he had to offer. The government could spare no arms or munitions; in fact it could spare no equipment at all. The ex-major would have to scrape together what he could find in Texas on his own, then make up the balance out of enemy stores from the forts he took as he marched upriver. No matter how fruitful the project promised to be, it would have to be self-sustaining: Davis made that quite clear at the outset, before granting the authority.

In early July, two weeks before Manassas, Sibley was made a brigadier and assigned to command the Department of New Mexico. Like much of his equipment, the department itself was still in Union hands; but that would be corrected, too, when he had accomplished the first stage of the plan he had outlined in the President's office. Davis wished him Godspeed, and Sibley re-

---

"If an old woman with a broomstick should come with full authority from the state of Texas to demand the public property, I would give it to her."

— David E. Twiggs

---

turned at once to Texas, where he recruited a brigade of three mounted regiments by the end of the year and set out for El Paso, the jump-off point for his campaign to control the Rio Grande.

Two men, David E. Twiggs and John R. Baylor, had accomplished much for him already, before and since his trip to Richmond. Twiggs, a Federal brigadier in command of the Texas Department during the secession furor, had repeatedly asked Washington for instructions through that stormy time. Receiving none, he acted in accordance with a statement he had made: "If an old woman with a broomstick should come with full authority from the state of Texas to demand the public property, I would give it to her." He did just that, surrendering all the troops, forts, and equipment in his charge, not to an old woman, but to a posse of citizens who styled themselves a "committee for public safety." Northern howls of "treason to the flag" went up, and Twiggs, being summarily dismissed from the U.S. Army, repaired forthwith to New Orleans, where he was solaced and rewarded with a commission as a Confederate major general.

In time, a portion of this surrendered equipment was inherited by

★

Sibley, who needed it badly. Meanwhile Baylor, his other helper, had kept as busy as the first. Issuing a blanket invitation to whoever would join him on what he announced as a 1000-man "buffalo hunt" in Old Mexico, he showed his commission as a Confederate lieutenant colonel to the 350 volunteers who turned up, swore them in, organized them into a regiment called the Texas Mounted Rifles, and marched them to El Paso in time to receive the surrender of Fort Bliss, across the river from the Mexican hamlet.

Upstream the Rio Grande was divided like the nation, north and south, and Baylor saw in this a chance to accomplish a great deal more. For some time now there had been a movement among New Mexicans to split the territory along the 34th parallel and detach the southern portion as Arizona. Since in general the people of this lower region favored the Confederacy, he decided to go up there and help them, adding thereby a future new state to his new nation. There was one problem. Forty miles upriver from El Paso, just this side of the village of Mesilla, Fort Fillmore blocked the way, its garrison of 700 U.S. regulars commanded by Major Isaac Lynde, a veteran of thirty-four years in the infantry. Undeterred at being thus outnumbered two-to-one, Baylor spent no time musing on the odds. In mid-July — while Sibley was on the final leg of his round-trip journey to Richmond — the Texan led his Mounted Rifles north.

On the night of the 24th, though the Federals had been warned that he was coming, he camped unmolested within 600 yards of the fort on the opposite bank of the river, then next morning splashed across and occupied Mesilla. When Lynde at last marched out to challenge the invaders, the townspeople, who had greeted Baylor with vivas and hurrahs, climbed a nearby hill to watch the contest. After demanding an immediate surrender, and receiving an immediate refusal, the gray-bearded major sent one squadron forward in a tentative, head-on charge that was repulsed with four men killed and seven wounded. As a battle it wasn't much; but it was quite enough for Lynde. Abandoning any notion of holding the fort, he fired a few short-falling rounds in the direction of the hill where the ungrateful — and unarmed — men, women, and children were cheering the secessionists, then ordered a retreat northeast to Fort Stanton, 150 sandy miles beyond the Organ Mountains.

Next day, displaying what one of his officers called "a sublimity of majestic indifference," he was taking lunch at San Augustín Springs when he discovered that the empty fort had been no more than a tub to Baylor's whale. The Texan wanted the soldiers, too, and was there at hand, demanding their surrender or a fight. Lynde decided the former would be best. After paroling the 492 officers and men taken here — the other 200-odd had already been picked up as stragglers — Baylor returned to Mesilla and on August 1 issued a proclamation establishing the Confederate Territory of Arizona, with the 34th parallel as its northern boundary and himself as its military governor. Rich-

mond quickly sustained his action, and Congress welcomed the delegate who
soon arrived to represent the new far-western territory.

Such, then, was the situation Sibley found awaiting him when he
reached Fort Bliss in mid-December with his newly recruited brigade. Between
them, in their different ways, Twiggs and Baylor had accomplished much of his
project for him already, supplying his men with surrendered equipment and
clearing the Rio Grande well beyond the Texas border. Fort Stanton's garrison
had withdrawn to Albuquerque, while the Unionists at Fort Thorn, fifty miles
above Mesilla, had retreated eighty miles upriver to Fort Craig, which now remained the only prepared defensive position in Federal hands below the boundary parallel. Once it fell, the others to the north should fall like toppled blocks:
Albuquerque, Santa Fe, and Fort Union, eastward beyond the foothills of the
Sangre de Cristo Mountains. At Fort Craig, he knew, 4000 troops were preparing to move against him, with perhaps as many more in support beyond the parallel. He himself had 3700, including Baylor's.

Yet he was no more discouraged by these odds than Baylor had been
by longer ones. Three days after New Year's he marched northward, four regiments in a long, mounted column, and within the week he occupied Fort
Thorn. The rest of the month was spent developing the situation. Then on February 7 he set out for Fort Craig, where the Federals were massing. His purpose
was offensive; he did not intend to surrender the initiative. On the 19th, after a
series of probing actions by his scouts, the main body came up and made camp
on an open plain across the river from the fort on the west bank. The stage was
set for the first major clash to determine who would control the Rio Grande.

★ ★ ★ *T*hat night, when the wind was from the east, Confederate voices could be heard across the water by the troops
inside the fort. Colonel Edward R. S. Canby was in command,
not only of the fort but also of the whole department, and this was only the latest of his trials since the advent of secession. He had taken over by appointment
upon the departure into enemy ranks of the previous commander, W. W. Loring,
the one professional in the quartet of prima donnas who brought grief to
R. E. Lee in West Virginia. Indiana-born, tall, clean-shaven and soldierly-
looking, with mild manners and a big nose that dominated his otherwise surprisingly delicate features, Canby was a year younger than Sibley and had finished at
West Point a year behind him. Thrust into command at the outbreak of hostili-
ties, he had about 1000 territorial militia, poorly armed and even more poorly
trained, to supplement the scattering of peacetime regulars stationed at the various posts and forts in his department. Supplies were as scarce as distances were
vast. Consequently, while Baylor took Fort Bliss and then Fort Fillmore, Canby
could do nothing but work with what he had in an attempt to strengthen his

defenses, meanwhile sending out repeated calls for volunteers. All this time, Sibley was raising soldiers down in Texas: for what purpose his opponent knew all too well for his mind's ease. By the end of the year Canby had five regiments, recruited by prominent New Mexicans — Kit Carson was one — and sent them out to bolster such remaining scattered strongpoints as had not been abandoned or surrendered during the build-up.

All through January he continued his preparations to move southward from Fort Craig. Perhaps he might even have done so, in time, if Sibley had not spared him the risk and trouble by moving north against him, arriving February 19 and making camp within earshot of the fort on the opposite bank of the Rio Grande. In expectation of a siege, Canby spent the night making his strong position even stronger, preparing to repulse the attack which he believed would come at dawn. It did not come. Instead, as the light grew, he looked across the river and saw, between him and the rising sun, enemy wagons rolling north: Sibley was by-passing the fort, leaving it — and the Federals inside it — to wither on the vine, while he moved northward into the unprotected region on beyond the parallel, the region whose protection was Canby's primary assignment. What he had seen, out there between him and the rising sun, left the Union commander no choice. He himself would have to attack, to fight without the defensive advantage of the adobe walls he had been strengthening all this time. Accordingly, he sent a regiment up the western bank, under orders to cross the river five miles upstream and charge the rebels, who he believed were moving north across the mesa of Valverde in march column.

In this he was mistaken. Sibley had not intended to go north without at least an attempt to cripple any enemy force he left behind. He was maneuvering for a crossing and an assault against the fort. But now that Canby had obliged him by coming out for a fight in the open, Sibley was appreciative and ready. Crashing through the rust-colored reeds on the eastern bank, then charging up the slope onto the mesa, the Federals found the Texans waiting with double-shotted guns. Cannon and rifle fire broke up the attack in short order, the blue troopers scattering for what little cover they could find. They clung there, under sniper fire through what was left of daylight, and withdrew after dark to report to their commander that the rebels were still there: very much so, in fact. The two-day Battle of Valverde was half over.

For Canby, that first day had begun in error and ended in repulse. Now at least, as dawn of the second came glimmering through, there would be no error in estimating the enemy situation. Sibley was there, outnumbered, and he would attack him. He sent three more regiments up to join the first, with orders to force the crossing in strength and whip the rebels, still drawn up on the mesa within musket range of the river. He had not wanted this kind of fighting; these 4000 men were all he had to protect the whole Southwest. But now that it could no longer be avoided, he was determined to make the work as short and decisive as possible, no matter how bloody.

It was far from short work, but it turned out bloody enough. After losing a good many men at the crossing—they came under a galling fire and the bodies of men and horses floated slowly downstream, bumping along in the shallow water—they managed to get their guns across and with them knock the enemy back into the sandy ridges at the far edge of the mesa. From there, the Texans tried cavalry charges against the flanks and dismounted charges against the center, the sand-polished rowels of their spurs as big and bright as silver dollars. Past midday the charges continued; all were repulsed. Then at 2.45 Canby himself came up from the fort, bringing the remaining regiment. He assumed command just as Colonel Tom Green, on the other side, took over from Sibley, who had become indisposed—from the heat, some said, while others said from whiskey. Whichever it was, it was a Confederate advantage: Green was an all-out fighter. He put his cavalry out front, massing behind them all the dismounted men he could lay hands on, and sent them charging all together against a six-gun battery at the north end of the Federal line. For eight minutes, one participant said, the fighting was "terrific beyond description." By then Green's men were among the guns; the battery officers and cannoneers were dead. When the Texans turned the captured pieces against the line they had so lately been a part of, it broke badly, one Confederate declaring that the Northerners, in their haste to reach the west bank of the river, became "more like a herd of frightened mustangs than men." Once again there was slaughter at the crossing and more bodies floating sluggishly downstream in the blood-stained water.

Green was reassembling his elated troopers, preparing to use what was left of the short hot winter day to butcher or capture what was left of the rattled Federal army before it could reach the fort five miles downstream. He got his men together and was about to charge the enemy drawn up shakily on the opposite bank, when a truce party came forward under a white flag: Canby requested an armistice, time to care for the wounded and bury the dead. His chivalry thus appealed to, Green agreed to the cease fire, and while the defeated New Mexicans retreated under its protection to the adobe fastness of Fort Craig the victorious Texans rifled the knapsacks of the fallen, bolting "Yankee light-bread and other most delicious eatables," washed down with whiskey found in the canteens of the Union dead. Darkness fell; the battle was over. The men poured the sand from their boots and took their rest.

Recovered from his indisposition next morning, Sibley found that Green had left it to him to decide whether to go after the survivors in the fort, bagging the lot, or turn his back on them and continue the march northward. Federal casualties had been 263, Confederate 187, but the victory had been even more decisive as to proof of who would fight and who would panic under pres-

★

Edward Canby, having lost to the Confederates at Valverde, adopted a "scorched earth" policy, allowing a lack of supplies and the terrain to defeat his enemy.

sure. The opening phase of the campaign to seize the Southwest as a base for operations farther west had been accomplished; ahead lay the chief cities of the region, Albuquerque and Santa Fe. As Sibley saw it, such poor soldiers as Canby's were not worth the time that would be spent in completing their destruction. He gave his Texans a full day's rest as a reward for their exertions, then pressed on north without delay.

Within a week, having paused to establish a hospital for his wounded at Socorro, just beyond the boundary parallel, he had covered the hundred-odd miles to Albuquerque. He had good reason for haste. This was desert country, where loss of a canteen or a last handful of crackers could be as fatal as a bullet through the heart, and he had left Valverde with only five days' rations in his train. Fortunately, he had encountered no enemy soldiers on the way; apparently they had heard what had happened to their friends the week before and were falling back from contact. Then, as he came within sight of Albuquerque, he saw something that affected him worse than if he had seen a whole new Federal army drawn up for battle on the outskirts. Three great columns of smoke stood tall and black above the town. Anticipating his arrival, and his hunger, the Union garrison had set fire to their rich depot of supplies when they fell back on Santa Fe that morning.

He moved in unopposed and took the place, scraping together what few provisions he could buy or commandeer in order to continue the movement north. Four days later, March 5, he occupied the capital. Here too he was unopposed; the garrison pulled out on the eve of his arrival. All Sibley and his Texans got of the Santa Fe depot was its ashes.

★ ★ ★ *T*he burnings had been done under orders from Canby. When he fell back on Fort Craig under cover of the flag of truce on the night of his defeat, he sent couriers to the northward posts with instructions that all public properties, "and particularly provisions," were to be destroyed as soon as the invaders seemed about to come within reach. He knew this country and what it could do to an army without supplies. Having tried stand-up fighting at Valverde, and having lost, he adopted now a "scorched earth" policy, one not difficult to apply in a region where the earth was already scorched enough to burn the sole off a boot in a morning's walk.

Sibley's men were already feeling the pinch. Nor were the discomforts of short rations, threadbare clothes, and sand-leaking boots relieved by any considerable sympathy from the people of Albuquerque or Santa Fe. Expecting cheers and volunteers at the end of their long victory march, the Texans instead had found the atmosphere definitely unfriendly ever since they crossed the parallel. The southern commander's prediction that troops of sympathizers would come marching in to join him, miners and trappers from Utah Territory and beyond, had by no means been fulfilled; in fact, there were rumors that groups there were organizing to join the other side. Sibley was finding that all he won with victory was miles and miles of sand. Still, he had done nearly all of what he set out to do in preparing a base for the conquest of the Far West. Those miles and miles included the Rio Grande and the territorial capital. Except for the stunned remnant of Canby's army, still cowering inside the adobe protection of Fort Craig, all that remained was Fort Union, sixty miles east of Santa Fe, beyond the foothills of the Sangre de Cristo Mountains, so called because their slopes were the color of blood each day at sunset.

Fort Union had been the rallying point for all the garrisons Sibley had flushed from their accustomed posts. By now, he knew, it was held in strength, and he figured he would have to fight to take it. Preparing to do so, he advanced a picket of 600 men from Santa Fe twenty miles southeast to the mouth of Apache Canyon, which led on to Las Vegas, the new capital, and Fort Union. They were to hold the canyon mouth, preventing any Federal advance, while the rest of the

★

Confederates were being assembled to join them; then they would all go forward together to wipe out the final enemy stronghold. Preparations continued through most of March. Then, on the 26th, the picket got word that a small force — "200 [New] Mexicans and about 200 regulars" — was coming through the canyon for an attack on Santa Fe. It sounded too good to be true, but the Texans were not missing any chance to give the Yankees another drubbing. They mounted up and rode forward, taking two guns along for good measure.

Four miles up the canyon they caught sight of what they had been told to expect: a column of 400 Union troopers riding foolhardily within gun range of a body of seasoned Confederates who had them outnumbered three-to-two. There in the rocky trough of the pass the Texans formed their line for slaughter. Slaughter it was, but not as had been intended. Suddenly, one wrote his wife, Federal infantry "were upon the hills on both sides of us, shooting us down like sheep." They had been sucked into an ambush. As they fell back, startled, they could see up on the overhead ledges enemy sharpshooters "jumping from rock to rock like so many mountain sheep." Losing men at every attempt to take up a new position, they were near panic, not only because of the bullets, but also from sheer astonishment. New Mexicans — "Mexicans," they called them, with all the contempt a Texan could put into the word — had never fought like this. Then they discovered something else, which startled them even more. "Instead of Mexicans and regulars, they were regular demons . . . in the form of Pike's Peakers, from the Denver City gold mines."

That was what they were, all right, recruits from frontier mining towns; 1st Colorado, they called themselves, 1342 volunteers, with one battery of field guns and another of mountain howitzers. They had made a long cold wet march to reach Fort Union on the same day Sibley pulled into Santa Fe at the end of his long hot dry one. After two weeks of sandy drill in the vicinity of the fort, they felt ready and came looking for a fight. Now they had it, here in Apache Canyon. The Texans had finally rallied and were making a last-ditch stand near the mouth of the canyon. Drawn up in a strong position behind the moat of a dry streambed, they felt ready at last for whatever came. What came was the Federal cavalry. Released from decoy duty, they came riding fast, leaped the arroyo, and landed among the defenders, hacking and shooting. The Texans broke and fled, all but 71 who surrendered, bringing their casualties to 146 in all. The Coloradans had lost a total of 19.

While the Federals withdrew to meet reinforcements from Fort Union, the Confederate survivors sent out news of the disaster, which brought two regiments hurrying next day to their support. By dawn of the third day, March 28, the main bodies of both armies were moving through the canyon from opposite directions. An hour before noon they met at Glorieta Pass: "a terrible place for an engagement," a northern lieutenant afterward remembered, "a deep gorge, with a narrow wagon-track running along the bottom, the ground rising precipitously on each side, with huge bowlders and clumps of stunted cedars interspersed." Maneuver was impossible. All the two forces could do was scramble for cover and start banging away, the tearing rattle of pistol and rifle fire punctuated cacophonously by the deeper booms of cannon. Neither could advance, yet both knew that to fall back would be even more fatal than to stay there. For five hours the fighting continued in a boiling cloud of rock dust. Then an armistice was called to permit care for the wounded and burial of the dead.

The Texas commander had proposed it, and during the lull he received word of a calamity in his rear. A party of 300 Coloradans, led by a former preacher, had circled around behind the hills and come down upon the Confederate supply train, capturing the guard, burning the 85 provision-laden wagons, and bayoneting the nearly 600 horses and mules. In addition to Yankees, the Texans now would be fighting thirst and starvation. Against those odds they pulled back under cover of the truce and got away, out of the canyon and up the road to Santa Fe. The Federals, who had inflicted 123 casualties at a cost of 86, were all for going after them, up to the gates of the capital itself. But word had come from Canby at Fort Craig. He feared an attack on Fort Union by some roundabout route, perhaps across the eastern plains from the Texas panhandle. They were to hold that final stronghold "at all hazards, and to leave nothing to chance." Grudgingly the Coloradans obeyed, retracing their steps back through the canyon where they had fought and won two battles.

Four days later, April 1—the day McClellan took ship at Alexandria for his overnight voyage to the Peninsula—Canby left Fort Craig at last, marching north on Sibley's five-weeks-old trail. He was a brigadier general now, promoted as of the day before. On the 8th he arrived before Albuquerque. Sibley was ready for him, having been there all the while with half his army.

The two exchanged artillery salvos, and Canby retired beyond the nearby Sandía Mountains, calling for the Fort Union garrison to come out and reinforce him. Sibley likewise sent word for the Glorieta survivors, licking their wounds in Santa Fe, to join him there on the banks of the Rio Grande. Both armies thus were concentrating within one day's march of each other. The great winner-take-all battle of the Southwest, to which all that had gone before would have served as prologue, seemed about to be fought near Albuquerque.

It was never fought, either there or elsewhere, and for several reasons — mostly Sibley's. The countryside was too poor to support an invading army without the help of the people living there or supply lines leading back to greener regions, and he had neither. Rather, the inhabitants were unexpect-

*M*en of the 1st Colorado are seen at left drilling in the Colorado mining town of Empire as locals look on. Carrying the flag above, they marched into New Mexico to defeat the Confederates at Glorieta Pass.

edly hostile, more inclined to cache their scant provisions than to exchange them for Confederate money, which they considered worthless. Sibley's artillery ammunition was nearly exhausted and his wagon train had been destroyed. The recruits he expected had not appeared, or if they had — the Pike's Peakers, for example — they came against him wearing blue, so that the numerical odds were even longer now than they had been at the outset. Perceiving all this, he saw his dream dissolve in the encroaching gloom. There was but one thing left for him to do with his ragged, ill-fed, weary army: get it out of there and back to Texas. He was by no means certain that he could manage this, however, depending as it did on whether he would have the coöperation of his opponent.

He got it in full. Canby, having fought once at Valverde, wanted no more fighting he could possibly avoid. Sibley began his retreat on April 12, crossing the river with his main body to make camp that night, twenty miles south, on the west bank at Los Lunas. Next day, having stayed behind to bury their brass field pieces, for which they had neither shells nor powder, the remainder followed down the east bank to Peralta, nearly opposite. Canby marched in pursuit, his reinforcements having arrived that day from Fort Union. He was not trying to cut the rebels off and then destroy them. The last thing he wanted, in fact, was for them to turn and fight or even stop to catch their breath. What he wanted was for them to leave, the sooner the better; he wanted them out of the territory for whose protection he was responsible. At Peralta, coming upon the smaller Confederate segment, he gave it a nudge. "As we galloped across the bottom toward them they fluttered like birds in a snare," a Coloradan wrote. But that was all. When they scurried across the river, then turned south with the main body to continue the retreat, Canby turned south, too, but he remained on the eastern bank. For two days the retreat continued in this fashion, the two armies marching in plain view of each other, often within cannon range, on opposite banks of the fordable Rio Grande. Canby's men were outraged, shouting for him to send them across the river to slaughter the tatterdemalions who had been so arrogant two months before, when they were headed in the opposite direction. The northern commander was deaf alike to protests and appeals, however passionate. If there was to be any killing done, he would rather let the desert do it for him.

Beginning with the third day, the desert got its chance. When the Federals woke to reveille that morning near La Joya, they could see campfires burning brightly across the river. Dawn showed no signs of life in the camp, however, and after waiting a long while for the Texans to begin their march Canby sent some scouts across, who returned with news that the camp was abandoned; the rebels had left in the night. Sibley, it appeared, had wanted a battle even less than Canby did. Approaching Socorro, with Fort Craig only a

Texan Alfred Peticolas drew this sketch showing the Confederate retreat through the harsh terrain of West Texas in June 1862.

day's march beyond, he had left under cover of darkness in an attempt to shake his pursuers and swung westward on a hundred-mile detour to avoid a clash with whatever troops the fort's commander might have left to garrison it. Canby did not pursue. He knew the country Sibley was taking his men through, out there beyond the narrow valley benches. It was all desert, and he was having no part of it. He marched his troopers leisurely on to the safety and comfort of Fort Craig, arriving April 22. By that time Sibley's Texans were at the midpoint of their detour. Canby was content to leave their disposal to the desert.

It was one of the great marches of all time, and one of the great nightmares ever after for the men who survived it. They had no guide, no road, not even a trail through that barren waste, and they began the ten-day trek with five days' poor rations, including water. What few guns they had brought along were dragged and lowered up- and downhill by the men, who fashioned long rope harnesses for the purpose. For miles the brush and undergrowth were so dense that they had to cut and hack their way through with bowie knives and axes. Skirting the western slopes of the Magdalenas, they crossed the Sierra de San Mateo, then staggered down the dry bed of the Palomas River until they reached the Rio Grande again, within sight of which the Texans sent up a shout like the "Thalassa!" of Xenophon's ten thousand. From start to finish, since heading north at the opening of the year, they had suffered a total of 1700 casualties. Something under 500 of these fell or were captured in battle, and of the remaining 1200 who did not get back to Texas, a good part crumpled along the wayside during this last one hundred miles. They reached the river with nothing but their guns and what they carried on their persons. A northern lieutenant, following their trail a year later, reported that he "not infrequently found a piece of a gun-carriage, or part of a harness, or some piece of camp or garrison equipage, with occasionally a white, dry skeleton of a man. At some points it seemed impossible for men to have made their way."

Sibley reached Fort Bliss in early May, with what was left of his command strung out for fifty miles behind him. Here he made his report to the Richmond government, a disillusioned man. He did not mention the California gold fields or the advantages of controlling the Pacific Coast. He confined his observations to the field of his late endeavor, and even these were limited to abuse: "Except for its geographical position, the Territory of New Mexico is not worth a quarter of the blood and treasure expended in its conquest. As a field for military operations it possesses not a single element, except in the multiplicity of its defensible positions. The indispensable element, food, cannot be relied on." Nor did he express any intention of giving the thing another try. The grapes had soured in the desert heat, setting his teeth on edge. "I cannot speak encouragingly for the future," he concluded, "my troops having manifested a dogged, irreconcilable detestation of the country and the people."

The report was dated May 4. Ten days later he assembled the 2000 survivors on the parade ground, all that were left of the 3700 Texans he had taken north from there four months ago. After thanking them for their devotion and self-sacrifice during what he called "this more than difficult campaign," he continued the retreat to San Antonio, where he took leave of them and they disbanded. It was finished. All his high hopes and golden dreams had come to nothing, like the newly founded Territory of Arizona, which had gone out of existence with his departure. Any trouble the Unionists might encounter in the upper Rio Grande Valley from now on would have to come from rattlers and Apaches; the Confederates were out of there for good. As far as New Mexico and the Far West were concerned, the Civil War was over.

★ ★ ★   **A**ll this time, while Sibley and Van Dorn were undergoing their defeats and suffering frustration of their plans, Beauregard kept busy doing what he could to shore up the western flank of the long line stretching eastward from the Mississippi River. Loss of Henry and Donelson, along with the troops who were charged with their defense, had irreparably smashed its center, throwing left and right out of concert and endangering the rear. "You must now act as seems best to you," Johnston had told him. "The separation of our armies is for the present complete." He was alone.

Gloomily the Creole left Nashville on February 15. Two days later—the day after Donelson fell—he passed through Corinth, the northeast Mississippi railroad nexus, on his way to inspect Polk's dispositions at Columbus, but his sore throat got sorer from anxiety and exposure, forcing him off the train at Jackson, Tennessee. From a hotel bed he summoned the bishop-general to join him for a conference. Waiting, he was downcast. Now indeed, as he had said, the ship of state was "on the breakers." When Polk arrived Beauregard informed him that Columbus must be abandoned.

The bishop protested. He had spent the past five months strengthening "the Gibraltar of the West" for just such an emergency, he said. But his fellow Louisianian explained that the manpower expense was too great. The 17,000-man garrison must fall back to New Madrid, forty miles downriver near the Tennessee line, where the swampy terrain would require less than half as large a defensive force, freeing the balance to assist in restoring the shattered center. In desperation Polk then offered to hold Columbus with 5000 men. Beauregard shook his head. It would not do. They would be by-passed and captured at leisure, cut off from assisting in the defense of Memphis, which seemed next on the Federal list of major downriver objectives, or from coöperating with Johnston, who was retreating southwest with Hardee's troops for a possible conjunction. Polk returned to his fortified bluff, as heavy-hearted now as his commander, and set about dismounting his heavy guns and packing his wagons. Orders were orders; he would retreat—but not without every ounce of equipment charged against his name.

Beauregard's new line, covering Memphis and the railroads running spokelike from that hub, extended generally north-northwest along the roadbed of the Mobile & Ohio, from Corinth on the right, through Jackson and Humboldt, Tennessee, to the vicinity of New Madrid on the left. To defend this 150-mile air-line stretch he had only such men as would be available from Polk's command when they pulled out of Columbus. As he examined the maps in his sickroom he saw that, despite the renewed advantage of a railroad shuttle from flank to flank of his line, he was worse off, even, than Johnston had been in Kentucky. However, his spirits rose as his health improved, until presently he had recovered his accustomed Napoleonic outlook. Back in Nashville he had seen the problem: "We must defeat the enemy *somewhere*, to give confidence to our friends. . . . We must give up some minor points, and concentrate our forces, to save the most important ones, or we will lose all of them in succession." To relieve what he called his "profound anxiety," he addressed on the 21st a confidential circular to the governors of Louisiana, Alabama, Mississippi, and Tennessee, unfolding for them a plan that would transmute disaster into glorious success by turning the tables on the Yankees. If the governors would send him reinforcements to bring his strength to 40,000 he would take the offensive forthwith. He would march on Paducah, then on Cairo, and having taken those two points he would lay St Louis itself under siege. This last would involve Van Dorn, across the river. Describing the project and invoking his assistance, the Creole general inquired of the Mississippian: "What say you to this brilliant programme?"

Van Dorn's reply came two weeks later, in the form of a dispatch giving news of his defeat at Elkhorn Tavern. This ruled out any chance of his coöperating in an advance against St Louis, even if the governors east of the river had been able to send the troops requested; which they had not. But Beauregard did not relapse into his former depression. He kept busy, issuing rhetorical addresses to his soldiers and rallying the populace to "resist the cruel invader." In an attempt to repair his shortage of artillery, for example, he broadcast an appeal to the planters of the Mississippi Valley for brass and iron bells to provide metal for casting cannon: "I, your general, intrusted with the command of the army embodied of your sons, your kinsmen, and your neighbors, do now call on you to send your plantation bells to the nearest railroad depot, subject to my order, to be melted into cannon for the defense of your plantations. Who will not cheerfully and promptly send me his bells under such circumstances? Be of good cheer; but time is precious." This produced more poetry in southern periodicals than bells in Confederate foundries, but the general refused to let his spirits be dampened, even by such taunts as the one his appeal provoked in the pro-Union Louisville *Courier*: "The rebels can afford to give up all their church bells, cow bells and dinner bells to Beauregard, for they never go to church now, their cows have all been taken by foraging parties, and they have no dinner to be summoned to."

Polk meanwhile was completing his preparations to evacuate Columbus, working mainly at night to hide his intentions from prying enemy eyes. This was no easy task, involving as it did the repulse of a gunboat reconnaissance on the 23d and the removal of 140 emplaced guns and camp equipment for 17,000 men, but he accomplished it without loss or detection. By March 2, the heaviest guns and 7000 of his soldiers having been sent downriver to New Madrid, he was on his way south with the remainder. Within the week he reached Humboldt, the crossing of the Mobile & Ohio and the Memphis & Louisville Railroads, where he stopped. From here, his 10,000 troops could be hurried to meet whatever developed in any direction, either up where they had just come from, or down at Corinth, or back in Memphis. Little as he approved of retreat in general, the militant churchman had shown a talent for it under necessity.

The detached 7000 saw less cause for gladness on occupying the post assigned them around New Madrid. Rather, it seemed to them on arrival

Leonidas Polk, Confederate general and Episcopal bishop, spent five months fortifying Columbus before Beauregard ordered him to abandon that Kentucky stronghold.

that they had been sent to the swampy back-end of nowhere. After they had been there a while, however, they began to appreciate that the difficulty of the terrain was what made the position especially suitable for defense. Both banks of the river were boggy swamps, impenetrable to marching men; besides which, the Mississippi itself collaborated with the defenders to render its placid-looking, chocolate surface something less than convenient as a highway for invaders. As it approached the Kentucky-Tennessee line, several miles upstream, the river began one of its compass-boxing double twists, like a snake in convulsions, describing an S drawn backwards and tipped on its face, so that two narrow peninsulas lay side by side, the one to the west pointing north, the other south. Off the tip of the former, across the river in Missouri, lay the town of New Madrid, whose three forts, mounting seven guns each, commanded the second bend. At the tip of the other peninsula, nearer the Tennessee bank, was Island Ten — so called because it was the tenth such in the forty winding miles below the mouth of the Ohio — whose 39 guns, including a 16-gun floating battery tied up off the foot of the island, commanded the straight stretch of river leading into the first bend. Beauregard placed much reliance on those 60 guns; they constituted the twin-fluked, left-flank anchor of his tenuous line. The next defensible position was Fort Pillow, another hundred miles downriver. Engineers had been ordered there to constrict the fortifications so that they could be held by 3000 troops instead of the 10,000 for which they had been designed in the palmier days just past. That would take time, however. For the present, as Beauregard saw it, the fall of the batteries at New Madrid and Island Ten "must necessarily be followed immediately by the loss of the whole Mississippi Valley to the mouth of the Mississippi River." His instructions were that they were to be "held at all costs," which in soldier language meant that those guns were worth their weight in blood and must be served accordingly.

Polk thought so too. Forwarding heavy guns and reinforcements, he expressed his hopes and confidence to a colonel whose regiment had been stationed in the area all along: "Your position is a strong one, which you have well studied, and I have no doubt of the vigor and efficiency of your defense. Keep me informed."

★ ★ ★ Another who agreed was Commodore Andrew Foote. He agreed, in fact, with both of them: with Beauregard in stressing the importance to the Confederates of their river-line defense, and with Polk in expecting that it would be conducted with vigor and efficiency, taking full account of all the advantages in their favor. The Federal flag officer had had time to think the problem over. After the sudden victory at Henry and the abrupt repulse at Donelson, he had returned to Cairo for badly needed repairs, both to his battered gunboats and to himself. The fall of the forts having delivered the whole Tennessee-Cumberland water system into Union hands, he could now give full attention to the western navy's primary assignment: the clearing of the Father of Waters, all the way to the Gulf.

This would be a much harder job than what had gone before, and the commodore knew it. For one thing, there was the distance. From the mouth of the Ohio to the mouth of the Mississippi was about 500 crowflight miles, but it was well over twice that far by the twisting course his boats would have to take. A tawny vastness lay before him, winding south beyond the enemy horizon, with various obstacles in and on and around it, natural and man-made. For another, there was the difference in the rivers themselves. The Mississippi ran

★

swifter—and it ran the other way. This meant that he would have to fight downstream, in which case even a slight mishap, such as a fouled rudder or a sudden loss of steam, could lead to destruction or capture. Highly vulnerable except from dead ahead, his ironclads carried little armor back from the prow and none at all at the stern. What was more, experiments conducted on the Mississippi during the refitting showed that they could not maintain station under reverse power, even with the help of anchors, which could get no firm purchase

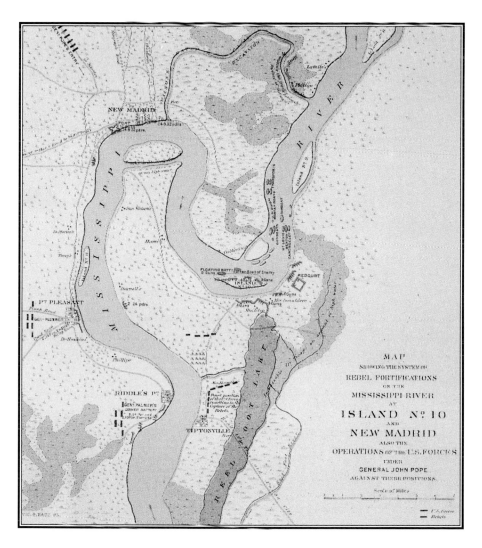

A map of Madrid Bend shows the combatants' positions in March 1862, after the Federals completed the channel (top) past Island Ten.

on the river's slimy bottom. If one of them went out of control in a downstream fight, through breakdown or damage to her engine or her steering apparatus, she would not drift rearward to safety — as three out of four had done in the upstream fight just past — but forward, under enemy guns and into enemy hands. Consideration brought doubts. When his brother, a judge in Ohio, reminded him that the public expected "dash and close fighting, something sharp and decisive," Foote replied: "Don't you know that my gunboats are the only protection you have upon your rivers . . . that without my flotilla everything in your rivers, your cities and your towns would be at the mercy of the enemy? My first duty then is to care for my boats, if I am to protect you." He had not spoken thus before the point-blank assault on Donelson. But now, with the wound in his ankle not yet healed and the sound of breaking armor still loud in his memory of that repulse, the commodore took counsel of his fears.

"Don't you know that my gunboats are the only protection you have upon your rivers . . . that without my flotilla everything in your rivers, your cities and your towns would be at the mercy of the enemy?"

— Andrew H. Foote

Despite his qualms, Foote set off downriver before daylight, March 4, prepared to assault the Columbus bluff with all seven of his ironclads. Arriving he found the fortress strangely silent, no stir of life on the ramparts and no metal frowning down from the embrasures. Two officers and thirty men, covered by all the guns of the fleet, made a dash for shore in a tug — and presently returned, more sheepish than exultant, with word that the Union flag had been flying there since yesterday. Out on a scout, four companies of Illinois cavalry had found the place deserted, then trooper-like had settled down and made themselves at home, rooting into the conglomerate litter Polk's men had left behind. Foote went ashore for a look at the fortifications, wrote a formal report on their capture, supervised further repairs to his gunboats — necessary because the armor above the Texas decks was so badly cracked and buckled that the civilian pilots refused to continue downriver until it had been replaced — then finally, on the 17th, set off again for his next objective: Island Ten.

Arriving that day, he moored his flotilla against the Missouri bank, three miles above the head of the fortified island, and began lobbing shells across the low-lying southern tip of the first peninsula. His fire was not very effective at that range, but neither was the enemy's, which was the commodore's main concern in his present frame of mind. In fact he had come prepared for this style of fighting. His seven ironclads were supplemented by eleven strange vessels, compressed hexagons 60 feet long and 25 feet wide, each with a single 13-inch mortar bolted to its deck. Originally there had been doubts as to whether they would stand the recoil, but three of the gunboat captains had settled that by firing the first shot: in spite of which they were still suspected of being about as dangerous at one end of the trajectory as the other. When the piece was loaded, the crew slipped through a door cut in one end of the surrounding seven-foot armored bulwark and stood on tiptoe on the outer deck, hands over ears, mouths agape, knees flexed against the concussion, until it was fired; then they would hurry back inside for the reloading. Foote at least was happy with them, despite the doubts and drawbacks. As soon as he got within range of the island he had them towed to the head of the column and started them firing in the direction of the nearest Confederate batteries, two air-line miles away.

Army men, who had been on the scene for two weeks now, anticipating the arrival of the gunboats with their Sunday punch, were much less happy about these new-style naval tactics, so different from what had gone before. At Henry the navy had taken the lead, leaving the landsmen with little to do, and now that the case was more or less reversed, the army howled with resentment. As time went by, the commodore refusing to budge from his upstream station, the howls took on a note of shrill derision. One exasperated colonel, when asked just what the flotilla was accomplishing, replied contemptuously, "Oh, it is still bombarding the state of Tennessee at long range."

None among the soldiers was more critical of the navy than their commander, Brigadier General John Pope. In protesting against caution he stood on solid ground. His notion of the way to fight a war was to locate the enemy and then go after him, preferably point-blank. These tactics were especially valid when operating, as Pope was here, with the advantage of three-to-one numerical odds, and he had proceeded to put them into practice. A forty-year-old West Pointer with a robust physique to match his positive manner, he had brought his four divisions overland down the right bank of the river, arriving March 3, and moved without delay against New Madrid and Point Pleasant, eleven miles below. Within ten days—four days before the navy's tardy arrival—he had captured both places, along with 25 heavy guns and quantities of equipment and supplies, when the defenders retreated to the security of the east bank and the fastness of Island Ten. He would have taken that place, too—he knew exactly how to go about it—except that he could not effect a crossing without protection for his transports. Confederate batteries commanded the river from the opposite bank, and even worse there was a motley collection of makeshift rebel gunboats on patrol. Neither of these deterrents would be much of a problem for even a single ironclad, Pope declared, if Foote would only send it. But this the naval commander would not do. Any attempt to run the gauntlet of the island batteries, he replied, "would result in the sacrifice of the boat, her officers and men, which sacrifice I would not be justified in making."

Pope was more vexed than discouraged. A week after his capture of New Madrid, in recognition of his hard-hitting competence, he had been made a major general. He would keep up the pressure, hoping in time to stiffen the navy's backbone. Meanwhile he had the rebels in a cul-de-sac, backed up against the swamps that lay between Reelfoot Lake and the river. There was no way out for them, and no way in for supplies, except along the road leading south through Tiptonville. Once the Federals were astride the river, the road would be cut; he could bag the lot by quick assault or, at the worst, by siege. All he wanted was a chance to ferry his men across with a fair degree of safety. Suspecting that the navy would never get up nerve enough to run past Island Ten, he began to construct a navy of his own: high-sided barges armored with boiler plate, designed to accommodate field guns. He kept busy in other ways as well, manning the captured heavy guns to strengthen his domination of Madrid Bend and bringing down supplies and reinforcements from upriver. This last took ingenuity, for the right-bank swamps blocked the direct route, but the general had that too. He had his engineers cut a channel (a canal, it was called, 50 feet wide, 9 miles long, and 4½ feet deep — this being the depth at which the flooded trees were sawed off under water) connecting the river, five miles north of the gunboat station, with Wilson's Bayou, which gave down upon New Madrid, thus by-passing the bend commanded by the guns on Island Ten. Shallow-draft transports got through with another whole division, bringing Pope's total strength to 23,000, but not the gunboats, whose bottoms would have been torn out by the stumps. Their only way led down past the cannon-bristled island, which Foote believed would sink in short order whatever came within range.

All but one of the gunboat captains agreed with the flag officer's estimate as to the outcome of a downstream fight or a try at running the batteries. That one was Commander Henry Walke, skipper of the *Carondelet.* For two weeks now the diurnal mortar bombardment had continued, and except for a single boat expedition, which spiked some guns in an abandoned battery on All Fools' Night, all that had been accomplished by the navy was a heavy expenditure of ammunition. A fifty-four-year-old Virginia-born Ohioan and a veteran of all the river engagements from Belmont on, Walke was touched in his pride, and had been so ever since Donelson, when, as last boat out of the fight, he had retreated firing blindly in an attempt to hide in the gunsmoke. It was his belief that the run could be made with a good chance of success, provided it was made in silence and by the dark of the moon. If the rebels did not know he was there, they would not shoot; or if they knew he was there, but could not see him, they would not be likely to hit him. At any rate he was willing to give it a try, and he said so at a conference on the flagship in late March. Foote was pleased to hear that someone thought the run could be made, though he himself was doubtful. The army gibes had begun to sting, and there were reports that the Confederates were building a fleet of giant ironclads at Memphis: he might soon have a downstream fight on his hands, against much longer odds, whether he wanted it or not. He asked Walke if he would be willing to back up his opinion by trying the run in the *Carondelet*. Walke said he would, emphatically. Foote said all right, go ahead. He would not order a man to try what he himself had already said was too risky, but he would approve it on a volunteer basis. Walke began his preparations at once.

The moon would be new and early-down on the night of April 4, which left him just under a week for getting ready. During this time he piled his decks with planks from a wrecked barge to give protection from plunging shot, coiled surplus chain in vulnerable spots, and wound an 11-inch hawser round and round the pilot house as high up as the windows. Cordwood barriers were built to inclose the boilers, and a coal barge loaded with bales of hay was lashed to the port side, which caused an observer to remark that the gunboat resembled "a farmer's wagon prepared for market." The only light she carried would be a lantern in the engine room, invisible from outside, and to

Federals use a saw mounted on a rocker arm to cut trees below the water line and open a channel by-passing Island Ten.

Henry Walke (left) commanded the U.S.S. Carondelet (below) on her daring downriver run, through a thunderstorm, past the guns of Island Ten.

ensure silence the engines were muffled by piping the escape steam through the paddle-wheel housing instead of through the stacks as usual. The one thing Walke was to avoid beyond all others was being captured; fighting upstream in rebel hands, the *Carondelet* might be a match for all her sister ships combined. To guard against this, the crew was armed with cutlasses, pistols, and hand grenades; two dozen volunteer sharpshooters were taken aboard; hot-water hoses were connected to the boilers for the purpose of scalding boarders; and if all else failed, Walke's orders were that she was to be sunk beneath their feet. Through the early evening of April 4 the sickle moon shone brightly, if inter-

mittently, over and under a scud of black clouds racing past. Then came moon-set, 10 o'clock; Walke passed the word, "All ready," and the gunboat slipped her moorings. The muffled engines merely throbbed; the gathering clouds had masked the stars. So absolute were the darkness and the silence as the *Caron-delet* stood out for New Madrid, the officers on deck asked through the speaking pipes if the engineer was going ahead on her.

It was not so for long. Just as she cleared the line of mortar rafts at the head of the moored column, the storm broke with tropical fury. Vast and vivid streaks of lightning split the sky, so that to one who watched it was as if the gates of hell "were opened and shut every instant, suffering the whole fierce reflection of the infernal lake to flash across the sky." Thunder crashed and rumbled and the rain came down in gulfs. The river ahead was an illuminated highway, with Island Ten looming in ominous silhouette, its drowsy lookouts no doubt startled into wide-eyed action at seeing the Yankee gunboat bearing down on them like something on a brightly lighted stage. Yet apparently not: Walke held his course past the first battery without being fired on — when suddenly, of her own accord, the *Carondelet* signaled her presence to her enemies ashore. Dry soot in her chimneys, normally kept wet by the escape steam, took fire and shot five-foot torches from their crowns, bathing with a yellow glare the upper deck and everything around. That did it. Ashore, there were cries of alarm and an officer shouting, "Elevate! Elevate!" and then the crash of gunfire through the thunder.

Carondelet went with the current, a leadsman knee-deep in muddy foam on her bow to sing out the soundings. The coal barge lashed alongside impeded her speed, but was no less welcome for that, coming as it did between the batteries and their target. Shells shrieked overhead or were heard plunging into the water as the island guns were echoed by others along the Tennessee bank. Wallowing in the wind-whipped waves, still under the crash and flash of thunder and lightning, the little ironclad held her course and took no hits. Clear of the island, she still had the floating battery to pass, but the final six shots from there were misses, like the rest. She had made it. Pulling up to the New Madrid landing, where army cannoneers were giving the navy its due at last by tossing their caps and cheering, Walke proudly took up a speaking trumpet and announced his arrival to those on bank, then turned to his bosun's mate and authorized the sounding of "grog, oh." Against regulations, the main brace then was spliced.

Pope at last had what he had been saying was all he needed, a gunboat south of Island Ten; and presently he had two. Learning of the *Caron-delet*'s successful run — she had taken two hits after all, it turned out: one in the coal barge, one in a bale of hay — Foote sent the *Pittsburg* down to repeat the performance on the night of the 6th, which was also dark and stormy. The makeshift rebel flotilla scattered, awed, and the ironclads knocked out the batteries opposite Point Pleasant. Pope put his men on transports and had the gunboats herd them over. The Tiptonville road was cut within an hour of the unopposed landing. All he had to do then was put his hand out; the 7000 Confederates were in it, along with more than a hundred pieces of light and heavy artillery, 7000 small arms, horses and mules by droves, mounds of equipment including tents for 12,000 men, and several boatloads of provisions.

It was all over before the dawn of April 8, accomplished without the loss of a single man in combat. The North had another hero: bluff John Pope. A forthright combination of ingenuity and drive — large-bodied, with stolid eyes and a full beard that spread down over his upper chest, his broad, flat face framed by dark brown hair brushed straight back from the bulging expanse of forehead and falling long at the sides — he commanded confidence by his very presence. Once he saw what he wanted, he went after it on his own, unflinchingly. The military worth of such a man was clear for all to see, including his commander. Halleck wired, exuberant: "I congratulate you and your command on your splendid achievement. It excels in boldness and brilliancy all other operations of the war. It will be memorable in military history and will be admired by future generations. You deserve well of your country."

Thus Halleck rejoiced and Pope basked in well-earned laudation, while their opponent Beauregard experienced quite opposite emotions. Once more on the eve of scoring what he had hoped would be "a beautiful *ten strike*," he was suddenly faced instead with the imminent testing of his prediction that the fall of New Madrid and Island Ten would mean the immediate loss of the whole Mississippi Valley. For him this meant the loss of the war, and he was correspondingly cast down. Midway of the campaign, which was stretching his nerves to the breaking point — one fluke of his left-flank anchor had snapped, and the other seemed about to snap as well — he wrote to a friend in Congress, inquiring distractedly: "Will not heaven open the eyes and senses of our rulers? Where in the world are we going to, if not to destruction?"

★ ★ ★

*Federal artillerists fire
point-blank at charging Confederates in the Hornets Nest, a Union
defensive position held during most
of the first day at Shiloh.*

Halleck-Grant, Johnston-Beauregard: Shiloh

1862 ★ ★ ★ ★ ★ **G**ood news was doubly welcome in St Louis, where Halleck had sat desk-bound all this time, scratching his elbows and addressing his goggle-eyed stare in the general direction of the back-area correspondents who came clamoring for information he could not give because he did not have it. The month between the mid-February capture of Fort Donelson and the mid-March fall of New Madrid had been for him a time of strain, one in which he saw his probable advancement placed in precarious balance opposite his probable stagnation. He had come out top man in the end, but the events leading up to that happy termination — as if, perversely, the fates had established a sort of inverse ratio between the success of Federal arms and the rise of Henry Halleck — had contained, for him, far more of anguish than of joy. There was small consolation in realizing later that the fates had been with him all along, that the cause for all that anguish had existed only in his own mind, as a product of fear and suspicion.

His first reaction, the day after the fall of the Cumberland fortress, was to request promotions for Buell, Grant, and C. F. Smith — and advancement for himself. "Give me command of the West," he wired McClellan. "I ask this in return for Forts Henry and Donelson." His second reaction, following hard on the heels of the first, was fear that Grant's victory might sting the Confederates into desperation. Even now perhaps they were massing for a sudden all-or-nothing lunge, northward around Grant's flank. Beauregard's plan for an attack on Paducah and Cairo had not gone beyond the dream stage, but Halleck feared it quite literally, and called urgently for Buell to come help him. Buell replied in effect that he had troubles of his own, and Halleck was even more firmly convinced of the necessity for authority to bend him to his will. "I must have command of the armies of the West," he told McClellan in a second wire, sent three days after the first, which had gone unanswered. "Hesitation and delay are losing us the golden opportunity. Lay this before the President and the Secretary of War. May I assume command? Answer quickly." This time McClellan did answer quickly, but not as his fretful subordinate had hoped. Replying that he believed Buell could handle his own army better from Bowling Green than Halleck could do from St Louis, he declined to lay Old Brains' self-recommendation on the presidential desk.

Perhaps it was what Halleck had expected. At any rate he had already put a second string to his bow, forwarding for Stanton's out-of-channels approval a plan for reorganizing the western department under his command. February 21, the day after McClellan's refusal, Stanton replied that he liked the plan, "but on account of the domestic affliction of the President" — Willie Lincoln had died the day before and was lying in state in the White House — "I have not yet been able to submit it to him." Halleck's hopes took a bound at this. Determined to strike while the iron was hot, he wired back that same day, urging the won-over Secretary to break in on the President's family trouble, whatever it was. "One whole week has been lost already by hesitation and delay," he complained. "There was, and I think there still is, a golden opportunity to strike a fatal blow, but I can't do it unless I can control Buell's army. . . . There is not a moment to be lost. Give me the authority, and I will be responsible for results." Stanton's reply came the following day, and Halleck's hopes hit bottom with a thud. The Secretary had gotten to Lincoln, but "after full consideration of the subject," he telegraphed, "[the President] does not think any change in the organization of the army or the military departments at present advisable."

Halleck's bow was completely unstrung; there was no one left to appeal to, either in or out of channels. After two days spent absorbing the shock, he replied with what grace he could muster: "If it is thought that the present arrangement is best for the public service, I have nothing to say. I have done my duty in making the suggestions, and I leave it to my superiors to adopt or reject them." For others closer at hand, however, he either had less grace to spare or else it was exhausted. Encountering signs of paperwork confusion down at Cairo that same day, he testily informed his chief of staff: "There is a screw loose in that command. It had better be fixed pretty soon, or the command will hear from me."

That was still his irascible, sore-pawed frame of mind the following week, when his worst fears in regard to Grant appeared to have been realized. At

Thought by some to be "the best all-around soldier in the army," Charles F. Smith (left) temporarily succeeded Grant at the start of the Shiloh campaign.

a time when Halleck was most concerned about a possible rebel counterattack, launched with all the fury of desperation, Grant and his 30,000 soldiers — the combat-hardened core of any defense the department commander might have to make — lost touch with headquarters, apparently neglecting to file reports because he was off on a double celebration of victory and promotion. The former alcoholic captain was now a major general, tenth-ranking man in the whole U.S. Army; Lincoln had signed the recommendation on the night of the day the Donelson news reached Washington, and the Senate had promptly confirmed it as of the Unconditional Surrender date. Halleck himself had urged the promotion, but not as warmly as he had urged several others, and he had yet to congratulate Grant personally for the capture of the forts. Other promotions were in the mill, soon to be acted on — Buell and Pope were to be major generals within a week, along with others, including Smith — but Grant would outrank them, which was not at all what Halleck had intended or expected. The fact was, absorbed as he had been in his rivalry with Buell, he was beginning to see that he had raised an even more formidable hero-opponent right there in his own front yard. Donelson having caught the public fancy, the public in its short-sighted way was giving all the credit to the general on the scene, rather than to the commander who had masterminded the campaign from St Louis. Irked by this, he then was confronted with what he considered the crowning instance of Grant's instability. Having won his promotion, the new hero apparently thought himself above the necessity for filing reports as to his whereabouts or condition. Where he was now, Halleck did not know for sure; but there were rumors.

On March 3 McClellan received a dispatch indicating that Halleck's sorely tried patience at last had snapped: "I have had no communication with General Grant for more than a week. He left his command without my authority and went to Nashville. His army seems to be as much demoralized by the victory of Fort Donelson as was that of the Potomac by the defeat of Bull Run. It is hard to censure a successful general immediately after a victory, but I think he richly deserves it. I can get no returns, no reports, no information of any kind from him. Satisfied with his victory, he sits down and enjoys it without any regard to the future. I'm worn-out and tired with this neglect and inefficiency." McClellan, whose eye for a possible rival was quite as sharp as Halleck's own, was sudden in reply: "Generals must observe discipline as well as private soldiers. Do not hesitate to arrest him at once if the good of the service requires it.... You are at liberty to regard this as a positive order if it will smooth your way."

Halleck did not hesitate. The order went by wire to Grant at once: "You will place [Brig.] Gen. C. F. Smith in command of expedition, and remain yourself at Fort Henry. Why do you not obey my orders to report strength and positions of your command?" The question was largely rhetorical; Halleck believed he already knew the answer, and he gave it in a telegram informing McClellan of his action in the matter: "A rumor has just reached me that since the taking of Fort Donelson, General Grant has resumed his former bad habits. If so, it will account for his neglect of my often-repeated orders." To anyone with an ear for army gossip, and McClellan's was highly tuned in that respect, this meant that Grant was off on a bender. "I do not deem it advisable to arrest him at present," Halleck continued, "but have placed General Smith in command of the expedition up the Tennessee. I think Smith will restore order and discipline."

Grant had been guilty of none of these things, and he said so in a telegram to Halleck as soon as he had complied with the instructions to turn over his command: "I am not aware of ever having disobeyed any order from headquarters — certainly never intended such a thing." The communications hiatus was explained by the defection of a telegraph operator who took Grant's dispatches with him, unsent, when he deserted. It was true, Grant said, that he had been to Nashville, but that was because Halleck had told him nothing; he had gone there to meet Buell and work out a plan for coöperation. When Halleck still showed resentment at having been left in the dark, Grant observed that there must be enemies between them, and asked to be relieved from further duty in the department. Halleck refused to agree to this, but continued to bolster his case by forwarding an anonymous letter charging that the property captured at Fort Henry had been questionably handled. His dander really up now, Grant replied: "There is such a disposition to find fault with me that I again ask to be relieved from further duty until I can be placed right in the estimation of those higher in authority."

Suddenly, incredibly, all was sweetness and light at Halleck's end of the wire. "You cannot be relieved from your command," he answered. "There is no good reason for it.... Instead of relieving you, I wish you as soon as your new army is in the field to assume command and lead it on to new victories."

There were a number of reasons behind this sudden change in attitude and disposition, all of which had occurred between the leveling and the

---

"There is such a disposition to find fault with me that I again ask to be relieved from further duty until I can be placed right in the estimation of those higher in authority."

— Ulysses S. Grant

---

withdrawing of the charges against Grant. First, the evacuation of Columbus had relieved Halleck's fears that the Confederates were about to unleash an attack on Cairo or Paducah, and while Curtis was stopping Van Dorn at Elkhorn Tavern, Pope was applying a bear hug on New Madrid. Then, just as he was congratulating himself on these improvements in the tactical situation, a stiff letter came from the Adjutant General, demanding specifications for the vague charges he had been making against his new major general. Trial-by-rumor would not do, the army's head lawyer informed him. "By direction of the President, the Secretary of War desires you to ascertain and report whether General Grant left his command at any time without proper authority, and, if so, for how long; whether he has made to you proper reports and returns of his force; whether he has committed any acts which are unauthorized or not in accordance with military subordination or propriety, and, if so, what." To reply as directed would be to give Grant what he had been seeking, a chance to "be placed right in the estimation of those higher in authority." Besides, Halleck had no specifications to report, only rumors. Instead, he replied that he was "satisfied" Grant had "acted from a

Federal soldiers mill about the dockside and aboard the side-wheeler Aleck Scott at Cairo, Illinois, a staging area for Union thrusts into Kentucky and Tennessee and down the Mississippi Valley.

praiseworthy although mistaken zeal. . . . I respectfully recommend that no further notice be taken of it. . . . All these irregularities have now been remedied."

However, there was something more behind this sudden volte-face, this willingness to bury the hatchet he had been flourishing lately. March 11— the day after the Adjutant General's call for specifics, and two days before he blandly informed Grant that there was "no good reason" for relieving him— the fond hope for which he had labored in and out of channels all these months was realized. He got the West. His command, which was called the Department of the Mississippi and extended for better than 500 miles eastward, from Kansas to a north-south line through Knoxville, was awarded him by Lincoln in the same War Order that deposed McClellan as general-in-chief and recalled Frémont to active duty. Receiving it that way, out of the blue, after two solid weeks of despair, Halleck was in no mood to quarrel with anyone, not even Grant: in fact, especially not Grant. Beauregard was reported to be intrenching around Corinth, reinforced to a strength of 20,000 men. "If so, he will make a Manassas of it," Halleck said. That meant hard fighting: in which case he wanted his hardest-fighting general in command: and that meant Grant, whatever his instability in other respects. "The power is in your hands," Halleck told him. "Use it, and you will be sustained by all above you."

So Grant got aboard a steamboat at Fort Henry and went up the Tennessee to rejoin his army.

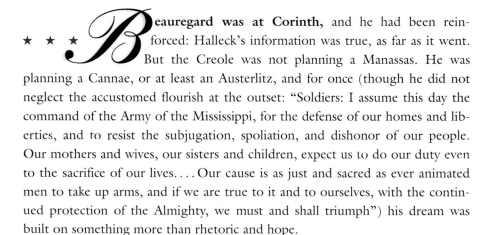

★ ★ ★ **B**eauregard was at Corinth, and he had been rein-forced: Halleck's information was true, as far as it went. But the Creole was not planning a Manassas. He was planning a Cannae, or at least an Austerlitz, and for once (though he did not neglect the accustomed flourish at the outset: "Soldiers: I assume this day the command of the Army of the Mississippi, for the defense of our homes and liberties, and to resist the subjugation, spoliation, and dishonor of our people. Our mothers and wives, our sisters and children, expect us to do our duty even to the sacrifice of our lives. . . . Our cause is as just and sacred as ever animated men to take up arms, and if we are true to it and to ourselves, with the continued protection of the Almighty, we must and shall triumph") his dream was built on something more than rhetoric and hope.

Recent and looming disasters at last had jarred the Richmond government into action. The fall of Henry and Donelson, followed at once by the loss of Kentucky and Middle Tennessee, now threatened the railroad leading eastward from Memphis, through Corinth and Tuscumbia, to Chattanooga, where it branched south, through Atlanta, to Charleston and Savannah, and north, through Knoxville, to Lynchburg and Richmond. "The vertebrae of the Confederacy," former War Secretary L. P. Walker called it, and rightly; for once this only east-west all-weather supply line was cut, the upper South would be divided—as prone for conquest as a man with a broken backbone. Now when Beauregard cried wolf, as he had done unheeded so often before, the authorities listened. Without Major General Braxton Bragg and the 10,000 soldiers he commanded at Mobile and Pensacola, the southern coast would be wide open to amphibious attack, but under the press of necessity the dispersed defensive was out, no matter the risk; Bragg and his men were ordered north to Corinth. So were Brigadier General Daniel Ruggles and his 5000 from New Orleans, though their departure left the South's chief city without infantry to defend it. By early March they were with Beauregard, absorbed into the Army of the Mississippi. Combined with Polk's 10,000—so that in point of fact it was they who did the absorbing—they brought the expansive Creole's total strength to 25,000 men.

His spirits were lifted toward elation by this considerable transfusion of troops from his native shore—including one elite New Orleans outfit which carried his name on its roster as an honorary private; "Pierre Gustave Toutant Beauregard!" rang out daily at roll call, like the sudden unfurling of a silken banner; "Absent on duty!" the color-sergeant proudly answered for him. He looked forward to combinations and maneuvers that would be nothing less than Napoleonic in concept and execution. Johnston by now was across the Tennessee, marching westward from Decatur with the remnant of what had been the Army of Kentucky. Floyd's brigade had been sent to Chattanooga, but Forrest's troopers had caught up with the column, bringing Hardee's total to 15,000. When they arrived there would be 40,000 soldiers around Corinth, exactly the number the impatiently waiting general had said would allow a strike at Cairo and Paducah. Nor was that all. Van Dorn's 15,000, licking their Elkhorn Tavern wounds in Arkansas, had been alerted for an eastward march that would bring them across the Mississippi at Memphis, where they would find boxcars waiting to bring them rapidly down the vital railroad line to Corinth. The total then would soar to 55,000. Any twinge of regret for the 20,000 lost at Donelson and penned up now on Island Ten was quickly assuaged by the thought that, even without them, the Army of the Mississippi would not only be the largest any Confederate had ever commanded, but in fact would be almost twice as large as the combined force that had covered itself and its generals—particularly Beauregard—with glory at Manassas. As he waited now for Johnston he rehearsed in his mind the recommendations he would make for the utilization of this strength.

Scouts had been bringing him full reports of the enemy situation all this time. Grant's army was twenty-odd miles to the north, in camp on the left bank of the Tennessee, awaiting the arrival of Buell's army, which was moving west from Nashville. Even with the addition of Van Dorn and Johnston, the southern army would not be as large as the two northern armies combined, but it would be larger than either on its own. The answer, then — provided the gray-clad reinforcements won the race, which seemed likely, since the Yankees marching overland from Nashville were encountering various obstacles such as

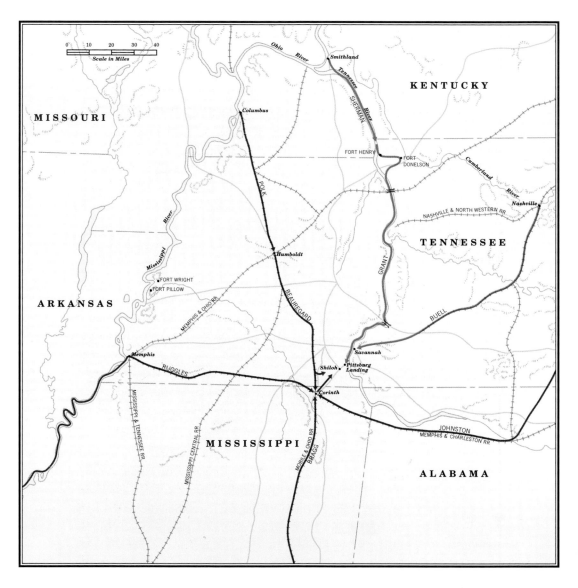

*Johnston concentrated his Confederates
(red arrows) at Corinth, and Halleck (blue) moved
to Pittsburg Landing. They would meet at Shiloh.*

burned bridges—was a slashing attack. If Van Dorn and Johnston reached Corinth before Buell reached the Tennessee, the superior Confederate army would pounce on Grant and accomplish his destruction, then fall in turn on Buell and treat him likewise, after which the way to Louisville and St Louis would lie open. Beauregard saw and rehearsed it thus in his mind, complete no doubt with the final surrender ceremonies at the point of deepest penetration, wherever that might be. When Johnston arrived on the 24th at the head of the column which now reached the end of its long retreat from Bowling Green, he considered the race half won.

The tall, handsome Texan, who had set out seven months ago, buoyed up by the confident hopes of the South that he would drive the blue invaders from the soil of his native Kentucky, now came back to Mississippi oppressed by the seething resentment of those who had cheered him loudest then. He took it calmly, the flared mustache and deep-set eyes masking whatever hurt the barbs of criticism gave him. "What the people want is a victory," he had said, and he welcomed Beauregard's proposal—the more so since it coincided with plans he had made on the march—as a chance to give them one. In fact, as a sign of appreciation for all the Louisiana general had done in the trying past few weeks, Johnston made the gesture of offering him command of the army for the coming battle; he himself would act as department commander, he said, with headquarters at Memphis or at nearby Holly Springs. Beauregard's heart gave a leap at this, touching his fiery ambition as it did, but he recognized a gesture when he saw one, and declined. Then the two got down to preparing the army for combat, prescribing rigid training schedules for the soldiers, who being raw needed all the instruction they could possibly absorb, and reorganizing them into four corps: 10,000 under Polk, 16,000 under Bragg, 7000 under Hardee, and 7000 under Breckinridge. (The last was designated as Crittenden's at first, but he was presently removed to suffer demotion for the Fishing Creek debacle.) The 15,000 under Van Dorn would add a substantial fifth corps when they got there, but even without them the army was about as large as the one Grant had in camp on the near bank of the Tennessee, twenty-two miles to the north.

★ ★ ★   The reinstated Federal commander had been with his army a week by the time Johnston joined Beauregard at Corinth. After the hundred-mile boat ride Grant came ashore at Savannah, a hamlet on the east bank, where C. F. Smith, an old soldier who never neglected the creature comforts, had established headquarters in a fine private mansion overlooking a bend of the Tennessee. One division was at Crump's Landing, three miles upstream on the opposite bank, and as Grant arrived the other five were debarking at Pittsburg Landing, six miles farther south and also on the west side of the river. The site had been recommended by the commander of one of the new divisions; a "magnificent plain for camping and drilling," he called it, "and a military point of great strength."

This was Tecumseh Sherman. He too had been reinstated, Halleck having decided that he was not really insane after all, just high-strung and talkative; besides, he had a brother in the Senate. Grant, for one, thought highly of him. During the Donelson campaign Sherman had worked hard, forwarding reinforcements and supplies and offering to waive his then superior rank for a chance to come up and join the fighting. But the men assigned to him were not so sure, not at the outset anyhow. Red-headed and gaunt, with sunken temples and a grizzled, short-cropped ginger beard, he had a wild expression around his eyes and a hungry look that seemed to have been with him always. "I never saw him but I thought of Lazarus," one declared. His shoulders twitched and his hands were never still, always picking at something, twirling a button or fiddling with his whiskers. They had not fancied getting their first taste of combat under a man who had been sent home such a short while back under suspicion of insanity. Three days before Grant's arrival, though at first their fears were intensified, they learned better. Smith sent them south for a try at breaking the vital Memphis & Charleston Railroad, down across the Mississippi line.

They came off the transports at midnight in a blinding rain. By daylight they were far inland, and still the rain came pouring. Bridges were washed out, so that the cavalry, scouting ahead, lost men and horses, drowned while trying to ford the swollen creeks. Behind them, the Tennessee was rising fast, threatening to cut them off by flooding the bottom they had marched across. At this point, just when things were at their worst, Sherman ordered them back to the transports. It had been a nightmare operation, and probably they had done no earthly good; they were wet, tired, hungry, cold; for the most part they had been thoroughly frightened. But curiously enough, when they were back aboard the transports, drinking hot coffee and snuggling into blankets, they felt fine about the whole thing. They had been down into enemy country, the actual Deep South—a division on its own, looking for trouble: that gave them the feeling of being veterans—and they had seen their commander leading them. Sherman was not the same man at all. He was not nervous; his shoulders did not twitch; he was calm and confident, and when he saw the thing was impossible he did not hesitate to give it up. Whatever else he might be, he certainly was not crazy. They knew that now, and they were willing to follow wherever he led them.

Grant too had changed, the veterans saw when he came up to Pittsburg to inspect them. Mostly it was the aura of fame that had been gathering around him in the month since the news from Donelson first set the church bells ringing. He was Unconditional S. Grant now, and his picture was on the cover of *Harper's Weekly*. There was a hunger for particulars about him, for instance how he "generally stood or walked with his left hand in his trousers pock-

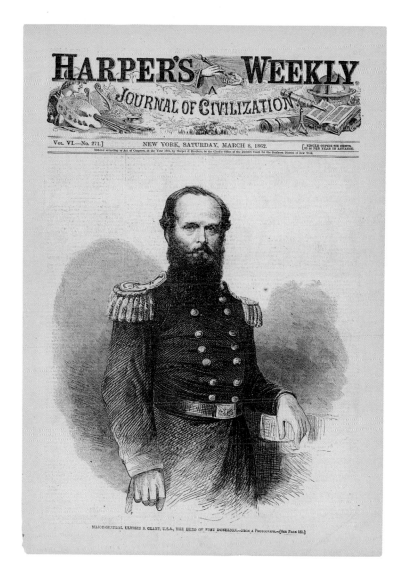

*Harper's ran this inaccurate portrait of
Grant, "The Hero of Fort Donelson," to show
the nation its new western idol.*

et, and had in his mouth an unlighted cigar, the end of which he chewed restlessly." The cigar was an example of the change that stemmed from fame. Learning that he had kept one clamped in his teeth that critical afternoon at Donelson, whenever he was not using it like a marshal's baton to point the direction for attack, readers had sent him boxes of them to express their admiration, and since Grant had never been one to waste things, least of all good tobacco, the long-stemmed meerschaum that had given him so much satisfaction in the past was put away while he concentrated on smoking up those crates of gift cigars. One other change he had made on his own. His beard, which formerly had reached down past the second button on his coat, had been clipped short. It seemed to the soldiers, observing him now, a gesture not unlike that of a man rolling up his sleeves in preparation for hard work.

For him, work meant fighting; that was his trade, the only one he had ever been any good at or able to earn a living by, and he wanted to be at it right away. Restrained by Halleck, however — "We must strike no blow until we are strong enough to admit no doubt of the result," the department commander warned — all Grant could do now was prepare for the attack he would launch when Buell got there. Meanwhile the position appeared to him to be about as good as Sherman had reported. A hundred-foot yellow-clay bluff rose abruptly from the narrow shelf of the landing, where steamboats had unloaded peacetime cargoes for Corinth, to a plateau eroded by gullies and covered with second-growth timber exccpt for scattered clearings cut by farmers for orchards and grain fields. It was not quite a "magnificent plain," but it did have points of military strength, the flanks being protected by Lick and Snake Creeks, which emptied into the Tennessee above and below the landing. The area between them, a quadrilateral varying roughly from three to five miles on a side, gave plenty of room for drilling the five divisions camped there and was conveniently cross-hatched by a network of wagon trails leading inland and connecting the small farms. But Grant's primary interest was on the main road leading southwest to Corinth, one hard day's march away. That was the one he would take when the time came: meaning Buell. Halleck reported him nearing Waynesboro, forty miles away, but cautioned Grant: "Don't let the enemy draw you into an engagement now. Wait till you are properly fortified and receive orders."

This raised another question; for the position had not been fortified at all. Smith had already expressed an opinion on that. The crusty general had been put to bed with an infected leg, having skinned his shin on the sharp edge of a rowboat seat, but he was quite undaunted. "By God," he said, "I ask nothing better than to have the rebels come out and attack us! We can whip them to hell. Our men suppose we have come here to fight, and if we begin to spade it will make them think we fear the enemy." Grant agreed and left things as they were, despite the warning. The war was on its last legs, he told Halleck, and the enemy too demoralized to constitute a danger: "The temper of the rebel troops is such that there is but little doubt but that Corinth will fall much more easily than Donelson did when we do move. All accounts agree in saying that the great mass of the rank and file are heartily tired."

One man at least did not agree at first, and that was Sherman. Privately he was telling newsmen, "We are in great danger here." But when asked why he did not protest to those in charge, he shrugged; "Oh, they'd call me crazy again." As time went by, however, and no attack developed, he became as complacent as the rest. Before the end of March he wrote gaily to an army friend in Cairo: "I hope we may meet in Memphis. Here we are on its latitude, and you have its longitude. Draw our parallels, and we breakfast at the Gayoso, whither let us God speed, and then rejoice once more at the progress of our cause."

Already there had been cause for rejoicing by some of his fellow generals, promotions having come through on the 21st for the three who commanded divisions at Donelson. Smith received his in bed—his leg was getting worse instead of better—but McClernand took his step-up with the continuing belief that other advancements were in store, and Lew Wallace was now the youngest major general in the army. Smith's division was placed in charge of W. H. L. Wallace, an Ohio lawyer who had won his stars at Donelson. Two of the three divisions added since were led by brigadiers who had moved to Illinois from the South and stood by the Union when trouble came: Benjamin M. Prentiss, a Virginia-born merchant, and Stephen A. Hurlbut, a lawyer originally from Charleston, South Carolina. Sherman, commanding the remaining green division, had had less combat experience than any of them—none at all, in fact, since that grievous July afternoon on the banks of Bull Run in far-away Virginia, where McClellan, now that April was at hand, was boarding a steamer to go down the coast and join his army for an advance up the James peninsula—but he was the only one of the six who was regular army, and Grant left the tactical arrangements in general to him, commuting daily by steamboat from the Savannah mansion, nine miles away.

Between them, these six commanded eighteen brigades: 74 regiments containing 42,682 soldiers, some raw, some hardened by combat. Green or seasoned, however, they approved to a man of their commander's intention to march down to Corinth, as soon as Buell arrived with 30,000 more, and administer another dose of the medicine they had forced down rebel throats the month before.

★ ★ ★ *J*ohnston had sixteen brigades, 71 regiments with a total strength of 40,335. But even apart from the day-to-day danger of Buell's reaching Pittsburg Landing with three fourths that many more, the present near-equality in numbers was considerably offset by a contrasting lack of combat experience. Two thirds of Grant's men had been in battle—in fact had been victorious in battle—whereas in Johnston's army, except for Forrest's troopers and the handful Polk had sent to Pillow's aid five months ago at Belmont, few had heard a shot fired in anger, and only Hardee's men had even done much real marching. Bragg referred to the forces around Corinth as "this mob we have, miscalled soldiers," and complained that a good part of them had never done a day's work in their lives. Johnston of course was aware of these

★

shortcomings, but his scouts having kept him well informed he counted much on the element of surprise. He knew what he would find up there: an army camped with its back to a deep river, unfortified, hemmed in by boggy creeks, disposed for comfort, and scattered the peacetime way. Meanwhile, drill and instruction were repairing the Confederate flaws Bragg had pointed out so harshly. He would strike as soon as he felt it possible. The question was, how long would he have before Buell got there or Grant saw the danger and corrected his dispositions or, worse, moved out and beat him to the punch?

Late at night, April 2, a telegram from Bethel, twenty miles north on the M & O, seemed to Beauregard to confirm the last and worst of these fears: Lew Wallace was maneuvering in that direction. Taking this for the beginning of a full-scale attack on Memphis, he forwarded the message to Johnston after writing on the bottom: "Now is the moment to advance, and strike the enemy at Pittsburg Landing." Johnston read it, then crossed the street to confer with Bragg, who had been made chief of staff in addition to his other duties under last week's reorganization. Johnston wanted more time for drilling his army and awaiting the arrival of Van Dorn, but Bragg was insistent in support of Beauregard's indorsement. Whatever this latest development meant, Buell was drawing closer every day. It had to be now or never, he said, and Johnston at last agreed. Ready or unready, Van Dorn or no Van Dorn, they would go up to Pittsburg and attack the Federal army in its camp. Within an hour of the telegram's midnight arrival, orders went out for the four corps commanders to "hold their commands in hand, ready to advance upon the enemy in the morning by 6 a.m. with three days' cooked rations in haversacks, 100 rounds of ammunition for small arms, and 200 rounds for field-pieces."

Early next morning Beauregard's chief of staff got to work, preparing the march instructions from notes the general had made on scraps of paper during the night. As he worked he had at his elbow Napoleon's Waterloo order, using it as a model despite the way that battle had turned out for the one who planned it. Since this would require considerable time — first the writing, then the copying and the distribution — Beauregard called Hardee and Bragg to his room to explain the march routes verbally; their corps would lead the way, and the written instructions could be delivered after they got started. As he spoke he drew a crude map on the top of a camp table, indicating distances and directions.

Two roads ran from Corinth up to Pittsburg. On the map they resembled a strung bow leaned sideways, curved side up, with the two armies at the top and bottom tips. The lower route, through Monterey, was the string; the upper route, through Mickey's, was the bow. Bragg and Breckinridge were to travel the string, Hardee and Polk the bow, in that order. Hardee was to reach Mickey's that night, bivouac, then at 3 a.m. pass on and form for battle in the

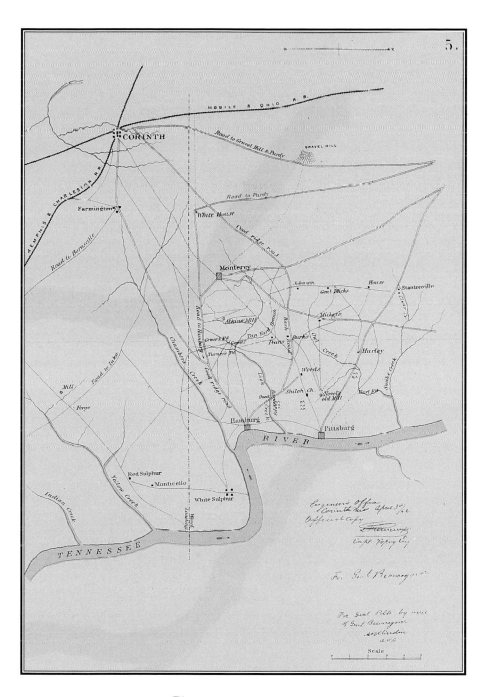

*Polk's copy of a map prepared for
Confederate corps commanders shows the approaches
to Pittsburg Landing from Corinth.*

fields beyond. Polk was to wait while Bragg marched up the road from Monterey and cleared the junction at Mickey's, then follow him into position, clearing the way for Breckinridge in turn. They were to regulate their columns so as not to delay each other, keeping their files well closed and the various elements properly spaced. So much for the march order; the battle order followed.

Beyond Mickey's, within charging distance of the enemy outposts, they were to form for battle in successive lines, Hardee across the front with one brigade from Bragg, who was to form a second line five hundred yards in rear. Polk and Breckinridge were to mass their corps to the left and right, a half-mile behind Bragg, so that when he went forward, following Hardee, Polk could spread out wide in his support, leaving Breckinridge in column as the general reserve. The flanks of the army, with the three lead corps extending individually across the entire front, rested on the creeks that hemmed Grant in. As they advanced, each line would thus support the one in front, and the reserve corps would feed troops from the rear toward those points where resistance turned out stiffest. The attack on the right was intended to move fastest, bearing generally left in a long curve, first along the watershed of Lick Creek and then down the west bank of the Tennessee, so as to sweep the Federals clear of the landing and drive them back against the boggy northward loop of Snake Creek, where they could be destroyed.

Today was Thursday, April 3. According to schedule, the troops would complete the twenty-mile approach march and be deployed for battle no later than midmorning tomorrow. But when the council broke up at 10 o'clock, already four hours past the starting time, and the generals dispersed to get their columns on the road, troops and wagons quickly snarled to a standstill, blocking the streets of Corinth. Polk at last got clear of the jam, but had to wait while Hardee doubled his column and took the lead. By then it was late afternoon, and Polk was held up till after sunset. When he stopped for the night he had covered a scant nine miles. Down on the lower road, Bragg's unwieldy column did no better. Manifestly, the schedule would have to be revised. Beauregard set it forward a whole day, intending now to be deployed in time to strike the Federals early Saturday morning.

But if Thursday had been like a bad dream, Friday was a nightmare. The march, which had seemed so easy to regulate on the flat, uncluttered table-top, turned out to be something quite different on the ground, which was neither flat nor uncluttered—nor, as it turned out, dry. The abrupt, thunderous showers of a Mississippi April broke over the winding column, and soon the wagon and artillery wheels had churned the roads into shin-deep mud. There were halts and unaccountable delays, times when the men had to trot to keep up, and times when they stood endlessly in the rain, waiting for the file ahead to stumble into motion. In their wake, the roadsides

★

were littered with discarded equipment, overcoats and playing cards, bowie knives and Bibles. A more welcome delay was the rest halt given each regiment while its colonel read the commanding general's address, written in Corinth while they were assembling for the march.

> *Soldiers of the Army of the Mississippi:*
>
> *I have put you in motion to offer battle to the invaders of your country. With the resolution and disciplined valor becoming men fighting, as you are, for all worth living or dying for, you can but march to a decisive victory over the agrarian mercenaries sent to subjugate and despoil you of your liberties, property, and honor. Remember the precious stake involved; remember the dependence of your mothers, your wives, your sisters, and your children on the result; remember the fair, broad, abounding land, the happy homes and the ties that would be desolated by your defeat.*
>
> *The eyes and hopes of eight millions of people rest upon you. You are expected to show yourselves worthy of your race and lineage; worthy of the women of the South, whose noble devotion in this war has never been exceeded in any time. With such incentives to brave deeds, and with the trust that God is with us, your generals will lead you confidently to the combat, assured of success.*
>
> *A. S. JOHNSTON, General*

It was delivered in various styles, ranging from the oratorical, with flourishes, to the matter-of-fact, depending on the previous civil occupation of the reader. The troops cheered wildly or perfunctorily, depending on their degree of weariness and in part on how the address was read, then fell back into column on the muddy roads for more of the stop-and-go marching.

★

But the one who had it worst that day was Bragg. He too had made a late start out of Corinth, and the head of his oversized column did not reach Monterey, where it should have bivouacked the night before, until near midday.

One of his divisions was lost somewhere in the rear, perhaps sidetracked, and he had had no word from Breckinridge at all. As a result, though Hardee and Polk were marching hard to make up for yesterday's wasted time, the latter was held up short of Mickey's, waiting for Bragg to clear the junction, and the former had no sooner got past it than he received a message asking him to call a halt so that Bragg's dragging column could close the expanding gap. Bragg was a tall, gangling man, a West

A native North Carolinian, lately a Louisiana sugar planter, in his middle forties but looking ten years older because of chronic stomach trouble and a coarse gray-black beard which emphasized his heaviness of jaw and sternness of aspect . . .

Pointer and a Mexican War hero — "A little more grape, Captain Bragg," Zachary Taylor was supposed to have told him at Buena Vista, as every schoolboy knew (though what he really said was, "Captain, give 'em hell") — a native North Carolinian, lately a Louisiana sugar planter, in his middle forties but looking ten years older because of chronic stomach trouble and a coarse gray-black beard which emphasized his heaviness of jaw and sternness of aspect; not that the latter needed emphasis, already having been rendered downright ferocious by the thick bushy eyebrows which grew in a continuous line across the bottom of his forehead. It galled him to have to send that message to Hardee, amounting as it did to an admission of being to blame for the delay; for he was a strict disciplinarian, and like most such he was quick to lose his temper when things went wrong.

Still jammed on the roads leading into and out of Mickey's, when they should have been moving into the final position where they would deploy for the attack tomorrow morning, the weary and bedraggled troops were caught that night in the same thunderstorm that attended the *Carondelet* on her run past Island Ten, just over a hundred miles away. All semblance of order dissolved under torrents of rain. When Johnston and Beauregard rode into Mickey's soon after sunrise, expecting to find the army arrayed for combat — they had left Corinth the day before and spent the night at Monterey — the rain had stopped and the sun was shining bright on the flooded fields, but the army was far from arrayed. In fact, most of it had not even arrived. Hardee was approximately in position, but he was waiting for the brigade from Bragg that would complete his line. By the time it got there, the sun was already high in the sky and Beauregard was fuming. He had cause. As they marched forward to file into line, the men began to worry about the dampness of the powder in their rifles; but instead of drawing the charges and reloading, they tested them by snapping the triggers; with the result that, within earshot of the Federal outposts, there was an intermittent banging up and down the columns, as rackety as a sizeable picket clash. Nor was that all. The returning sun having raised their spirits, the men began to tune up their rebel yells and practice marksmanship on birds and rabbits.

For two hours then, with Johnston and Beauregard standing by, Bragg continued to deploy the remainder of his corps — all but the rear division, which still had not arrived. When Johnston asked where it was, the harassed Bragg replied that it was somewhere back there; he was trying to locate it. Johnston waited, his impatience mounting, then took out his watch: 12.30. "This is perfectly puerile! This is not war!" he exclaimed, and set off down the road himself to look for the missing division. He found it wedged behind some of Polk's troops, who had not been willing to yield the right of way. The daylight hours were going fast. By the time Johnston got the road cleared and the last of Bragg's men passed to the front, his watch showed 2 o'clock. Polk's deployment used up another two hours, and Breckinridge, who had come up at last, was still to be brought forward. The shadows were getting longer every minute. It was not until about 4.30, however, that Johnston received the worst shock of all.

Riding forward he came upon a roadside conference between Beauregard and Polk and Bragg. The Creole's big sad bloodhound eyes were rimmed with angry red and his hands were fluttering as he spoke. He was upset: which was understandable, for it was already ten hours past the time when he expected to launch the attack. He favored canceling the whole movement and returning at once to Corinth. In his mind, surprise was everything, and what with the delay piled on the previous postponement, the constant tramping back and forth and the racket the men had been making, all chance for surprise had been forfeited. He knew this, he said, because at one point that afternoon he had heard a drum rolling, but when he sent to have it silenced, the messenger came back and reported that it could not be done; the drum was in the Union camp. Beauregard reasoned that if he could hear enemy drumtaps, there was small doubt that the Federals had heard the random firing and whooping in the Confederate columns. Besides, ten southern troopers had been captured in a cavalry clash the night

*Confederate Generals Beauregard, Polk,
Breckinridge, Johnston, Bragg, and Hardee (left
to right) confer on the eve of their attack at Shiloh.*

before; surely by now they had been questioned, and one at least had talked.

"There is no chance for surprise," he ended angrily. "Now they will be intrenched to the eyes."

Johnston heard him out, then turned to Polk, his West Point roommate. The bishop disagreed. His troops were eager for battle; they had left Corinth on the way to a fight, he said in that deep, pulpit voice of his, and if they did not find one they would be as demoralized as if they had been whipped. Bragg said he felt the same way about it. While he was speaking Breckinridge rode up. Surprised that withdrawal was even being considered, he sided with Polk and Bragg, declaring that he would as soon be defeated as retire without a fight. Hardee was the only corps commander not present, but there was no doubt which side he would favor; he was already formed for battle, anxious to go forward. The vote was in, and Johnston made it official. There would be another delay, another postponement, but there would be no turning back.

"Gentlemen, we shall attack at daylight tomorrow," he said.

He told the corps commanders to complete the deployment and have the troops sleep on their arms in line of battle. Beauregard was protesting

★

that Buell most likely had come up by now, bringing the Federal total to 70,000. But that made no difference either: not to Johnston, who had reached what he believed would be his hour of vindication after his long retreat. As he walked off he spoke to one of his staff. "I would fight them if they were a million," he said. "They can present no greater front between those two creeks than we can, and the more men they crowd in there, the worse we can make it for them."

While the army completed its deployment, the troops bedding down so that when they woke in darkness they would already be in line for the dawn assault, the sun set clear and red beyond the tasseling oaks. There was a great stillness in the blue dusk, and then the stars came out, dimming the pale sickle moon already risen in the daylight sky. Mostly the men slept, for they were weary; but some stayed awake, huddled around fires built in holes in the ground to hide them. In part they stayed awake because of hunger, for it was a Confederate belief that rations carried lighter in the stomach than in a haversack, and they had consumed their three days' rations at the outset. The nearest of them could hear Yankee bugles, faint and far like foxhorns three fields off, sounding out of the dark woods where tomorrow's battle would be fought. "The elephant," veterans called combat, telling recruits the time had come to meet the elephant.

★ ★ ★   *S*trictly speaking, Beauregard was right, at least in part. Buell had arrived—that is, he slept that night on the outskirts of Savannah, intending to confer with Grant next morning —but with only one of his divisions, the others being scattered along twenty miles of the road back toward Nashville. They would arrive tomorrow and the next day. Grant, being informed of this, could go to bed that night rejoicing that things had worked out so well at last. He intended to send Buell's men upstream to Hamburg. The road from there to Corinth was a mile shorter than the one leading down from Pittsburg, and the two converged eight miles this side of the objective. Conditions thus were ideal for his intention, which was to attack as soon as Buell's army could be transferred to the west bank for coöperation with his own. Irksome as the delay had been, it had given him time to study the terrain and whip his reinforcements into shape, including even some seasoning clashes with rebel cavalry who ventured up to probe the rim of his camp at Pittsburg Landing.

The men themselves were feeling good by now, too, though at the outset they had had their doubts and discomforts. They had spent a rough first week clearing campsites, a week full of snow and sleet and a damp cold that went through flesh to bone. "The sunny South!" they jeered. All night, down the rows of tents, there was coughing, a racking uproar. Diarrhea was another evil, but they made jokes about that too; "the Tennessee quickstep," they called it, laughing ruefully on sick call when the surgeons advised them to try the application of red-hot pokers. Then suddenly the weather faired, and this was the sunny South indeed; even the rain was warm. By the end of March Grant was reporting, "The health of the troops is materially improving under the influence of a genial sun which has blessed us for a few days past."

He knew because he had been among them, making his daily commuter trip by steamboat from Savannah. Mostly, though, he kept his mind on the future, the offensive he would launch when Buell got there. He left the present—the defensive—largely to Sherman, who had kept busy all this time confirming his commander's high opinion of him. The red-haired Ohioan's green division was the largest in the army, and he had awarded it the position of honor, farthest from the landing. Three miles out, on the Corinth road, his headquarters tent was pitched alongside a rude log Methodist meeting-house called Shiloh Chapel. Two of his brigades were in line to the west of there, extending over toward Owl Creek, which flowed into Snake Creek where it turned northwest, a mile from the river, leaving Owl Creek to protect the army's right flank south of the junction. His third brigade was east of the chapel, and his fourth was on the far side of the position, beyond Prentiss's two brigades, whose camp was in line with his own. The others were three-brigade divisions: McClernand's just in rear of Sherman's, Hurlbut's and W. H. L. Wallace's well back toward the landing, and Lew Wallace's five miles north, beyond Snake Creek. It was not so much a tactical arrangement, designed for mutual support, as it was an arrangement for comfort and convenience, the various positions being selected because of the availability of water or open fields for drilling. In Sherman's mind, as in Grant's, the main concern was getting ready to move out for Corinth as soon as Buell arrived. He had long since got over his original concern, privately admitted, that the army was "in great danger here."

The same could not be said for all his officers. One in particular, the colonel of the 53d Ohio, had sounded the alarm so often that his soldiers were jeered at for belonging to what was called the Long Roll regiment. High-strung and jumpy—like Sherman himself in the old days—he was given to imagining that the whole rebel army was just outside his tent flap. During the past few days his condition had grown worse. Friday, April 4, he lost a picket guard of seven men, gobbled up by grayback cavalry, and when he advanced a company to develop the situation they ran into scattered firing and came back. All day Saturday he was on tenterhooks, communicating his alarm to Sherman. That afternoon he piled on the last straw by sending word to headquarters that a large force of the enemy was moving on the camp. Sherman mounted and rode out to confront him. While the colonel told excitedly of the hordes of rebels out there in the brush, Sherman sat with his mouth clamped down, looking into the empty woods. At last the man stopped talking. Sherman sat glaring down at him, then jerked the reins to turn his horse toward camp. "Take your damned regiment back to Ohio," he said, snapping the words. "Beauregard is not such a fool as to leave his base of operations and attack us in ours. There is no enemy nearer than Corinth."

★

A Mexican War veteran, merchant, and Republican politician, Benjamin Prentiss (left) commanded a Federal division that bore the brunt of the Confederate assault.

So he said, adding the final remark to sharpen the sting of the rebuke, though actually he knew better. This was but one of several such clashes, including one the previous evening in which ten rebel prisoners were taken, and just this morning he had notified Grant: "The enemy has cavalry in our front, and I think there are two regiments of infantry and one battery of artillery about 2 miles out. I will send you 10 prisoners of war and a report of last night's affair in a few minutes."

There was a need for frequent reports, for Grant would not be coming up to visit the camps today. He had sprained his ankle during the violent thunderstorm the night before, when his horse slipped and fell on his leg. The soft ground had saved him from serious injury, but his boot had had to be cut off because of the swelling and he was limping painfully on crutches. The first dispatch from Sherman had opened, "All is quiet along my lines," and presently there was another, apparently sent after he got back from administering the stinging rebuke to the Ohio colonel: "I have no doubt that nothing will occur today more than some picket firing. The enemy is saucy, but got the worst of it yesterday, and will not press our pickets far.... I do not apprehend anything like an attack on our position."

The prisoners, if sent, went unquestioned. What could they possibly have to say that would interest a man who had already made up his mind that if he was to have a battle he would have to march his soldiers down to Corinth and provoke it? Sustained in his opinion by reports such as these two from Sherman, Grant refused to be disconcerted by incidentals. Besides, the staff officer who was best at conducting interrogations was at Hamburg, inspecting the campsite selected for Buell's army. No time was to be lost now, for the lead division had arrived at noon, along with a note from Buell: "I shall be in Savannah tomorrow with one, perhaps two, divisions. Can I meet you there?" The note was dated yesterday; "tomorrow" meant today. But Grant either did not observe the heading (another incidental) or else he was in no hurry. "Your dispatch received," he replied. "I will be there to meet you tomorrow" — meaning Sunday.

Ever since his run-in with Halleck, regarding the alleged infrequency of his reports, he had kept the St Louis wire humming. Before he went to bed tonight in the fine big house on the bluff at Savannah, with nothing to fret him but the pain in his swollen ankle, he wrote a letter informing his chief that Buell's lead division had arrived; the other two were close on its heels and would get there tomorrow and the next day. He told him also of yesterday's picket clash. "I immediately went up," he said, "but found all quiet." Then he added: "I have scarcely the faintest idea of an attack (general one) being made upon us, but will be prepared should such a thing take place."

Next morning at breakfast he heard a distant thunder from the south. The guns of Shiloh were jarring the earth.

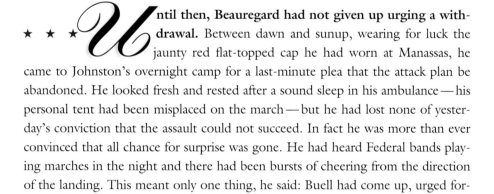

★ ★ ★ *U*ntil then, Beauregard had not given up urging a withdrawal. Between dawn and sunup, wearing for luck the jaunty red flat-topped cap he had worn at Manassas, he came to Johnston's overnight camp for a last-minute plea that the attack plan be abandoned. He looked fresh and rested after a sound sleep in his ambulance — his personal tent had been misplaced on the march — but he had lost none of yesterday's conviction that the assault could not succeed. In fact he was more than ever convinced that all chance for surprise was gone. He had heard Federal bands playing marches in the night and there had been bursts of cheering from the direction of the landing. This meant only one thing, he said: Buell had come up, urged forward by the alerted Grant, and now there were 70,000 men in the Union camp, intrenched and expectant, waiting for the Confederates to walk into the trap.

The reply came not from Johnston, who stood with a cup of coffee in his hands, sipping from it as he heard him out, but from the army itself. The Creole was caught in midsentence by a rattle of musketry from dead ahead, a curious ripping sound like tearing canvas. Staff officers looked in that direction, then back at Johnston, who was handing the half-empty cup to an orderly. "The battle has opened, gentlemen," he said. "It is too late to change our dispositions." Beauregard mounted and rode away; the argument was no longer a matter for words. Johnston swung onto his horse and sat there for a long moment, his face quite grave. Then he twitched the reins, and as the big bay thoroughbred began to walk toward the sound of firing, swelling now across the front, the general turned in the saddle and spoke to his staff: "Tonight we will water our horses in the Tennessee River."

★ ★ ★   The opening shots had been fired ahead of schedule because one of Prentiss's brigade commanders, sleepless and uneasy in the hours before dawn, had sent a three-company reconnaissance out to explore the woods to his front. Encountering a portion of Hardee's skirmish line, which had not yet gone forward, they mistook it for a scouting party and attacked with spirit, driving the skirmishers back on the main body. Repulsed in turn by heavy volleys, they fell back to give the alarm that the enemy was moving in strength against the Federal position. Prentiss thus was warned of what was coming before it got there, and turned his green division out to meet the shock.

Sherman too was warned, but took no heed because the alarm was sounded by the same colonel he had rebuked for crying wolf the day before. A man had stumbled out of a thicket into the Ohio camp, holding a wound and crying, "Get in line! The rebels are coming!" A captain who went to investigate quickly returned shouting, "The rebs are out there thicker than fleas on a dog's back!" But when the colonel sent a courier to inform Sherman, word came back: "You must be badly scared over there."

Presently, though, riding forward with an orderly to where the colonel was shakily getting his men into line, he saw for himself the Confederates advancing across a large field in front, the skirmishers holding their rifles slantwise like quail hunters and the main body massed heavily behind them. The sun, which had risen fast in a cloudless sky — "the sun of Austerlitz," Southerners called it, seeing in this a Napoleonic omen — flashed on their bayonets as they brought their rifles up to fire. "My God, we're attacked!" Sherman cried, convinced at last as the volley crashed and his orderly fell dead beside him. "Hold your position; I'll support you!" he shouted, and spurred away to send up reinforcements. But: "This is no place for us," the colonel wailed, seeing his general head for the rear, and went over and lay face-down behind a fallen tree. His men were wavering, firing erratically at the attackers. When the next enemy volley crashed, the colonel jumped up from behind the tree; "Retreat! Save yourselves!" he cried, and set the example by taking off rearward at a run.

Most of his men went with him, believing they knew a sensible order when they heard one, but enough stayed to give Sherman time to warn the brigades on his other flank to drop their Sunday breakfast preparations and brace themselves for the assault. They formed in haste along the ridge where their tents were pitched, looking out over a valley choked with vines and brambles, and began to fire into the wave of gray that was surging out of the woods on the far side. Green as they were, they held their ground against four successive charges, firing steadily until the fifth swept up the slope, then gave way in tolerable good order to take up a second position farther back. The 6th Mississippi, for one, could testify to the accuracy of their fire; for it started across that valley with 425 men and reached the tented ridge with just over 100; the rest lay dead or wounded among the brambles. So thick they lay, the dead of this and the other four regiments in those charges, that one observer remarked that he could have walked across that valley without touching his feet to the ground; "a pavement of dead men," he called it.

Prentiss was fighting as doggedly on the left, and McClernand had marched to the sound of guns, filling the gap between the two divisions, so that the three were more or less in line, resisting stubbornly. All three were leaking men to the rear, the faint-hearted who sought safety back at the landing under the bluff, but the ones who stayed were determined to yield nothing except under pressure that proved itself irresistible. By the time Sherman's soldiers got settled in their second position, waiting for what came next, they had the feel of

*After the first Confederate attack,
thousands of terrified Federals flee to hide
under the bluffs of the Tennessee River.*

being veterans. Whatever came next could not possibly be worse than what had gone before, and having their commander move among them added to their confidence. He had been hit twice already, but gave no sign of even considering leaving the field. The first time was in the hand; he wrapped it in a handkerchief and thrust it into his breast, never taking his eyes off the enemy. The other bullet clipped a shoulder strap, nicking the skin, but that did not seem to bother him much either. When a headquarters aide came riding up to ask how things were going, he found Sherman leaning against a tree, propped on his uninjured hand, watching the skirmishers. "Tell Grant if he has any men to spare I can use them," he said, still narrow-eyed. "If not, I will do the best I can. We are holding them pretty well just now. Pretty well; but it's hot as hell."

By midmorning Grant himself was at his lieutenant's elbow, amid the bursting shells and whistling bullets. Brought to his feet by the rumble of guns from the south, he had left the breakfast table and gone aboard his steamer at the wharf below the mansion, pausing only long enough to send two notes. One was to Buell, canceling their meeting in Savannah, and the other was to Brigadier General William Nelson, whose division had arrived the day before, directing him to "move your entire command to the river opposite Pittsburg." On the way upstream—it was now about 8.30—he found Lew Wallace waiting for him on the jetty at Crump's. The firing sounded louder; Pittsburg was definitely under attack, but Grant still did not know but what a second attack might be aimed in this direction. Without stopping the boat he called out to Wallace as he went by, "General, get your troops under arms and have them ready to move at a moment's notice." Wallace shouted back that he had already done so. Grant nodded and went on.

When he docked and rode his horse up the bluff from the landing, a crutch strapped to the saddle like a carbine, the tearing rattle of musketry and the steady booming of cannon told him the whole trouble was right here in the three-sided box where his main camp had been established. Wounded men and skulkers were stumbling rearward, seeking defilade, and beyond them the hysterical quaver of the rebel yell came through the crash of gunfire and the deeper-throated shouts of his own soldiers. Grant's first act was to establish a straggler line, including a battery with its guns trained on the road leading out of the uproar. Then he went forward to where W. H. L. Wallace and Hurlbut had formed ranks and by now were sending reinforcements to the hard-pressed divisions on the far edge of the fight. The situation was critical, but Grant kept as calm as he had done at Donelson in a similar predicament. This time, though, he had reserves, and he sent for them at once. A summons went to Lew Wallace, five miles away, instructing him to join the embattled army. Another went to Nelson, presumably already toiling across the boggy stretch of land between Savannah and the river bank opposite Pittsburg, urging him to "hurry up your command as fast as possible."

By 10 o'clock he was up front with Sherman. One of the Ohioan's brigades had disintegrated under fire, but the other two were resisting heavy pressure against their second position, half a mile back from the ridge where their tents were pitched. He said his biggest worry was that his men would run out of ammunition, but Grant assured him that this had been provided for; more was on the way. Satisfied that Sherman could look out for himself, the army commander then visited McClernand, fighting as hard in rear of Shiloh Chapel, and finally Prentiss, whose division had been repulsed by the fury of the initial onslaught, but in falling back across the open field had come upon an eroded wagon trail which wound along the edge of some heavy woods on the

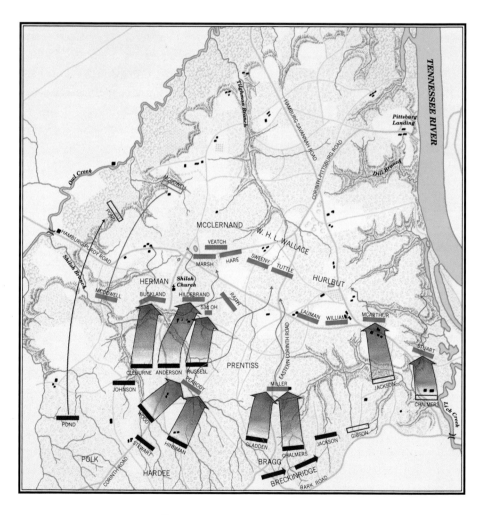

At dawn on April 6, the Confederate attack (red arrows) drove the surprised Federals back to the northeast.

far side. They had got down into the shallow natural trench of this sunken road to make a stand, and that was what they were doing when Grant arrived. In fact they were doing a thorough job of it, dropping the Confederates in windrows as they charged across the fields. Approving of this execution, Grant told Prentiss to "maintain that position at all hazards." Prentiss said he would try.

He not only tried, he did maintain that position against repeated headlong charges delivered without apparent concern for loss. Elsewhere, however, conditions were much worse. At noon, when Grant returned to his headquarters near the rim of the bluff, he found the fugitives streaming rearward thicker than ever, through and past the straggler line, white-faced and unmindful of the officers who tried to rally them. Bad news awaited him: Sherman and McClernand had been forced back still farther. Both were retiring sullenly, fighting as they did so, but if either division broke into a rout, the rebels would come whooping down on the landing and the battle would be over. W. H. L. Wallace and Hurlbut had committed all their troops, and nothing had been heard from Lew Wallace, who should have completed his five-mile march before now, nor from Nelson across the river. There was no reserve at hand to block a breakthrough. In desperation Grant sent two staff officers beyond Snake Creek to hurry Wallace along and a third across the Tennessee with a note for Nelson, worded to show the urgent need for haste: "If you will get upon the field, leaving all your baggage on the east bank of the river, it will be a move to our advantage, and possibly save the day to us. The rebel force is estimated at over 100,000 men."

★ ★ ★ **B**eauregard had taken over the log church called Shiloh, and from this headquarters he performed for the army commander the service the other Johnston had performed for him at Manassas, exercising control of the rear area and forwarding reinforcements to those points where additional strength was needed. Thus Johnston was left free to move up and down the line of battle, encouraging the troops, and this he did. Some he sought to steady by speaking calmly. "Look along your guns, and fire low," he told them. Others he sought to inspirit with fiercer words: "Men of Arkansas, they say you boast of your prowess with the bowie knife. Today you wield a nobler weapon: the bayonet. Employ it well!" Whichever he did, or whether he did neither, but merely rode among them, tall and handsome on his tall, handsome horse, the men cheered at the sight of their commander exposing himself to the dangers he was requiring them to face. This was indeed his hour of vindication.

His men swept forward, overrunning the enemy's front-line camps and whooping with elation as they took potshots at the backs of fleeing Yankees. Where resistance stiffened, as along the ridge where Sherman's tents were pitched, they matched valor against determination and paid in blood for the resultant gain. Not that there were no instances of flinching at the cost. An Arkansas major reported angrily that a Tennessee regiment in front of his own "broke and ran back, hallooing 'Retreat, retreat,' which being mistaken by our own men for orders of their commander, a retreat was made by them and some confusion ensued." No sooner was this corrected than the same thing happened again, only this time the major had an even more shameful occurrence to report: "They were in such great haste to get behind us that they ran over and trampled in the mud our brave color-bearer." There were other, worse confusions. The Orleans Guard battalion, the elite organization with Beauregard's name on its muster roll, came into battle wearing dress-blue uniforms, which drew the fire of the Confederates they were marching to support. Promptly they returned the volley, and when a horrified staff officer came galloping up to tell them they were shooting at their friends: "I know it," the Creole colonel replied. "But dammit, sir, we fire on everybody who fires on us!"

Such mishaps and mistakes could be corrected or even overlooked by the high command. More serious were the evils resulting from straggling, caused mainly by hunger and curiosity. When some Northerners later denied that they had been surprised at Shiloh, a Texan who had scalded his arm in snatching a joint of meat from a bubbling pot as he charged through one of the Federal camps replied that if Grant's army had not been surprised it certainly had "the most devoted mess crews in the history of warfare." Sunday breakfasts, spread out on tables or still cooking over campfires, were more than the hungry Confederates could resist. Many sat down, then and there, to gorge themselves on white bread and sweet coffee. Others explored the Yankee tents, foraging among the departed soldiers' belongings, including their letters, which they read with interest to find out what northern girls were like. Hundreds, perhaps thousands, were lost thus to their comrades forging ahead, and this also served to blunt the impetus of the attack which in its early stages had rolled headlong over whatever got in its way.

Most serious of all, though, were the flaws that developed when the attack plan was exposed to prolonged strain. Neatly efficient as the thing had looked on paper, it was turning out quite otherwise on the rugged plateau with its underbrush and gullies and its clusters of stubborn blue defenders. Attacking as directed — three corps in line from creek to creek, one behind another, each line feeding its components piecemeal into the line ahead — brigades and regiments and even companies had become so intermingled that unit commanders lost touch with their men and found themselves in charge of strangers who never before had heard the sound of their voices. Coördination was lost. By noon, when the final reserves had been committed, the army was no longer a clockwork aggregation of corps and divisions; it was a frantic mass of keyed-up men crowded into an approximate battle formation to fight a hundred furious skirmishes strung out in a crooked line. Confusing as all this was to those who fought thus to the booming accompaniment of two hundred guns, it was perhaps even more confusing to those who were trying to direct them. And indeed how should they have understood this thing they had been plunged into as if into a cauldron of pure hell? For this was the first great modern battle. It was Wilson's Creek and Manassas rolled together, quadrupled, and compressed into an area smaller than either. From the inside it resembled Armageddon.

Attempting to regain control, the corps commanders divided the front into four sectors, Hardee and Polk on the left, Bragg and Breckinridge on the right. Coördination was lacking, however, and all the attacks were frontal. Besides, compliance with Johnston's original instructions — "Every effort will be made to turn the left flank of the enemy, so as to cut off his line of retreat to the Tennessee River and throw him back on [Snake] Creek, where he will be forced to surrender" — was being frustrated by Prentiss, who stood fast along

---

For this was the first great modern battle.
It was Wilson's Creek and Manassas
rolled together, quadrupled, and compressed
into an area smaller than either.
From the inside it resembled Armageddon.

---

the sunken road. "It's a hornets' nest in there!" the gray-clad soldiers cried, recoiling from charge after charge against the place. When Sherman and McClernand gave way, taking up successive rearward positions, the Confederate left outstripped the right, which was stalled in front of the Hornets Nest, and thus presented Johnston with the reverse of what he wanted. He rode toward the far right to correct this, carrying in his right hand a small tin cup which he had picked up in a captured camp. Seeing a lieutenant run out of one of the tents with an armload of Yankee souvenirs, Johnston told him sternly: "None of that, sir. We are not here for plunder." Then, observing that he had hurt the young man's feelings, which after all was a poor reward for the gallantry shown in the capture, by way of apology he leaned down without dismounting and took the tin cup off a table. "Let this be my share of the spoils today," he said, and from then on he had used it instead of a sword to direct the battle. He used it so now, his index finger hooked through the loop of the handle, as he rode toward the right where his advance had stalled.

At this end of the battle line, on the far flank of the Hornets Nest, there was a ten-acre peach orchard in full bloom. Hurlbut had a heavy line of infantry posted among the trees, supported by guns whose smoke lazed and swirled up through the branches sheathed in pink, and a bright rain of petals fell fluttering like confetti in the sunlight as bullets clipped the blossoms overhead. Arriving just after one of Breckinridge's brigades had recoiled from a charge against the orchard, Johnston saw that the officers were having trouble getting the troops in line to go forward again. "Men! they are stubborn; we must use the bayonet," he told them. To emphasize his meaning he rode among them and touched the points of their bayonets with the tin cup. "These must do the work," he said. When the line had formed, the soldiers were still hesitant to reënter the smoky uproar. So Johnston did what he had been doing all that morning, all along the line of battle. Riding front and center, he stood in the stirrups, removed his hat, and called back over his shoulder: "I will lead you!" As he touched his spurs to the flanks of his horse, the men surged forward, charging with him into the sheet of flame which blazed to meet them there among the blossoms letting fall their bright pink rain.

This time the charge was not repulsed; Hurlbut's troops gave way, abandoning the orchard to the cheering men in gray. Johnston came riding back, a smile on his lips, his teeth flashing white beneath his mustache. There were rips and tears in his uniform and one bootsole had been cut nearly in half by a minie bullet. He shook his foot so the dangling leather flapped. "They didn't trip me up that time," he said, laughing. His battle blood was up; his eyes were shining. Presently, however, as the general sat watching his soldiers celebrate their capture of the orchard and its guns, Governor Isham Harris of Tennessee, who had volunteered to serve as his aide during the battle, saw him reel in the saddle.

"General — are you hurt?" he cried.

"Yes, and I fear seriously," Johnston said.

None of the rest of his staff was there, the general having sent them off on various missions. Riding with one arm across Johnston's shoulders to prevent his falling, Harris guided the bay into a nearby ravine, where he eased the pale commander to the ground and began unfastening his clothes in an attempt to find the wound. He had no luck until he noticed the right boot full of blood, and then he found it: a neat hole drilled just above the hollow of the knee, marking where the femoral artery had been severed. This called for a knowledge of tourniquets, but the governor knew nothing of such things. The man who knew most about them, Johnston's staff physician, had been ordered by the general to attend to a group of Federal wounded he encountered on his way to the far right. When the doctor protested, Johnston cut him off: "These men were our enemies a moment ago. They are our prisoners now. Take care of them." So Harris alone was left to do what he could to staunch the bright red flow of blood.

He could do little. Brandy might help, he thought, but when he poured some into the hurt man's mouth it ran back out again. Presently a colonel, Johnston's chief of staff, came hurrying into the ravine. But he could do nothing either. He knelt down facing the general. "Johnston, do you know me? Johnston, do you know me?" he kept asking, over and over, nudging the general's shoulder as he spoke.

But Johnston did not know him. Johnston was dead.

Confederate General A. S. Johnston (left) lies bleeding to death at Shiloh (below) after being wounded on the first day of fighting.

* * * It was now about 2.30. When the command passed to Beauregard—who in point of fact had been exercising it all along, in a general way, from his headquarters at Shiloh Chapel—his first order was that news of Johnston's death was to be kept from the men, lest they become disheartened before completing the destruction of the northern army. There would be no let-up; the attack was to continue all along the line, particularly against the Hornets Nest, whose outer flank was threatened now by the Confederates who had flung Hurlbut's men gunless out of the orchard and taken their place. After a lull, which allowed for the shifting of troops to strengthen the blow, the line was ready to go forward. A dozen separate full-scale assaults had been launched against the sunken road, each one over a thickening carpet of dead and wounded. All twelve had failed; but this one would not fail. Pressure alone not having been enough, now pressure was to be combined with blasting. At point-blank range, with Beauregard's approval, Dan Ruggles had massed 62 guns to rake the place with canister and grape.

When those guns opened, clump by clump, then all together, blending their separate crashes into one continuous roar, it was as if the Hornets Nest exploded, inclosing its defenders in a smoky, flame-cracked din of flying clods, splintered trees, uprooted brush, and whirring metal. Elsewhere on the field that morning a wounded soldier, sent to the rear by his company commander, had soon returned, shouting to be heard above the racket: "Captain, give me a gun! This durn fight aint got any rear!" Presently this was quite literally true for Prentiss, who held fast along the sunken road. On the flanks, the men of Hurlbut and W. H. L. Wallace scrambled backward to get from under the crash. The line was bent into a horseshoe. Then Wallace fell, cut down as he tried to rally his men, and they gave way entirely, running headlong. Hurlbut's followed suit. Only Prentiss's troops remained steadfast along the sunken road, flanked and then surrounded. The horseshoe became an iron hoop as the Confederates, pursuing Hurlbut and the remnants of Wallace around both flanks of Prentiss, met in his rear and sealed him off.

He could hear them yelling back there, triumphant, but he fought on, obedient to his strict instructions to "maintain that position at all hazards." The dead lay thick. Every minute they lay thicker. Still he fought. By 5.30—two long hours after Ruggles' guns began their furious cannonade—further resistance became futile, and Prentiss knew it. He had the cease-fire sounded and surrendered his 2200 survivors, well under half the number he had started with that morning. Sherman and McClernand on the right, and Hurlbut to a lesser degree on the left, had saved their divisions by falling back each time the pressure reached a certain intensity. Prentiss had lost his by standing fast: lost men, guns, colors, and finally the position itself: lost all, in fact, but honor. Yet he had saved far more in saving that. Sherman and McClernand had saved their divisions by retreating, but Prentiss had saved Grant by standing fast.

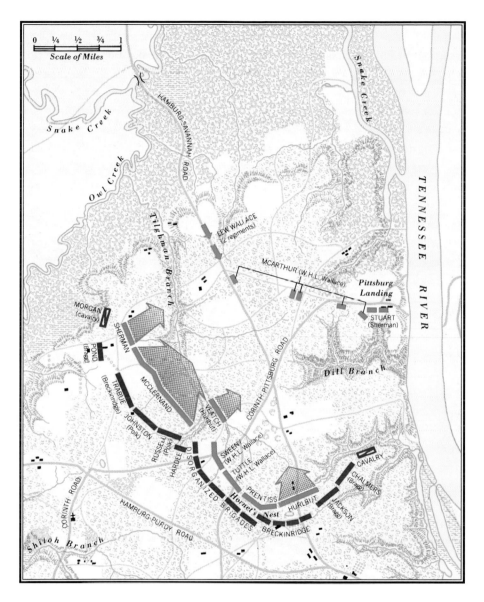

*Federals, regrouping after the initial
attack, held in the Hornets Nest until they
were again forced to withdraw.*

Beauregard saw it otherwise. During twelve hours of fighting, in addition to much other booty found in the captured camps, his army had taken 23 cannon, exclusive of those surrendered by Prentiss, and flushed the Northerners from every position they had chosen to try for a stand. The Hornets Nest, if the toughest of these, was merely one more in a series of continuing successes. Now that the sunken road lay in rear of the advance, the shortened line could be strengthened for the final go-for-broke assault that would shove what was left of Grant's army over the bluff and into the Tennessee. So he thought, at any rate; until he tried it. On the left, Hardee and Polk were pecking away at Sherman and McClernand, but the attacks were not delivered with spirit or conviction. Too many of their men had died or straggled, and those who stayed were near exhaustion. On the right, where more could be expected in the wake of the recent collapse, Bragg and Breckinridge fared even worse. Their casualties had been about as high and the number of stragglers was even higher; hundreds stayed behind to gawk at the captured thousands, including one real live Yankee general, who came marching out of the Hornets Nest under guard. Two of Bragg's brigades—or the remnants—tried an assault on the left flank of the Federals, who were crowded into a semicircular position along the road that led from the landing to the bridge

---

Here on the battlefield which took its name from the log church called Shiloh—interpreted by Bible scholars to mean "the place of peace"—those who could found shelter in the Federal camps and had their dreams invaded by the drum of rain on canvas.

---

that spanned Snake Creek. However, it was delivered across a ravine knee-deep in backwater, and when the weary troops emerged on the far side they were met by massed volleys almost as heavy as those that had shattered Prentiss. They ran back, scrambling for cover, and the long day's fight was over.

The sun was down. Beauregard merely made the halt official when he sent couriers riding through the gathering twilight with orders for the attacks to be suspended and the men brought back to rest for the completion of their work tomorrow morning. Much of the Yankee army might escape under cover of darkness, but it could not be helped. The lesson of Manassas was repeated. For green troops, victory could be as destructive of effective organization as defeat, and even more exhausting. As the men withdrew, a patter of rain began to sound. The rumble of heavy guns, fired intermittently from beyond the bluff, was mixed with peals of thunder. Lightning flashed; the rain fell harder. A hundred miles northwest, the *Pittsburg*'s crew was thankful for the storm as they prepared to make their run past Island Ten; the *Carondelet* was waiting. Here on the battlefield which took its name from the log church called Shiloh — interpreted by Bible scholars to mean "the place of peace" — those who could found shelter in the Federal camps and had their dreams invaded by the drum of rain on canvas. Others slept in the open, where the rain fell alike on the upturned faces of the dead and of those who slept among them, inured by having seen so much of death that day already, or else just made indifferent by exhaustion.

★ ★ ★   **onfidence south of the battle line,** that when the attack was renewed tomorrow the Federals would be driven into the river, was matched by confidence north of it, at least on the part of the northern commander, that the reverse would rather be the case. Surrounded by his staff Grant sat on horseback just in rear of the guns whose massed volleys had shattered the final rebel assault. His army had been driven two miles backward; one division had surrendered en masse; another had been demoralized, its commander killed, and the other three were badly shaken, bled to half their strength. So that when one of the staff officers asked if the prospect did not appear "gloomy," it must have seemed an understatement to the rest; but not to Grant. "Not at all," he said. "They can't force our lines around these batteries tonight. It is too late. Delay counts everything with us. Tomorrow we shall attack them with fresh troops and drive them, of course."

Fresh troops were the answer, and he had them; Buell's men were arriving as he spoke. By morning, 20,000 of them would have climbed the bluff in the wake of Nelson's lead brigade, which had been ferried across from the opposite bank in time to assist in repulsing the attack against the fifty guns assembled on the left. The navy, too, was in support and had a share in wrecking the last assault. Though all the ironclads were at Island Ten, two wooden gunboats were at Pittsburg, anchored where a creek ran out of the last-ditch ravine into the river, and thus were able to throw their shells into the ranks of the Confederates as they charged. Nor was that all. As twilight deepened into dusk, Lew Wallace at last came marching across Snake Creek bridge to station his division on the right flank of the army. He had marched toward what he thought was such a junction as soon as he received Grant's first order, but then had had to countermarch for the river road when he learned that the flank had been thrown back near the landing. Five hours behind schedule, he got jaundiced looks on arrival, but his 6000 soldiers, mostly Donelson veterans, were no less welcome for being late. Combined with Buell's troops and the survivors of the all-day fight, they meant that Grant would go into battle on the second day with more men than he had had at dawn of the first. Then too, well over half of them would be unworn by

★

fighting: whereas the Confederates would not only have been lessened by their casualties, but would most likely not have recovered from the weariness that dropped so many of them in their tracks as soon as the firing stopped.

Grant had another sizeable reserve — 6000 to 12,000 men, depending on various estimates — but he did not include them in his calculations. These were the skulkers, fugitives who took shelter along the river bank while the battle raged on the plateau overhead. Every man on the field had come up this way, debarking from the transports, so that when the going got too rough they remembered that high bluff, reared up one hundred feet tall between the landing and the fighting, and made for it as soon as their minds were more on safety than on duty. Some were trying to cadge rides on the ferries plying back and forth; others, more enterprising, paddled logs and jerry-built rafts in an attempt to reach the safety of the eastern bank. Still others were content to remain where they were, calling out to Buell's men as they came ashore: "We are whipped! Cut to pieces! You'll catch it! *You*'ll see!" Nelson, a six-foot five-inch three-hundred-pound former navy lieutenant, lost his temper at the sight. "They were insensible to shame and sarcasm," he later declared, "for I tried both; and, indignant of such poltroonery, I asked permission to fire on the knaves." However, the colonel who commanded the fuming general's lead brigade was more sickened than angered by the display. "Such looks of terror, such confusion, I never saw before, and do not wish to see again," he recorded in his diary.

Henri Lovie, a Federal eyewitness, sketched the chaos behind Grant's final line near Pittsburg Landing the evening of April 6.

Perhaps like the colonel Grant preferred to leave them where they were, out of contact with the men who had stood and fought today or were expected to stand and fight tomorrow. Fear was a highly contagious emotion, and even if threats or cajolery could have herded them back up the bluff, they would most likely run again as soon as the minies began whizzing. Perhaps, too, he saw them as a reproach, a sign that his army had been surprised and routed, at least to this extent, because its commander had left it unintrenched, green men to the front, and had taken so few precautions against an enemy who, according to him, was "heartily tired" of fighting. At any rate he allotted the skulkers no share in his

plans for tomorrow. Nor did he return to the fine big house nine miles downriver, or even seek shelter in one of the steamboat cabins. After inspecting his battle line — his four divisions would take the right, Buell's three the left — he wrapped himself in a poncho and lay down under a large oak to get some sleep. The rain had already begun, however, and presently it fell in torrents, dripping through the branches to add to the discomfort of his aching ankle. Unable to sleep, he wandered off to take refuge in a cabin on the bluff. But that would not do either. The surgeons had set up a field hospital there and were hard at work, bloody past the elbows. Driven out by the screams of the wounded and the singing of the bone-saws, Grant returned to his oak and got to sleep at last, despite the rain and whatever twinges he was feeling in his ankle and his conscience.

He had an insomniac counterpart beyond the line of battle. But Bedford Forrest's ankle and conscience were intact; his sleeplessness proceeded from entirely different causes. His regiment had been assigned to guard the Lick Creek fords, but after some hours of hearing the guns he had crossed over on his own initiative and claimed a share in the fighting. It stopped soon after sundown, but not Forrest. Out on a scout, he reached the lip of the bluff, south of the landing, and saw Buell's reinforcements coming ashore. For Forrest this meant just one thing: the Confederates must either stage a night attack or else get off that tableland before the Federals charged them in the morning. Unable to locate Beauregard, he went from camp to camp, telling of what he had seen and urging an attack, but few of the brigadiers even knew where their men were sleeping, and those who did were unwilling to take the responsibility of issuing such an order. At last he found Hardee, who informed him that the instructions already given could not be changed; the cavalryman was to return to his troops and "keep up a strong and vigilant picket line." Forrest stomped off, swearing. "If the enemy comes on us in the morning, we'll be whipped like hell," he said.

Unlocated and uninformed — he slept that night in Sherman's bed, near Shiloh Chapel — Beauregard not only did not suspect that Buell had arrived, he had good reason for thinking that he would not be there at all, having received from a colonel in North Alabama — it was Ben Hardin Helm, one of Lincoln's Confederate brothers-in-law — a telegram informing him that Buell had changed his line of march and now was moving toward Decatur. The Creole went to bed content with what had been done today and confident that Grant's destruction would be completed tomorrow. Before turning in, he sent a wire to Richmond announcing that the army had scored "a complete victory, driving the enemy from every position."

His chief of staff, sharing an improvised bed in the adjoining headquarters tent with the captured Prentiss, was even more ebullient, predicting that the northern army would surrender as soon as the battle was resumed. The distinguished captive, accepting his predicament with such grace as became a former Virginian, did not agree with his host's prognostication; nor was he reticent in protest. "You gentlemen have had your way today," he said, "but it will be very different tomorrow. You'll see. Buell will effect a junction with Grant tonight and we'll turn the tables on you in the morning." No such thing, the Confederate declared, and showed him the telegram from Helm. Prentiss was unimpressed. "You'll see," he said.

Outside in the rain, those who had been too weary to look for shelter, along with those who had looked without success, got what sleep they could, in spite of the 11-inch shells fired two every fifteen minutes by the gunboats. Their fuzes describing red parabolas across the starless velvet of the night, they came down steeply, screaming, to explode among the sleepers and the wounded of both sides; "wash pots" and "lampposts," the awed soldiers called the big projectiles. All night the things continued to fall on schedule. Dawn grayed the east, and presently from the direction of the sunrise came the renewed clatter of musketry, the crack and boom of field artillery. As it swelled quickly to a roar, Prentiss sat bolt upright on the pallet of captured blankets inside Sherman's headquarters tent, grinning at his Confederate bedmate. "There is Buell!" he cried. "Didn't I tell you so?"

★ ★ ★ *I*t was Buell, just as Prentiss said. His other two divisions, under Brigadier Generals Alexander D. McCook and Thomas L. Crittenden—the latter being the brother of the Confederate corps commander who had been relieved on the eve of battle—had come up in the night; he was attacking. Grant's four divisions—one hale and whole, if somewhat shamefaced over its roundabout march the day before, the others variously battered and depleted, but quite willing—took up the fire on the right, and at 7 o'clock the general sent a message to the gunboats. They were to cease their heavy caliber bombardment; the army was going forward.

Grant's orders, sent as soon as he rose at dawn from his sleep beneath the dripping oak, directed his generals to "advance and recapture our original camps." At first it was easy enough. The rebels, having broken contact the night before, were caught off balance and gave ground rapidly, surprised to find the tables turned by unexpected pressure. Wallace, Sherman, and McClernand, with Hurlbut's remnants in reserve, pushed forward to the vicinity of McClernand's camp before they ran into heavy artillery fire and halted, as Sherman said, "patiently waiting for the sound of General Buell's advance." They had not long to wait: Buell's men were taking their baptism of fire in stride. One Indiana colonel, dissatisfied with signs of shakiness when his men encountered resistance

—Sherman, who was looking on, referred to it as "the severest musketry fire I ever heard" (which would make it severe indeed, after all he had been through yesterday) — halted them, then and there, and put them briskly through the manual of arms, "which they executed," he later reported, "as if on the parade ground." Considerably steadied, the Hoosiers resumed their advance. By noon, Buell's men had cleared the peach orchard on the left and Grant's were approaching Shiloh Chapel on the right. There the resistance stiffened.

After the initial shock of finding Buell on the field after all, Beauregard recovered a measure of his aplomb and went about the task of preparing his men to receive instead of deliver an attack. This was by no means easy, not only because of the gallant rivalry which urged the two armies of Westerners forward against him, but also because his own troops had scattered badly about the blasted field in their search for food and shelter the night before. Polk, in fact, had misunderstood the retirement order and marched his survivors all the way back to their pre-battle camp on the Corinth road. Improvising as best he could, the Creole assigned Hardee the right, Breckinridge the center, and Bragg the left. When Polk returned, belatedly, he put him in between the last two. It was touch and go, however. Like Johnston, he found it necessary to set a spirited example for his men. Twice he seized the colors of wavering regiments and led them forward. Reproved for rashness by a friend who doubtless recalled what had happened to Johnston yesterday, Beauregard replied: "The order now must be 'Follow,' not 'Go'!"

At one point that afternoon he received a shock that was followed in quick succession by a hopeful surge of elation and a corresponding droop of disappointment. He noticed in some woods along his front a body of troops dressed in what appeared to be shiny white silk uniforms. At first he thought they were Federals who had breached his line, but when he saw that they were firing north, it occurred to him — though he had long since given up the notion that they could possibly arrive on time — that they might be the vanguard of Van Dorn's 15,000 reinforcements, hurried east by rail from Memphis. Certainly there were no such uniforms in the Army of the Mississippi, while there was no telling what outlandish garb the Elkhorn Tavern veterans might wear. Presently, however, a staff officer, sent to investigate, returned with the explanation. They were the general's own Orleans Guard battalion, who had turned their dress-blue jackets wrong side out to put an end to being fired on by their friends. Yesterday they had startled the defenders of the Hornets Nest by charging thus with the white silk linings of their coats exposed; "graveyard clothes," the Federals had called them.

The Confederates had their backs up and were holding well along the ridge where Sherman's tents were pitched; today as yesterday Shiloh Chapel was army headquarters. But the men were bone-weary. Clearly they had no chance of defeating the reinforced Federals now applying pressure all along the line, the breaking of a single link of which might prove disastrous to the whole. Not only were they weary: their spirits had flagged at the sudden frown of fortune, the abrupt removal of victory just as it seemed within their grasp. Governor Harris, still a volunteer aide, sensed this feeling of futility in the soldiers. Shortly after 2 o'clock, he expressed his fear of a collapse to the chief of staff, who agreed and

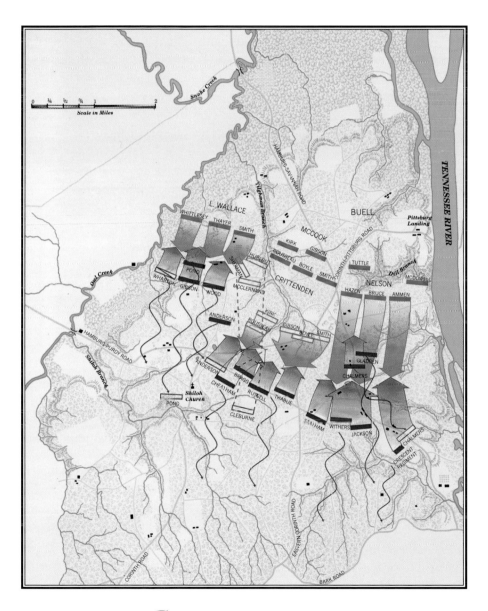

*R*einforced during the night by Buell,
Grant attacked (blue arrows) at dawn
April 7, turning the tide of the battle.

went to Beauregard with the question: "General, do you not think our troops are very much in the condition of a lump of sugar thoroughly soaked in water — preserving its original shape, though ready to dissolve? Would it not be judicious to get away with what we have?" Beauregard nodded, looking out over the field of battle. "I intend to withdraw in a few moments," he said calmly.

Couriers soon rode out with orders for the corps commanders to begin the retreat. Breckinridge was posted along the high ground just south of Shiloh Chapel, his line studded with guns which kept up a steady booming as the other corps retired. Executed smoothly and without disorder, the retrograde maneuver had been completed by 4 o'clock, with time allowed for captured goods to be gleaned from the field and loaded into wagons, including five stands of regimental colors and twenty-one flags of the United States. Hardee, Bragg, and Polk marched their men a mile beyond and camped for the night where they had slept on their arms two nights before, in line of battle for Sunday's dawn assault. Breckinridge stayed where he was, prepared to discourage pursuit. But there was none to discourage: Grant's men were content with the recovery of their pillaged camps.

All day there had been intermittent showers, brief but thunderous downpours that drenched the men and then gave way to steamy sunshine. That night, however, the rain came down in earnest. Privates crowded into headquarters tents and stood close-packed as bullets in a cartridge box, having lost their awe of great men. When Breckinridge moved out next morning to join the long Confederate column grinding its way toward Corinth, the roads were quagmires. The wind veered, whistling out of the north along the boughs of roadside trees, and froze the rain to sleet; the countryside was blanketed with white. Hailstones fell as large as partridge eggs, plopping into the mud and rattling into the wagon beds to add to the suffering of the wounded, who, as one of them said, had been "piled in like bags of grain." Beauregard doubled the column all day to encourage and comfort the men, speaking to them much as he would do on a visit to one of their camps a week later, when, seeing a young soldier with a bandaged head, he rode up to him, extended his hand, and said: "My brave friend, were you wounded? Never mind; I trust you will soon be well. Before long we will make the Yankees pay up, interest and all. The day of our glory is near." Cheered by the bystanders, he gave them a bow as he rode away, and that night the boy wrote home: "It is strange Pa how we love that little black Frenchman."

For the present, though, the cheers were mostly perfunctory along that column of jolted, sleet-chilled men. They had had enough of glory for a while. It was not that they felt they had been defeated. They had not. But they had failed in what they had set out to do, and the man who had led them out of Corinth to accomplish the destruction of "agrarian mercenaries" was laid out dead now in a cottage there. All the same, they took much consolation in the thought that they had held their lines until they were ready to leave, and then had done so in good order, unpursued.

They were not entirely unpursued. In the Federal camp the burial details were at work and the surgeons moved about the field, summoned by the anguished cries of mangled soldiers from both armies; but Sherman was not there. Prompted by Grant, he had moved out that morning with one brigade to make a show of pursuit, or at any rate to see that the Confederates did not linger. A show was all it was, however, for when he reached a point on the Corinth road, four miles beyond his camps, he was given a lesson hunters sometimes learned from closing in too quickly on a wounded animal.

The place was called the Fallen Timbers, a half-mile-wide boggy swale where a prewar logging project had been abandoned. The road dipped down, then crested a ridge on the far side, where he could see enemy horsemen grouped in silhouette against the sky. Not knowing their strength or what might lie beyond the ridge, he shook out a regiment of skirmishers, posted cavalry to back them up and guard their flanks, then sent them forward, following with the rest of the brigade in attack for-

*N*athan Bedford Forrest was severely wounded in his successful bid to stop the Union pursuit of the rebels at the Fallen Timbers.

mation at an interval of about two hundred yards. The thing was done in strict professional style, according to the book. But the man he was advancing against had never read the book, though he was presently to rewrite it by improvising tactics that would conform to his own notion of what war was all about. "War means fighting," he said. "And fighting means killing." It was Forrest. Breckinridge had assigned him a scratch collection of about 350 Tennessee, Kentucky, Mississippi, and Texas cavalrymen, turning over to him the task of protecting the rear of the retreating column.

As he prepared to defend the ridge, outnumbered five-to-one by the advancing blue brigade, he saw something that caused him to change his mind and his tactics. For as the skirmishers entered the vine-tangled hollow, picking their way around felled trees and stumbling through the brambles, they lost their neat alignment. In fact, they could hardly have been more disorganized if artillery had opened on them there in the swale. Forrest saw his chance. "Charge!" he shouted, and led his horsemen pounding down the slope. Most of the skirmishers had begun to run before he struck them, but those who stood were knocked sprawling by a blast from shotguns and revolvers. Beyond them, the Federal cavalry had panicked, firing their carbines wildly in the air. When they broke too, Forrest kept on after them, still brandishing his saber and crying, "Charge! Charge!" as he plowed into the solid ranks of the brigade drawn up beyond. The trouble was, he was charging by himself; the others, seeing the steady brigade front, had turned back and were already busy gathering up their 43 prisoners. Forrest was one gray uniform, high above a sea of blue. "Kill him! *Kill* the goddam rebel! Knock him off his horse!" It was no easy thing to do; the horse was kicking and plunging and Forrest was hacking and slashing; but one of the soldiers did his best. Reaching far out, he shoved the muzzle of his rifle into the colonel's side and pulled the trigger. The force of the explosion lifted Forrest clear of the saddle, but he regained his seat and sawed the horse around. As he came out of the mass of dark blue uniforms and furious white faces, clearing a path with his saber, he reached down and grabbed one of the soldiers by the collar, swung him onto the crupper of the horse, and galloped back to safety, using the Federal as a shield against the bullets fired after him. Once he was out of range, he flung the hapless fellow off and rode on up the ridge where his men were waiting in open-mouthed amazement.

Sherman was amazed, too, but mostly he was disgusted. As soon as he had gathered up his wounded and buried his dead, he turned back toward Pittsburg Landing. Snug once more in his tent near Shiloh Chapel, he wrote his report of the affair. It concluded: "The check sustained by us at the fallen timbers delayed our advance. . . . Our troops being fagged out by three days' hard fighting, exposure and privation, I ordered them back to camp, where all now are."

───────── ⁓⧝⁓ ─────────

★ ★ ★   **T**he ball now lodged alongside Forrest's spine as he followed the column grinding its way toward Corinth was the last of many to draw blood in the Battle of Shiloh. Union losses were 1754 killed, 8408 wounded, 2885 captured: total, 13,047 — about 2000 of them Buell's. Confederate losses were 1723 killed, 8012 wounded, 959 missing: total, 10,694. Of the 100,000 soldiers engaged in this first great bloody conflict of the war, approximately one out of every four who had gone into battle had been

★

killed, wounded, or captured. Casualties were 24 percent, the same as Waterloo's. Yet Waterloo had settled something, while this one apparently had settled nothing. When it was over the two armies were back where they started, with other Waterloos ahead. In another sense, however, it had settled a great deal. The American volunteer, whichever side he was on in this war, and however green, would fight as fiercely and stand as firmly as the vaunted veterans of Europe.

Now that this last had been proved beyond dispute, the leaders on both sides persuaded themselves that they had known it all along, despite the doubts engendered by Manassas and Wilson's Creek, which dwindled now by contrast to comparatively minor engagements. Looking instead at the butcher's bill — the first of many such, it seemed — they reacted, as always, according to their natures. Beauregard, for example, recovered his high spirits in short order. Two days after the battle he wired Van Dorn, still marking time in Arkansas: "Hurry your forces as rapidly as possible. I believe we can whip them again." He believed what he told the wounded soldier, "The day of our glory is near," and saw no occasion for retracting the announcement of "complete victory" sent to Richmond on the night of the first day. In fact, the further he got from the battle in time, the greater it seemed to him as a continuing demonstration of the superiority of southern arms. Nor did Davis retract the exultant message he sent to Congress in passing the telegram along. He was saddened, however, by other news it contained: namely, the loss of Albert Sidney Johnston. "When he fell," Davis wrote long afterward, "I realized that our strongest pillar had been broken."

Reactions on the other side were also characteristic. Once more Halleck saw his worst fears enlarged before his eyes, and got aboard a St Louis steamboat, bound for Pittsburg Landing, to take charge of the army himself before Grant destroyed it entirely. "Your army is not now in condition to resist an attack," he wired ahead. "It must be made so without delay." Grant tightened his security regulations, as instructed, but he did not seem greatly perturbed by the criticism. Now as always, he was a good deal more concerned with what he would do to the enemy than he was with what the enemy might try to do to him, and in any case he had grown accustomed by now to such reactions from above. The battle losses were another matter, providing some grim arithmetic for study. Total American casualties in all three of the nation's previous wars — the Revolution, the War of 1812, and the Mexican War: 10,623+6765+5885 — were 23,273. Shiloh's totaled 23,741, and most of them were Grant's.

Perhaps this had something to do with his change of mind as to the fighting qualities of his opponents. At any rate, far from thinking them "heartily tired" and ready to chuck the war, he later said quite frankly that, from Shiloh on, "I gave up all idea of saving the Union except by complete conquest."

★ ★ ★

★

*Cotton bales and steamboats
sit at a New Orleans dock in this
prewar photograph. In 1860,
thirty-three steamship lines served
the city, the largest in the South.*

Farragut, Lovell: New Orleans

1862 ★ ★ ★ ★ ★ While the ironclad gunboats of the western navy were pounding out their victories on the Tennessee, the Cumberland, and the mile-wide Mississippi — past Island Ten, they now were bearing down on undermanned Fort Pillow; Memphis, unbraced for the shock, was next on the list — the wooden ships of the blue-water navy were not idle in the east. Along the coasts of the Atlantic and the Gulf, where the thickened blockade squadrons hugged the remaining harbors and river outlets, the fall and winter amphibious gains had been continued and extended. Three times the *Monitor* had declined the *Merrimac-Virginia*'s challenge to single combat in Hampton Roads; if the rebel vessel wanted trouble, let her make it by trying to interfere with the *Monitor*'s task of protecting the rest of the fleet off Old Point Comfort. This she could not or would not do, and the *Monitor* maintained station in shoal water, content with a stalemate, while elsewhere other Federal warships were stepping up the tempo of Confederate disasters.

By mid-March the month-old Roanoke Island victory had been extended to New Bern and other important points around the North Carolina sounds, including control of the railroad which had carried men and supplies to the armies in Virginia. Simultaneously, down on the Florida coast, Fernandina was seized, followed before the end of the month by the uncontested occupation

★

of Jacksonville and St Augustine. Charleston and Savannah had been threatened all this time by the army-navy build-up at Port Royal. In April, while preparations were under way for a siege of the South Carolina city, an attack was mounted against Fort Pulaski, a stout brick pentagon on Cockspur Island, guarding the mouth of the Savannah River. Heavy guns and mortars knocked it to pieces, breaching the casemates and probing for the powder magazine. After thirty-odd hours of bombardment, the white flag went up and the blue-clad artillerists moved in to accept the surrender. Mostly they were New Englanders, and when a Georgian made the inevitable allusion to wooden nutmegs, a Connecticut man, pointing to a 10-inch solid shot that had pierced the wall, told him: "We don't make them of wood any longer."

Savannah itself was not taken, and indeed there was no need to take it. Sealed off as it was by the guns of Fort Pulaski, it was no more important now, at least from the naval point of view, than any other inland Confederate city which had lost its principal reason for existence. Wilmington, North Carolina, a much tougher proposition, with stronger and less accessible defenses, was presently the only major Atlantic port not captured or besieged by Union soldiers. Here the sleek low ghost-gray blockade-runners made their entrances and

Shallow-draft blockade-runners ride at anchor in a bustling Bermuda harbor, waiting for cargoes to smuggle into southern ports.

★

exits, usually by the dark of the moon, burning smokeless coal and equipped with telescopic funnels and feathered paddles to hide them from the noses, eyes, and ears of their pursuers. Martial and flippant names they had, the *Let Her Be* and *Let Her Rip*, the *Fox, Leopard, Lynx* and *Dream*, the *Banshee, Secret, Kate* and *Hattie*, the *Beauregard*, the *Stonewall Jackson*, the *Stag* and *Lady Davis*. The risks were great (one out of ten had been caught the year before; this year the odds were one-to-eight) but the profits were even greater. Two trips would pay the purchase price; the third and all that followed were pure gravy, as well as a substantial aid to the southern problem of supply. Last fall, one of the slim speedy vessels had steamed into Savannah with 10,000 Enfield rifles, a million cartridges, two million percussion caps, 400 barrels of powder, and a quantity of cutlasses, revolvers, and other badly needed materials of war. For all their reduction of the number of ports to be guarded, the blockade squadrons had their hands full.

Meanwhile, down along the Gulf, another Federal fleet was scoring corresponding successes to maintain the victory tempo set by its Atlantic rivals. At the mouth of the Florida river whose name it bore, Apalachicola fell in early April, followed in quick succession by the seizure of Pass Christian and Biloxi, on the Mississippi coast. These were bloodless conquests, the defenders having left to fight at Shiloh alongside the main body summoned north from Pensacola, which in turn was taken early the following month. Like Wilmington, Mobile remained — a much tougher proposition; but even before the capture of Pensacola, the Federals had made substantial lodgments on the coast of every southern state except Texas and Alabama.

Satisfying as all these salt-water victories were to the over-all command, the fact remained that, unlike the western navy on its way down the Mississippi, they had merely nibbled at the rim of the rebellion. Except for simplifying the blockade difficulties — which was much — they had accomplished very little, really, even as diversions. The problem, seen fairly clearly now by everyone, from Secretary Welles down to the youngest powder monkey, was conquest: *divide et impera*, pierce and strangle: which had been the occupation of the river gunboats all these months while the blue-water ships were pounding at the beaches. It was time for them, too, to try their hand at conquest by division instead of subtraction.

If the Mississippi could be descended, perhaps it could be ascended as well, so that when the salt- and fresh-water sailors met somewhere upstream like upper and nether millstones, having ground any fugitive elements of the enemy fleet between them, the Confederacy — and the task of its subjugation — would be riven. Much effort and much risk would be involved; the problems were multitudinous, including the fact that the thing would have to be done by wooden ships. But surely it was worth any effort, and almost any risk, considering the prize that awaited success at the very start: New Orleans.

★

★ ★ ★ *T*he Crescent City was not only the largest in the South, it was larger by population than any other four combined, and in the peacetime volume of its export trade, as a funnel for the produce of the Mississippi Valley, it ranked among the foremost cities of the world. Its loss would not only depress the South, and correspondingly elate the North; it would indicate plainly to Europe — especially France, where so many of its people had connections of blood and commerce — the inability of the rebels to retain what they had claimed by rebellion. In short, its capture would be a feather, indeed a plume, in the cap of any man who could conceive and execute the plan that would prise this chief jewel from the crown of King Cotton.

One man already had such a plan, along with an absolute ache for such a feather. Commodore David Porter had made naval history as captain of the *Essex* in the War of 1812, and his son David Dixon Porter, forty-eight years old and recently promoted to commander, was determined to have at least an equal share of glory in this one. What was more, in the case of New Orleans he knew whereof he spoke. Thirty trips in and out of the Passes during a peacetime hitch in the merchant marine had familiarized him with the terrain, and months of blockade duty off the river's four main mouths had given him a chance to talk with oystermen and pilots about recent developments in the city's defenses. He knew the obstacles, natural and man-made, and he believed he knew how to get around or through them. Nor was he one to wait for fame to find him. In late '61 he turned up in Washington to unfold his plan for the approval of the Navy Secretary.

New Orleans itself was a hundred miles upriver, but its principal defense against attack from below was a pair of star-shaped masonry works, Forts Jackson and St Philip, built facing each other on opposite banks of the river, just above a swift-currented bend three fourths of the way down. Formerly part of the U.S. system of permanent defenses, they had been taken over and strengthened by the Confederates. Fort Jackson, on the right bank, was the larger, mounting 74 guns; Fort St Philip, slightly upstream on the east bank, mounted 52. Between them, with a combined garrison of 1100 men and an armament of 126 guns, they dominated a treacherous stretch where approaching ships would have to slow to make the turn. Originally there had been doubt that all this strength would be needed, river men having assured the defenders that no deep-draft vessel could ever get over the bars that blocked the outlets. However, this had been disproved in early October when the commander of the Gulf Blockade Squadron, finding the task of patrolling the multi-mouthed river well-nigh impossible from outside, sent three heavy warships across the southwest bar and stationed them fifteen miles above, at the juncture called Head of the Passes, a deep-water anchorage two miles long and half as wide, where the river branched to create its lower delta. As long as those sloops and their frowning guns remained there, nothing could get in or out of the Passes; New Orleans would

★

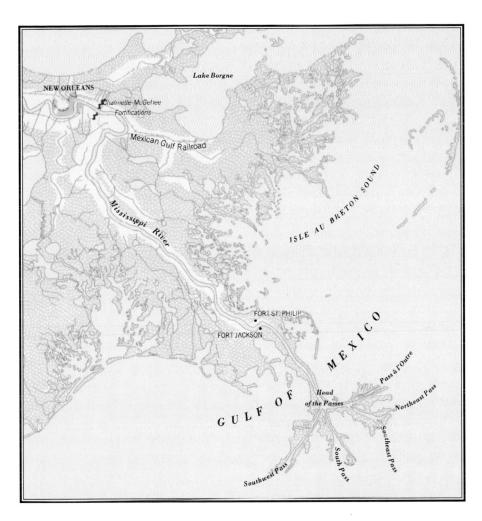

*Federals navigated intricate waterways
around Head of the Passes and took Forts
St Philip and Jackson to reach New Orleans.*

languish worse than ever, her trade being limited to what could be sneaked out by the roundabout route through Lake Pontchartrain and past the vigilant Federals on Ship Island, which had been seized the month before.

Clearly this was intolerable, and the city's defenders prepared to correct it at once. They had a makeshift fleet of four flat-bottomed towboats mounting two guns each, a seven-gun revenue cutter seized from Mexico before the war, under highly improbable charges of piracy, and a Boston-built seagoing tug covered over with boiler plate and equipped with an iron beak and a single 32-pounder trained unmovably dead ahead. Perhaps to offset her ugliness—all that metal caused her to ride so low in the water, she rather resembled a floating egg-plant—the authorities had given the ram the proud name *Manassas*. On the dark night of October 11, moving swiftly with the help of the four-knot current, she led the way downriver for an attack on the three big warships patrolling the Head of the Passes. Surprise was to be the principal advantage; the six-boat flotilla moved with muffled engines and no lights. To help offset the armament odds—16 guns, of moderate size or smaller, would be opposed by 51, over half of which were 8-inch or larger—tugs brought along three "fire-rafts," long flatboats loaded with highly combustible pine knots and rosin, which would be ignited and sent careening with the current when the time came. The plan was for the *Manassas* to make a ram attack in darkness, then fire a rocket as the signal for the fire-rafts to be lit and loosed and the gunboats to come down and join the melee.

The Federals had no lookout stationed, only the normal anchor watches they would have carried in any harbor. The first they knew of an attack

---

*As Beat-to-Quarters sounded there was a crash;
the Manassas had struck the 1900-ton flagship
Richmond, which now began firing indiscriminate
broadsides, like bellows of pain.*

---

was at 3.40 a.m. when a midshipman burst into his captain's cabin crying, "Captain, there's a steamer alongside of us!" On deck, the skipper barely had time to see "an indescribable object" emit a puff of smoke even darker than the night. As Beat-to-Quarters sounded there was a crash; the *Manassas* had struck the 1900-ton flagship *Richmond*, which now began firing indiscriminate broadsides, like bellows of pain, and hoisted three light-signals in rapid succession: ENEMY PRESENT. GET UNDER WAY. ACT AT DISCRETION. All three of the sloops were firing frantically, though none of them could see anything to aim at. The *Manassas* was groping blindly, filled with coal smoke. She had struck a barge lashed alongside the Federal flagship; the force of the blow had knocked her engines loose and a hawser had carried her stacks away, flush with the deck. In time she got the rocket off, however, and presently three distant sparks appeared upriver, growing in size as the rafts flamed higher and drew closer.

Aboard the sloops, delay had only served to increase the panic. PROCEED DOWN SOUTHWEST PASS. CROSS THE BAR, the flagship signaled, and all three

★

went with the current, the sluggish *Richmond* swinging broadside to it, helpless. One got over; the next lodged fast on the bar, stern upriver; then the *Richmond* struck and stuck, still broadside. The fire-rafts had run harmless against bank, but the Confederate gunboats, which up to now had not engaged, took the grounded sloops under fire with their small-caliber long-range Whitworths. Presently the Union flag-officer, Captain John Pope — called "Honest John" to distinguish him from the general who would win fame at Island Ten — was amazed to see the skipper of the other stranded vessel appear on the flagship's quarterdeck, wrapped in a large American flag. He had abandoned ship, bringing his colors with him, after laying and lighting a slow fuze to the powder magazine, intending thus to keep her from falling into the hands of the rebels.

After a long wait for the explosion — which would bring what an observer called "a shower of 1½-ton guns through the decks and bottom of almost any near-by ship" — it finally became evident that the sloop was not going to blow after all. Pope sent the flag-draped captain back to defend her and, if possible, get her afloat; which he subsequently managed to do by heaving most of her guns and ammunition over the side. (It later developed that the seaman charged with lighting the fuze had obeyed orders, but then, not being in sympathy with them, had cut off the sputtering end and tossed it overboard.) By now it was broad open daylight; the Confederates withdrew upstream, satisfied with their morning's work of clearing the Head of the Passes, and Pope made a tour of inspection to assess damages. Except for a small hole punched in the flagship when the *Manassas* struck the coal barge, there were none. Not a man had been hurt, not a hit had been scored; or so he thought until next morning, when he found a 6-pound Whitworth solid lodged in his bureau drawer. Explaining his performance, Honest John reported: "The whole affair came upon me so suddenly that no time was left for reflection." His request that he be relieved of command "on account of ill health" was quickly granted. "I truly feel ashamed for our side," one executive said when the smoke had cleared away.

Porter, on blockade duty outside the Southwest Pass at the time, expressed a stronger opinion. It was, he said, "the most ridiculous affair that ever took place in the American Navy." All the same, it helped in the formulation of his plan by showing what manner of resistance could be expected below New Orleans. In addition to the problem of getting across the bar and past the heavily gunned forts, he knew that the small Confederate flotilla would attempt to make up, in daring and ingenuity, for what it lacked in size. Besides, it might not be so small in time. There were reports of two monster ironclads, larger and faster than any the Federal navy had ever dreamed of, already under construction in the city's shipyards. Then too, there were land batteries at Chalmette, where Andrew Jackson's volunteers had stood behind a barricade of cotton bales and mowed down British regulars fifty years ago. The bars, the forts, the rebel boats, the batteries — these four, plus unknown others: but the greatest of these, as things now stood, was the problem of passing the forts. It was as a solution of this that Porter conceived and submitted his plan for the capture of New Orleans. The rest could be left to a flag-officer who, having done his reflecting beforehand, would not panic in a crisis.

The naval expedition, as Porter saw it, would have at its core a flotilla of twenty mortar vessels, each mounting a ponderous 13-inch mortar supplied with a thousand shells. Screened by intervening trees, they would tie up to bank, just short of the bend, and blanket the forts with high-angle fire while the seagoing sloops and frigates made a run past in the darkness and confusion. The fleet was to mount no fewer than 200 heavy guns, exclusive of the mortars, which would assure it more firepower than the enemy had in his forts and boats combined, with the Chalmette batteries thrown in for good measure. Once past the forts, it could wreck the rebel vessels and batteries by the sheer weight of thrown metal: New Orleans, under the frown of Federal warships, would have to choose between destruction and surrender. Army troops, brought along for the purpose — otherwise the show would be purely Navy — would go ashore to guard against internal revolt and outside attempts at recapture, thus freeing the fleet for other upriver objectives: Baton Rouge, Natchez, Vicksburg, and conjunction with Foote's ironclads steaming south. The Mississippi would be Federal, from Minnesota all the way to the Gulf.

By mid-November Porter was in Washington, submitting his proposal to the Secretary. Welles had small use for the commander personally — he had too much gasconade for the New Englander's taste, and before the war he had associated overmuch with Southerners — but the plan itself, coinciding as it did with some thinking Welles had been doing along this line, won his immediate approval. He took him to see the President, who liked it too. "This should have been done sooner," Lincoln said, and arranged a conference with McClellan, whose coöperation would be needed. McClellan saw merit in the plan, but raised some characteristic objections. In his opinion the expedition would entail a siege by 50,000 troops, for the heavy guns inside the forts would crush the wooden ships like eggshells. Bristling, Welles replied that the navy would do the worrying about the risk to its ships; all he wanted from the army was 10,000 men, to be added to the 5000 which Benjamin Butler, flushed by the recent amphibious victory at Hatteras Inlet, was raising now in Massachusetts for service down on the Gulf. When McClellan replied that he could spare that many — Butler in particular could be spared, along with his known talent for cabal — the conference at once got down to specifics.

Secrecy, a prime element of the plan, would be extremely difficult to maintain because of the necessarily large-scale preparations. However, if the expedition's existence could hardly be hidden, perhaps its destination could.

★

With this in mind, a new blockade squadron would be set up in the West Gulf, coincident with some loose talk about Pensacola, Mobile, Galveston — any place, in fact, except New Orleans. Next a roster of ships was drawn up, with an armament of about 250 guns. The choice of a fleet commander was left to Assistant Secretary G. V. Fox, himself a retired Annapolis man, who conferred with Porter on the matter, combing the list of captains. One after another they were rejected, either for being otherwise employed or else for being too much of the Honest John type. At last they came to David Glasgow Farragut, thirty-seventh on the list. Of Spanish extraction, sixty years old and sitting now as a

*David Glasgow Farragut was chosen
to lead the expedition against New Orleans
because of his self-reliance and audacity.*

★

member of a retirement board at Brooklyn Navy Yard, Farragut was a veteran of more than fifty years' active service, having begun as a nine-year-old acting midshipman aboard the *Essex*, whose captain, Porter's father, had informally adopted him and supervised his baptism of fire in the War of 1812. Here was a possibility. He was known to be stout-hearted and energetic; every year on his birthday he turned a handspring, explaining that he would know he was beginning to age when he found the exercise difficult. The trouble was he was southern born, a native of Knoxville, and southern married — twice in fact, both times to ladies from Norfolk — which raised doubts as to his loyalty and accounted for his present inactive assignment. Porter, on his way to New York to arrange for the purchase and assembly of the mortar flotilla, was instructed to call on his foster brother and sound him out.

The retirement board member was waiting for him, a smooth-shaven, square-built, hale-looking man with hazel eyes and heavy eyebrows, wearing his long side hair brushed across the top of his head to hide his baldness. Porter began by asking what he thought of his former associates now gone South. "Those damned fellows will catch it yet," Farragut replied. Asked if he would accept a command to go and fight "those fellows," he said he would. Porter then badgered him by pretending that the objective would be Norfolk, his wife's birthplace. Farragut jumped up crying, "I will take the command: only don't you trifle with me!"

Summoned to Washington, still without suspecting the purpose, he was questioned next by Fox, who asked — as if for a purely theoretical opinion — if he thought New Orleans could be taken from below. "Yes, emphatically," Farragut told him. "The forts are well down the river; ships could easily run them, and New Orleans itself is undefended. It would depend somewhat on the fleet, however."

"Well," Fox said, "— with such a fleet as, say, two steam frigates, five screw sloops of the cities class, a dozen gunboats, and some mortar vessels to shell the forts from high angle?"

"Why, I would engage to run those batteries with two thirds of such a force. . . . "

"What would you say if appointed to head such an expedition?"

"What would I say?" Farragut cried. He leaped to his feet and began to prowl about the room. Now he understood. The goal was to be New Orleans, which he knew well from years of living in it, and he was to have the flag. "What would I say?" he cried, and broke into exclamations of delight.

So it was settled. He received his orders during the last week of the year and began at once to fit out the eighteen warships assigned to his fleet, including two steam frigates, seven screw sloops, and nine gunboats, all of wood and mounting 243 guns, most heavy. Porter meanwhile had been assembling

★

his mortar flotilla of twenty schooners; the weapons themselves were cast in Pittsburgh, along with 30,000 bomb-shells, while the beds were manufactured in New York. In late January Farragut dropped down to Hampton Roads, Porter coming along behind, and by mid-February reached Key West, where final orders from Welles were broken open: "This most important operation of the war is confined to yourself and your brave associates. . . . If successful, you open the way to the sea for the great West, never again to be closed. The rebellion will be riven in the center, and the flag to which you have been so faithful will recover its supremacy in every State."

Convinced by inspection that the way to stop the small-time blockade runners working in and out of the coastal lakes and bayous was to intercept them with vessels adapted to the task, Farragut wrote to the Navy Department asking for some light ships of five-foot draft or less. Since he neglected to say what use would be made of them, Fox thought they were wanted for the upriver attack, which would have meant an unconscionable delay. Dismayed, the Assistant Secretary began to suspect that he had erred in his choice of a fleet commander. Instead of writing to Farragut, however, he wrote to Porter: "I trust that we have made no mistake in our man, but his dispatches are very discouraging. It is not too late to rectify our mistake. You must frankly give me your views . . . . I shall have no peace until I hear from you." Porter replied that it was too late for a change, but that he would do what he could to bolster the old man's shaky judgment. "Men of his age in a seafaring life are not fit for important enterprises, they lack the vigor of youth. He talks very much at random at times and rather underrates the difficulties before him without fairly comprehending them. I know what they are, and as he is impressible hope to make him appreciate them also." He added by way of consolation, "I have great hopes of the mortars if all else fails."

Happily unaware of the distrust of his superiors or the condescension of his adoptive brother, Farragut proceeded to Ship Island for refueling and refitting. By mid-March he was off the mouths of the Mississippi, maneuvering for an entrance, which was finally effected by sending Porter's mortars and the gunboats through Pass à l'Outre and taking the heavier frigates and sloops around to Southwest Pass. After much sweat and inch-by-inch careening— back-breaking labor that tried even Farragut's sunny disposition—all got over the bar except the largest, a 50-gun frigate, twenty of whose guns were distributed among the other vessels of the fleet now assembled at Head of the Passes. There the schooners discharged their seagoing spars and made ready for the work they had been built to do.

By mid-April the preparations were complete. Butler's soldiers were at hand: 18,000 of them, so persuasively had the former politician done his recruiting job in New England. The fleet was at anchor two miles below the bend where the mortar schooners had tied up to both banks, the tips of their masts disguised with foliage lest they show above the trees that screened the vessels from the forts. Ranges were quickly established: 2850 yards to Fort Jackson, 3680 to Fort St Philip. Farragut was somewhat doubtful as to the efficacy of the snub-nosed weapons, but Porter declared confidently that two days of mortar bombardment would reduce both forts to rubble. April 18 — Good Friday — he opened fire.

★ ★ ★ *H*oly Week was gloomy in New Orleans, the more so because of the contrast between the present frame of mind, with danger looming stark in both directions, and the elation felt six months ago at the comic repulse of the sloops from the Head of the Passes, which had seemed to give point to the popular conviction that "Nothing afloat could pass the forts. Nothing that walked could get through our swamps." Since then a great deal had happened, and all of it bad.

For one thing, the blockade had tightened. Roustabouts no longer swarmed on the levee, for there were no cargoes to unload; the wharves lay idle, and warehouses formerly bulging with cotton and sugar and grain yawned hollow; trade having come to a standstill, ready money was so scarce that there was a current joke that an olive-oil label would pass for cash "because it was greasy, smelt bad, and bore an autograph." For another, Foote's gunboats and Pope's soldiers were smashing obstacles so rapidly upriver that the danger seemed even greater from that direction, with neither forts nor swamps to slow them down. In the midst of these discouragements and fears, troops assigned to the city's defense were called north to fight at Shiloh, and all that returned from that repulse were the members of the honor guard with Sidney Johnston's body, following the muffled drums and the empty-saddled warhorse out St Charles Street to fire the prescribed three volleys across his crypt. Now there was this: Yankee ships once more across the bar, but in such strength that no small-scale attack, however ingenious and daring, could hope to budge them. For New Orleans, as for the South at large, the prospect was grim in this season of death and resurrection.

No one responsible for the city's defense was more aware of the danger than the man who was most responsible of all: Mansfield Lovell, a thirty-nine-year-old Maryland-born West Pointer who had resigned as New York Deputy Street Commissioner to join the Confederacy in September. Impressed with the Chapultepec-brevetted artilleryman's record as an administrator, Davis made him a major general and sent him to replace the over-aged Twiggs in New Orleans; which would not only give the city an energetic and efficient commander, but would also call widespread attention to the fact that willingness to fight for the South's ideals was by no means restricted to men of southern background, Lovell having spent most of his civilian years as a New Jersey ironworks executive. The new major general arrived in early October, and was appalled at the unpreparedness. There was plenty of Gallic enthusiasm, but it found release at champagne parties rather than at work. He wrote to Richmond, protesting that the city was "greatly drained of arms, ammunition, clothing, and supplies for other points." Presently it was drained of fighting men as well, leaving him with what he called a "heterogeneous militia" of 3000 short-term volunteers, "armed mostly with shotguns against 9- and 11-inch Dahlgrens."

The Creoles did not resent his criticisms. They found his intensity amusing and his presence ornamental. "A very attractive figure," one pronounced him, "giving the eye, at first glance, a promise of much activity." His horseman-ship was especially admirable; they enjoyed watching him ride dragoon-style "with so long a stirrup-leather that he simply stood astride the saddle, as straight as a spear." To add to the effect, he wore a facial ruff of hair much like Burn-side's, except that it was light brown and somewhat less flamboyant.

Despite his activity, no one was more surprised when the Union fleet showed its true intention. Not that he had not known it was assembling. Agents had kept him informed of its strength and location; but they had also relayed the loose talk about Mobile and Pensacola, and Lovell believed them — perhaps because he wanted to. What misled him most, though, was the presence of Ben Butler, who at the Democratic convention of 1860 had voted fifty-seven consec-utive times for the nomination of Jefferson Davis before switching over to Breckinridge with the majority. "I regard Butler's Ship Island expedition as a harmless menace so far as New Orleans is concerned," Lovell had told Rich-mond in late February. "A black Republican dynasty will never give an old Breckinridge Democrat like Butler command of any expedition which they had any idea would result in such a glorious success as the capture of New Orleans." Now he knew better; the warships were across the bar, above the Head of the Passes. But the knowledge came too late. He had been looking upriver all this time, where the Foote-Grant Foote-Pope amphibious teams were wrecking whatever stood in their way, ashore or afloat.

Hastening to meet the threat from above — his intelligence reports were quite good from that direction: too good, as it turned out — he had com-mandeered fourteen paddle-wheel steamers and converted them into one-gun gunboats, plating their outer bulwarks with inch-thick railroad iron to give them mass and rigidity for use as rams. Launched one by one between January and April, they made up the River Defense Fleet under J. E. Montgomery, a river captain, and were independent of Commander J. K. Mitchell, whose miniature flotilla had thrown such a scare into Honest John Pope six months before. Lovell did not like the command arrangement, which left him no real control over either. Besides, the new gunboats were put in the hands of a notoriously in-

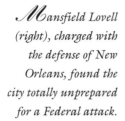

Mansfield Lovell (right), charged with the defense of New Orleans, found the city totally unprepared for a Federal attack.

dependent breed of men; "fourteen Mississippi river captains and pilots will never agree about anything once they get under way," he predicted. As fast as they came off the ways, eight of the boats were sent upriver to challenge the descending Union fleet at Memphis or Fort Pillow, though Lovell managed to hold onto six of them for the immediate protection of New Orleans. They would not amount to much in the way of a deterrent once the heavy-gunned armada below the forts broke into the clear, but anything that would delay or distract the Federal fleet, however briefly — even to the extent of making it pause to brush them aside — might be of enormous value because of something else that was going on inside the city. He had an ace in the hole; two, in fact. The question was whether he would have time to bring them out and play them.

Porter had heard aright in his talks with the pilots and oystermen; the Confederates were at work on two giant ironclads in the city's shipyards, each of them more formidable than the *Merrimac-Virginia*, which had just completed her work of destruction in Hampton Roads against vessels as stout as any in Farragut's fleet. The first, the *Louisiana*, mounting sixteen heavy rifles, had been launched and cased in a double row of T-shaped rails for armor, the inner rails bolted vertically to the bulwarks, the outer ones reversed and driven down the gaps. There had been various delays, including strikes — one lasted three full weeks — because the workers were unwilling to take Confederate bonds for pay, but the main trouble now was her power plant, which had been transferred from a steamboat. While Farragut was crossing the bar, mechanics were trying without success to coax the *Louisiana*'s engines into motion.

The other ironclad, the *Mississippi*, was an even more novel and formidable proposition, at least in prospect. Over 4000 tons in weight, 270 feet long and 58 feet in the beam, drawing only 14 feet and mounting 20 guns, she was a true dreadnought, designed to wear three-inch armor, have an iron snout set over a casing three feet thick, and be propelled by three engines at a speed of 14 knots; all of which would make her the most powerful and fastest warship ever built. The plan for her use was quite in scale with her proportions. She was to clear the Mississippi of enemy vessels, then the Gulf and the Atlantic, after which she would lay the northern coastal cities under levy. Improbable as this program sounded, it was by no means impossible; certainly nothing afloat or under construction could stand in her way. But first she would have to be finished, and she was still a considerable way from that. She had been launched, her timberwork completed, but so far she was armored only below the gun deck, and her vital 50-foot central drive shaft was too big a casting job for any southern rolling mill except the Tredegar in Richmond, which began work on the order in February. It would be weeks, or months, before delivery and installation of the shaft would permit her to move under her own power.

Time, then, was golden. Lovell bought what he could and tried to buy more by calling for the eight departed gunboats to be returned from upriver. This the government would not do, considering them more needed there to stem the rout at Island Ten and make a shield for Memphis; New Orleans would have to resist with what she had. Primarily then — with the Federal fleet already approaching the bend they guarded — that put the burden on Forts Jackson and St Philip, whose strength or vulnerability had become a subject of disagreement among the river men who had been so confident such a short time back. A chain boom, held afloat by cypress logs, spanned the Mississippi just below the forts, so that when the Yankees ran afoul of it or stopped to try and break it, plunging fire from the parapets would blow them out of the water like sitting ducks. So the river men had reckoned; but the March floods — the highest in anyone's memory — brought such a press of uprooted trees and brush against it that the boom gave way, depriving the gunners of their hope for stationary targets. Quickly the break was mended and the obstacle strengthened by adding a line of hulks to buoy it up. Now that it had broken once, however, there was considerable doubt that it would hold against the pressure, which was building up again.

In desperation Lovell ordered the *Louisiana* towed downstream, to be tied up to the east bank just above Fort St Philip. No less than fifty mechanics continued to tinker with her engines, but even if they never got them going she could serve as a floating battery, adding the weight of her bow and starboard guns

★

to those of the forts. Work continued aboard the *Mississippi*, too, on the outside chance that her drive shaft would arrive before the Federals did. It was Holy Week; Holy Wednesday and Thursday, then Good Friday, and a message arrived from downriver; both forts were under heavy bombardment, receiving two 200-pound mortar shells a minute. Lovell rode down to see for himself how bad it was.

★ ★ ★ *I*t was bad enough, or anyhow it seemed so. At the end of the first day's firing, the citadel and barracks of Fort Jackson were ablaze, rubble and sandbags thrown about and the protective levee cut, letting backwater into the place. "I was obliged to confine the men most rigidly to the casemates," the commandant reported, "or else we should have lost the best part of the garrison." They huddled there, white-faced with alarm, while the world outside seemed turned to flame and thunder. And yet it was by no means as bad as it seemed, being a good deal more spectacular than effective. Casualties were extremely low in both forts, and nothing really vital was hit in either. In fact, when Porter slowed the rate of fire at nightfall to give his weary crews some rest, his own men were rather more shaken up than those at the opposite ends of the looping trajectories. Soon after noon the lead east-bank schooner had taken a solid through her deck and bottom and had to be shifted down the line. What was more, the work itself was heavy, each piece being required to deliver a round every ten minutes, and the strain of absorbing the ear-pounding, bone-jarring concussions was severe. It was as if the bombardiers had spent those hours inside a tolling bell.

Porter had them back at their rapid-fire work by dawn. He had said he would silence the forts by sunset of the second day, and he intended to do it. All day the firing continued, but with less apparent effect than yesterday, the bursting shells having done all the superficial damage there was to do. At dusk the rebel casemate guns were still in action. Porter did not slacken fire. All night it continued; all Easter Day, all Easter night, all Monday; still the guns replied. In 96 hours — twice Porter's original estimate as to the time it would take to reduce them — the forts had absorbed over 13,000 shells, at a cost of only four men killed, fourteen wounded, and seven guns disabled. Porter's crews were near exhaustion, but he would not slacken fire. All Monday night, all Tuesday, Tuesday night, and Wednesday morning it continued; 16,800 shells had been pumped into the forts, which still replied. Then Farragut intervened. He had never placed much reliance on the mortars anyhow.

"Look here, David," he said. "We'll demonstrate the practical value of mortar work." He turned to his clerk. "Mr Osbon, get two small flags, a white one and a red one, and go to the mizzen topmasthead and watch the shells fall. If inside the fort, wave the red flag. If outside, wave the white one." In the beginning the fire had been accurate, but the gunners had been numbed into indifference by now; the white flag waved from the masthead far more often than the red. Farragut said calmly, "There's the score. I guess we'll go up the river tonight."

Porter protested, heart and soul. Even if the fleet got past the forts, it would leave them alive in its rear; how would the infantry manage the run in unarmed and unarmored transports? Besides, with the Federal warships gone upriver, what would prevent the surviving enemy gunboats from attacking the mortar flotilla? Farragut replied casually that Butler's men could make a roundabout trip, coming in through the Gulf bayous. As for the threat of rebel survivors, he didn't intend for there to be any; but if there were, then Porter would just have to look out for himself. He called his gig and made the rounds of all his ships, confirming the orders already issued for the run to be made that night. He would "abide by the result," he told them: "conquer or be conquered."

Crewmen of a Federal mortar schooner pose
on deck with their keglike, 25,000-pound
weapon, which fired 13-inch shells.

★

His two biggest worries — how to get across or through the boom and how to deal with fire-rafts — had already been lessened or disposed of. Sunday night two gunboats had gone forward under heavy fire and opened a gap by releasing the chain from one of the hulks. When the defenders responded by sending a fire-raft through the breach, flames leaping a hundred feet in the air, considerable frenzy had ensued, including a collision between two ships whose captains panicked at the threat of being roasted. However, by the time the current had carried the burning mass of pitch and pine harmlessly into the east bank, they knew better how to deal with or avoid them. Farragut had been for running the forts the following night, but a strong north wind had risen to slow him down. It blew through Tuesday; then Wednesday it died and he was ready,

---

As a final touch — one that never failed to provoke a sensation at the pit of every sailor's stomach, no matter how often he had seen it done before — the area around each gun was strewn with sand and ashes, so that when the fight grew hot the guncrews would not slip in their own blood.

---

having spent the interim preparing his wooden ships for the ordeal. Chains were looped down over the sides to protect the engines and magazines; Jacob's ladders were hung all round, so the carpenters could descend quickly and patch from the outside any holes shot in the hulls. Tubs of water were spotted about, and each ship had a well-drilled fire brigade equipped with grapnels for handling fire-rafts. The outer bulwarks were smeared with mud to hide the ships from the spotters in the forts, but the decks and the breeches of the guns were given a coat of whitewash to provide reflected light for nightwork. As a final touch — one that never failed to provoke a sensation at the pit of every sailor's stomach, no matter how often he had seen it done before — the area around each gun was strewn with sand and ashes, so that when the fight grew hot the guncrews would not slip in their own blood. That was all. Now there was only the waiting, which a gunner aboard the flagship thought the hardest job of all. "One has nothing to do to occupy the mind," he complained. "The mind runs on the great uncertainty about to take place, until it is a relief when the battle opens."

★

At 2 a.m. — it was Thursday now, the 24th — the hour being, as Farragut said, "propitious"— he had just received a signal that the gateway through the boom was still ajar   two red lanterns appeared at the *Hartford*'s mizzen peak, and the lead division began to move upstream. His original plan had been to lead the attack himself, aboard the flagship, but the senior captains, agreeing that the losses would be heavy, persuaded him that to risk losing the fleet commander at the outset would be to court disaster through confusion. So Farragut had arranged his seventeen warships in three divisions of eight, three, and six vessels, himself at the head of the second. It was a powerful aggregation, heavily gunned, and backed by the fire of the mortars. If the weight of thrown metal was to decide the issue, there could be but one result, for an entire round of projectiles from all the Federal guns would weigh more than ten tons, while one from all the Confederate guns, afloat and ashore, would weigh just three and a half. Farragut and his captains were not aware of these figures, however, or at any rate not the latter. All they knew was what they had been taught: that one gun ashore was worth four afloat. They knew, too, that the forts were built of brick and mortar, while the ships were built of wood. Farragut was confident, even cheerful, but when his clerk declared that he did not expect the fleet to lose beyond a hundred men, the Tennessee-born captain shook his head in doubt. "I wish I could think so," he said.

There were delays as the various sloops and gunboats jockeyed for position, each division moving in line ahead, breasting the broad dark current. Then at 340 the rebel lookouts spotted the lead division just as it reached the boom and started through the gap. Now delay was on the other side; the first eight ships were clear of the chain before the forts reacted. But when they did, according to an army man who had come up to watch the show, the effect was tremendous: "Imagine all the earthquakes in the world, and all the thunder and lightnings together in a space of two miles, all going off at once. That would be like it." Flaming brush-piles along the banks and fire-rafts on the river cast an eerie refulgence, pocked with rolling clouds of gunsmoke and the sudden scarlet of exploding shells. At this point the *Hartford*, leading the second division through the gap, made her entrance as if upon a brightly lighted stage.

It seemed to Farragut, high in the mizzen rigging, his feet on the ratlines and his back against the shrouds, "as if the artillery of heaven were playing on earth," but one of his gunners drew a comparison from the opposite direction: "My youthful imagination of hell did not equal the scene about us at this moment." Presently, however, there could be little doubt as to which description was more fitting. Attempting to dodge a fire-raft, the flagship's helmsman ran her into shallow water, directly under the guns of Fort St Philip. Farragut, who had descended to the quarterdeck just before a shellburst cut away most of the rigging where he had been standing, saw a mud flat dead ahead.

★

"Hard aport!" he shouted. Too late; she ran aground. Fortunately, the casemate gunners, expecting a landing party when they saw the *Hartford*'s bowsprit looming over their heads, deserted their pieces. But the fire-raft, pushed by a tug, changed course and rammed the flank of the grounded sloop, flames curling over the bulwarks and shooting up the rigging.

When Farragut saw his ship afire, his men giving back from the press of heat as the tug held the mass of burning pine firmly against her quarter, he threw up his hands and clasped them over his head in an anguished gesture. "My God, is it to end this way?" he cried. But he soon recovered his composure. Down on the gundeck, his clerk had conceived the notion of rolling some 20-pound shells onto the flaming raft, where they would explode and sink it. As he knelt to unscrew the fuze-caps Farragut saw him and mistook his attitude. "Come, sir, this is no time for prayer," he told him sternly, and called down also to the gunners, still holding back from the licking tongues of flame: "Don't flinch from that fire, boys. There's a hotter fire than that waiting for those who don't do their duty. Give that rascally little tug a shot!"

Then suddenly the worst was over. Catching the old man's spirit, despite the heat, the port crews returned to their guns and gave the tug two shots that hulled and sank her. The clerk got three of the shells uncapped and dropped them onto the blazing raft, which was torn apart by the explosion and went down in a hissing cloud of steam. While the fire brigade got busy with hoses and buckets, extinguishing the flames, the helmsman called for full power astern, and the ship careened off the mud flat, free to continue her course upriver and join in the destruction of the rebel flotilla.

Very little of it was left by now. When the skippers of the dozen Confederate vessels saw the northern warships clear the boom, run the gauntlet of fire from the forts, and head directly for them, apparently unscathed, big guns booming, they reacted with dismay—as well they might; all twelve of them together, with the immobilized *Louisiana* thrown in for good measure though only six of her 16 guns could be brought to bear, could not throw as much metal as a single Federal sloop. They scattered headlong, some for bank, where their crews set them afire and took to the swamps, while others tried for a getaway upriver. Three stayed to accept the challenge, upholding naval tradition by a form of naval suicide.

Two of the three were from the Confederate flotilla: the 7-gun former Mexican revenue cutter, which was reduced to kindling by the converging fire of three Union men-of-war as soon as she came within their range, and the low-riding armored ram *Manassas*, which headed downriver as soon as the guns began to roar and gave one of the heavy sloops an ineffectual glancing bump, firing her Cyclops cannon as she struck. (Aboard the sloop the cry went up, "The ram, the ram!" and the captain saw a rebel officer come out of the iron

The C.S.S. Governor Moore fires through her own bow into the U.S.S. Varuna in the fighting above Forts St Philip and Jackson.

hatch and run forward along the port gunnel to inspect the damage, if any. Suddenly he whirled with an odd, disjointed motion and tumbled into the water. Hardly able to believe his eyes, the captain called to the leadsman in the chains, asking if he had seen him fall. "Why, yes sir," he said: "I saw him fall overboard. In fact, I helped him; for I hit him alongside the head with my hand-lead.") The *Manassas* backed off and continued downriver, intending to do better with the next one, but took a terrific pounding from the guns of both forts, whose cannoneers mistook her for a disabled Federal vessel. She came about, staggering back upstream, her armor pierced, her engines smashed, and was pounded again by four of the enemy warships. Avoiding a fifth, which charged to run her down, she veered into bank and stuck there, smoke curling from her hatch and punctures. What was left of her crew jumped ashore and scurried to safety while the Union gunboats flailed the brush with canister and grape.

Third to accept the challenge was the unarmored sidewheel steamboat *Governor Moore*, one of two vessels sent by the state of Louisiana to make up a third division of the fleet defending New Orleans. When the firing began she moved upriver, adding rosin to her fires to get up steam before turning to join the fight. As she moved through the darkness she saw the 1300-ton screw steamer *Varuna*, the fastest ship in the Federal fleet, coming hard upstream in pursuit of the fugitive gunboats. The *Moore* carried two guns, one forward and one aft; the *Varuna* carried ten, eight of them 8-inchers; but the former, unde-tected against a dark backdrop of trees along the bank, had the advantage of surprise. She opened fire at a hundred yards — and missed. Startled, the Federal replied, strewing the steamboat's decks with dead and wounded. The *Moore* was now too close to bring her forward gun to bear, her bow being in the way, but the captain ordered the piece depressed and fired it through his own deck. The first shot was deflected by a hawse pipe, but the second, fired through the hole in the deck and bow, burst against the *Varuna*'s pivot gun, inflicting heavy casu-alties. The third came as the *Moore* rammed her opponent hard amidships, re-ceiving a broadside in return. She backed off, then fired and rammed again. That did it. The *Varuna* limped toward bank; whereupon one of the fleeing Confederate gunboats, seeing her distress, turned and gave her another bump before she made it. She went down quickly then, leaving her topgallant forecas-tle above water, crowded with survivors.

The *Moore*'s captain, having his blood up, ordered a downriver course, intending to take on the whole Yankee fleet with one broken-nosed steamboat. The crew seemed willing, what there was left — well over half were dead or dying — but the wounded first lieutenant at the helm had had enough. "Why do this?" he protested. "We have no men left. I'll be damned if I stand here to be murdered." And with that he slapped the wheel hard to starboard, making a run for the west bank. Five Union ships, within range by now, cut loose at her with all their guns; she seemed almost to explode. All told, her crew of 93, mostly infantry detachments and longshoremen, lost 57 killed and 17 wounded. The rest were captured or escaped through the swamps when she struck bank, already ablaze, her colors burning at the peak.

Dawn glimmered and spread through the latter stages of the fight-ing. When the sun came up at 5 o'clock the Federal ships broke out their flags to greet it and salute their victory. All being safely past the forts except the sunken *Varuna* and three of the lighter gunboats — one had taken a shot in her boiler, losing her head of steam; another had got tangled in the barri-cade; a third had turned back, badly cut up by the crossfire — Farragut or-dered them to anchor, wash down, and take count. Casualties were 37 dead and 149 wounded, nearly twice the clerk's hopeful estimate and more than three times the losses in the forts: 12 dead and 40 wounded. On the other hand, the Confederate flotilla was utterly destroyed, including the fleeing gunboat which had given the *Varuna* a final butt; her skipper burned her at the levee in New Orleans.

★

Below the boom, Porter's anxiety was relieved as he watched the charred remnants of the rebel fleet come floating down the river. When his demand for immediate surrender of the forts was declined, he put his mortar crews back to work, firing up the remainder of their shells.

★ ★ ★ *N*ew Orleans was in a frenzy of rage and disappointment at the news from downriver. Other cities might accept defeat and endure the aftermath in sullen silence; but not this one. All afternoon and most of the night, while crowds milled in the streets, brandishing knives and pistols and howling for resistance to the end, drays rattled over the cobbles, hauling cotton from the presses for burning on the quays, where crates of rice and hogsheads of molasses were broken open and thrown into the river. This at least won the people's approval; "The damned Yankees shall not have it!" they cried, and the night was hazed with acrid smoke that hid the stars.

They were no less violent next morning when they heard the guns of the enemy fleet make short work of the Chalmette batteries, then come slowly into view around Slaughterhouse Bend as a drizzle of rain began to fall; "silent, grim, and terrible," one among the watchers called the warships, "black with men, heavy with deadly portent." Their great hope had been the ironclads, built and launched in their own yards. One had already gone downriver, powerless, and been by-passed. Now here came the other, the unfinished *Mississippi*, drifting helpless, set afire to keep her from falling into Federal hands. The crowd howled louder than ever at the sight, shouting "Betrayed! Betrayed!" and screaming curses at the Yankee sailors who watched from the decks and yardarms. Aboard the *Hartford*, one old tar grinned broadly back at them as he stood beside a 9-inch Dahlgren, holding the lanyard in one hand and patting the big black bottle-shaped breech with the other. The rain came down harder.

Despite the threats and invective from the quay, Farragut's strength was so obvious that he didn't have to use it. Two officers went ashore and walked unescorted through the hysterical mob to City Hall, where the mayor was waiting for them. Lovell had retreated, leaving New Orleans an open city. However, if the citizens were willing to undergo naval bombardment, he offered to "return with my troops and not leave as long as one brick remained upon another." The offer was declined: as was the navy's demand for an immediate surrender. "This satisfaction you cannot obtain at our hands," the mayor told the two officers. He would not resist, but neither would he yield; if they wanted the city, let them come and take it.

Farragut wanted no pointless violence; he had had enough violence the day before, when, as he told a friend, "I seemed to be breathing flame." Saturday, while negotiations continued, he ordered his captains to assemble their crews at 11 o'clock the following morning and "return thanks to Almighty God for his great goodness and mercy for permitting us to pass through the events of the past two days with so little loss of life and blood. At that hour the Church pennant will be hoisted on every vessel of the fleet, and their crews assembled will, in humiliation and prayer, make their acknowledgments thereof to the Great Disposer of all human events." That would be ceremony enough for him, with or without a formal surrender by the municipal authorities.

Benjamin Butler (above) led the ground forces that occupied New Orleans and was named military governor of the city.

The occupation problem still remained, but not for long. Monday the garrisons of Forts Jackson and St Philip — they were "mostly foreign enlistments," the commandant said; "A reaction set in among them," he explained — mutinied, spiked the guns, and forced their officers to surrender. Still powerless, the *Louisiana* was blown up to forestall capture. Butler's 18,000 men ascended the river unopposed and marched into the city on the last day of the month. "In family councils," a resident wrote, "a new domestic art began to be studied — the art of hiding valuables" from looters under the general known thereafter as "Spoons" Butler. One cache he uncovered with particular satisfaction: 418 bronze plantation bells collected there in answer to Beauregard's impassioned pleas for metal. Sent to Boston, they sold for $30,000 to mock the rebels from New England towers and steeples. Other aspects of the occupation were less pleasant for the visitors. Not only was southern hospitality lacking, the people seemed utterly unwilling to accept the consequences of defeat: particularly the women, who responded to northern overtures with downright abuse. Butler knew how to handle that, however. "I propose to make some brilliant examples," he wrote Stanton

Farragut now was free to continue his trip upriver, and in early May he did so. Baton Rouge fell as easily as New Orleans, once the guns of the fleet were trained on its streets and houses; the state government had fled the week before to Opelousas, which was safely away from the river. Natchez was next, and it too fell without resistance. Then in mid-May came Vicksburg, whose reply to a demand for surrender was something different from the others: "Mississippians don't know, and refuse to learn, how to surrender to an enemy. If Commodore Farragut or Brigadier General Butler can teach them, let them come and try." The ranks were wrong; Butler was a major general, Farragut a captain; but the writer seemed to mean what he was saying. The guns frowned down from the tall bluff—"so elevated that our fire will not be felt by them," Farragut said—and there were reports of 20,000 reinforcements on the way from Jackson. Deciding to label this first attempt a mere reconnaissance, he left garrisons at Baton Rouge and Natchez, and was back in New Orleans before the end of May. Vicksburg was a problem that could wait. In time he intended to "teach them," but just now it needed study.

Welles was angry, hotly demanding to know why the attack against Vicksburg's bluff had not been pressed, but the feeling in the fleet was that enough had been done in one short spring by one upriver thrust. New Orleans was now in northern hands and a second southern capital had fallen—both delivered as outright gifts to the army from the navy. Southerners agreed that it was quite enough, though some found bitter solace in protesting that the thing had been done by mechanical contrivance, with small risk and no gallantry at all. The glory was departing. "This is a most cowardly struggle," a Louisiana woman told her diary. "These people can do nothing without gunboats. These passive instruments do their fighting for them. It is at best a dastardly way to fight." Then she added, rather wistfully: "We should have had gunboats if the Government had been efficient, wise or earnest."

★ ★ ★

Both sides used Corinth, Mississippi, seen here with piles of Union matériel after the Confederates evacuated in June 1862, as a staging area and supply depot.

Halleck, Beauregard · Corinth

1862 ★ ★ ★ ★ ★ The North had found a new set of western heroes—Farragut, Curtis, Canby, Pope, Ben Butler: all their stars were in ascendance—but some of the former heroes now had tarnished reputations: Grant, for instance. If the news from Donelson had sent him soaring like a rocket in the public's estimation, the news from Shiloh dropped him sparkless like the stick. Cashiered officers, such as the Ohio colonel who cried "Retreat! Save yourselves!" at first sight of the rebels, were spreading tales back home at his expense. He was incompetent; he was lazy; he was a drunk. Correspondents, who had come up late and gathered their information in the rear—"not the best place from which to judge correctly what is going on in front," Grant remarked—were soon in print with stories which not only seemed to verify the rumors of "complete surprise," but also included the casualty lists. Shocking as these were to the whole country, they struck hardest in the Northwest, where most of the dead boys were being mourned.

Hardest hit of all was Ohio, which not only had furnished a large proportion of the corpses, but also was smarting under the charge that several Buckeye regiments had scattered for the rear before firing a shot. Governor David Tod was quick to announce that these men were not cowards; they had been caught off guard as a result of the "criminal negligence" of the high command. By way of securing proof he sent the lieutenant governor down to talk with the soldiers in their camps. They agreed with the governor's view, and the envoy returned to publish in mid-April a blast against "the blundering stupidity and negligence of the general in command." He found, he said, "a general feeling among the most intelligent men that Grant and Prentiss ought to be court-martialed or shot." Grant himself was an Ohioan, but they disclaimed him; he had moved to Illinois.

Nor was Ohio alone in her resentment. Harlan of Iowa rose in Congress to announce that he discerned a pattern of behavior: Grant had blundered at Belmont until he was rescued by Foote's navy, had lost at Donelson until C. F. Smith redeemed him, and had been surprised at Shiloh and saved by Buell. "With such a record," Harlan declared, "those who continue General Grant in active command will in my opinion carry on their skirts the blood of thousands of their slaughtered countrymen."

Eventually the problem landed where the big ones always did: on the shoulders of Abraham Lincoln. Late one night at the White House a Pennsylvania spokesman made a summary of the charges. Grant had been surprised because of his invariable lack of vigilance and because he disregarded Halleck's order to intrench. In addition, he was reported drunk: which might or might not have been true, but in any case he had lost the public's confidence to such an extent that any future blood on his hands would be charged against the officials who sustained him. He had better be dismissed. Lincoln sat there thinking it over, profoundly alone with himself, then said earnestly: "I can't spare this man. He fights."

He was not fighting now, nor was he likely to be fighting any time in the near future. Halleck had seen to that by taking the field himself. As soon as he reached Pittsburg Landing, four days after the battle, he began reorganizing his forces by consolidating Grant's Army of the Tennessee and Buell's Army of the Ohio with Pope's Army of the Mississippi, summoned from Island Ten. When George Thomas, now a major general as a reward for Fishing Creek, arrived with Buell's fifth division — the other four, or parts of them, had come up in time for a share in the fighting — Halleck assigned it to Grant's army and gave Thomas the command in place of Grant, who was appointed assistant commander of the whole, directly under Halleck. That way he could watch him, perhaps use him in an advisory capacity, and above all keep him out of contact with the troops. Having thus disposed of one wild man, he attended to another. McClernand, with his and Lew Wallace's divisions, plus a third from Buell, was given command of the reserve. So organized, Halleck told his reshuffled generals, "we can march forward to new fields of honor and glory, till this wicked rebellion is completely crushed out and peace restored to our country." He was confident, and with good cause. His fifteen divisions included 120,172 men and more than 200 guns.

★

After Shiloh, Henry Halleck (left) took personal command of the western Union forces and moved on Corinth, Mississippi.

Thomas and Pope were pleased with the arrangement; but not Buell and McClernand. Buell, whose command was thus reduced to three green divisions while his former lieutenant Thomas had five, all veteran, protested: "You must excuse me for saying that, as it seems to me, you have saved the feelings of others very much to my injury." McClernand, too, was bitter. He saw little chance for "honor and glory," as Halleck put it, let alone advancement, when his army — if it could be called such; actually it was a pool on which the rest would call for reinforcements — did not even have a name. But the saddest of all was Grant. He had no troops at all, or even duties, so far as he could see. When he complained about being kicked upstairs into a supernumerary position, Halleck snapped at him with charges of ingratitude: "For the past three months I have done everything in my power to ward off the attacks which were made upon you. If you believe me your friend you will not require explanations; if not, explanations on my part would be of little avail."

C. F. Smith, who at Donelson had proved himself perhaps the hardest fighter of them all, was not included in the reshuffling because he was still confined to his sickbed in Savannah. After Shiloh, the infected shin got worse; blood poisoning set in. Or perhaps it was simply a violent reaction of the old man's entire organism, outraged at being kept flat on his back within earshot of one of the world's great battles. At any rate, he sickened and was dead before the month was out. Halleck ordered a salute fired for him at every post and aboard every warship in the department. The army would miss him, particularly the volunteers who had followed where he led, alternately cursed and cajoled, but always encouraged by his example. Grant would miss him most of all.

April 28, having completed the reorganization and briefed the four commanders, Halleck sent his Grand Army forward against Beauregard, who was intrenched at Corinth with a force which Halleck estimated at 70,000 men. Buell had the center, Thomas the right, and Pope the left; McClernand brought up the rear. Halleck intended to follow along, though for the present he kept his command post at Pittsburg. The great day had come, but he did not seem happy about it according to a reporter who saw him May Day: "He walks by the hour in front of his quarters, his thumbs in the armpits of his vest, casting quick looks, now to the right, now to the left, evidently not for the purpose of seeing anything or anybody, but staring into vacancy the while." Part of what was fretting him was the thing that had fretted Grant the year before, when he marched for the first time against the enemy and felt his heart "getting higher and higher" until it seemed to be in his throat. What Halleck felt was the presence of the enemy. "The evidences are that Beauregard will fight at Corinth," he wired Washington this same day.

Certain comparisons were unavoidable for a man accustomed to weighing all the odds. In the fight to come it would be Beauregard, who had co-directed the two great battles of the war, versus Halleck, the former lieutenant of engineers, who had never been in combat. True, he had written or translated learned works on tactics; but so had Hardee, waiting for him now beyond the woods. Bragg was there, grim-faced and wrathful, alongside Polk, the transfer from the Army of the Lord, and Breckinridge, an amateur and therefore unpredictable. So was Van Dorn, who had crossed the Mississippi with 17,000 veterans of Pea Ridge, where the diminutive commander had thrown them at Curtis in a savage double envelopment. It had failed because Curtis had kept his head while the guns were roaring. Could Halleck keep his? He wondered. Besides, Van Dorn might have learned enough from that experience to make certain it did not fail a second time.... For Halleck, the woods were filled with more than shadows.

Nevertheless, he put on a brave face when he wired Washington two days later: "I leave here tomorrow morning, and our army will be before Corinth tomorrow night."

Pope was off and running, in accordance with the reputation earned at New Madrid. Advancing seven miles from Hamburg on the 4th, he did not stop until he reached a stream appropriately called Seven Mile Creek, and from there he leapfrogged forward again to another creekline within two miles of Farmington, which in turn was only four miles from Corinth. He reported his position a good one, protected by the stream in front and a bog on his left, but he was worried about his other flank; "I hope Buell's forces will keep pace on our right," he told headquarters. It turned out he was right to worry. Buell was

---

"I leave here tomorrow morning, and our army will be before Corinth tomorrow night."

— Henry W. Halleck

---

not there. Lagging back, he was warning Halleck: "We have now reached that proximity to the enemy that our movements should be conducted with the greatest caution and combined methods." The last phrase meant siege tactics, and the army commander took his cue from that. "Don't advance your main body at present," he told Pope. "We must wait till Buell gets up."

Buell was back near Monterey, with Thomas conforming on his right. Presently Pope was back there, too: Beauregard made a stab at his front, and he had to withdraw to avoid an attempt to envelop the flank protected by the bog. In fact the whole countryside was fast becoming boggy. Assistant Secretary Thomas Scott, an observer down from the War Department, wired Stanton: "Heavy rains for the past twenty hours. Roads bad. Movement progressing slowly." Gloomily Halleck confirmed the report: "This country is almost a wilderness and very difficult to operate in." Scott attended a high-level conference and passed the word along: Halleck would continue the advance, and "in a few days invest Corinth, then be governed by circumstances." He made no conjecture as to what those circumstances might be, but Stanton could see one thing clearly. Last week's "tomorrow" had stretched to "a few days."

It was more than a few. Every evening the troops dug in: four hours' digging, six hours' sleep, then up at dawn to repel attack. The attack didn't come, not in force at least, but Halleck had every reason to expect one. Rebel deserters were coming in with eye-witness accounts of the arrival of reinforcements for the 70,000 already behind the formidable intrenchments. He took thought of the host available to Beauregard by rail from Fort Pillow, Memphis, Mobile, and intermediary points. No less than 60,000 could be sped there practically overnight, he computed, which would give the defenders a larger army than his own. Taking thought, he grew cautious; he grew apprehensive. "Don't let Pope get too far ahead," he warned, acutely aware by now that he had another wild man on his hands. "It is dangerous and effects no good."

He had cause for caution, especially since the accounts of deserters were confirmed by observers of his own. In mid-May the officer in charge of pickets reported that he had heard trains pulling into Corinth during the night. "Such trains were greeted with immense cheering on arrival," he declared. "The enemy are concentrating a powerful army." Next night it was repeated. A scout-

Federal troops under Halleck build breastworks as they stop for the night during their march toward Corinth in May 1862.

ing party, working near town, heard more trains arriving "and, after they stopped, marching music from the depot in the direction of the front lines." Intelligence could hardly be more definite, and Halleck found his apprehension shared. Indiana's Governor O. P. Morton, down to see how well his Hoosiers had recovered from the bloody shock of Shiloh, wired Stanton on May 22: "The enemy are in great force at Corinth, and have recently received reinforcements. They evidently intend to make a desperate struggle at that point, and from all I can learn their leaders have utmost confidence in the result.... It is fearful to contemplate the consequences of a defeat at Corinth." Halleck thought it fearful, too: the more so after McClernand capped the climax with a report he had from a doctor friend, captured at Belmont and recently exchanged. The Illinois general, fretting in his back-seat position, was finding "the amount of duty... very great, indeed exhausting, if not oppressive." Now he crowded into the frame of the big picture by passing along what he heard from the doctor, who had left Memphis on May 15. While there, he had spoken with some former classmates now in the rebel army, who "informed him that on that date the enemy's force at Corinth numbered 146,000." Other details were given, the doctor said, "prospectively increasing their number to 200,000." To palliate the shock of this, he added that "a considerable portion of the force... consists of new levies, being in large part boys and old men."

Two hundred thousand of anything, even rabbits, could make a considerable impression, however, if they were launched at a man who was unprepared: which was the one thing Halleck was determined not to be. Orders went out for the troops to dig harder and deeper, not only on the flanks, but across the center. They cursed and dug—the rains were over; summer was almost in—sweating in wool uniforms under the Mississippi sun. Only the Shiloh veterans, looking back, saw any sense in all that labor. Apparently all but four of the ranking generals shared their commander's apprehension: Pope, who chafed at restraint, bristling offensively on the left: Thomas, who did not have it in his nature to be quite apprehensive about anything: Sherman, who, happy over a pending promotion, called the movement "a magnificent drill": and Grant. Not even Shiloh had taught him caution to this extent. He suggested once to Halleck that he shift Pope's army from the left to the right, out of the swamps and onto the ridge beyond the opposite flank, then send it bowling directly along the high ground into the heart of Corinth. Halleck gave him a fish-eye stare of unbelief. "I was silenced so quickly," Grant said later, "that I felt that possibly I had suggested an unmilitary movement." He drew back and kept his own counsel. This was not his kind of war.

It was Halleck's kind, and he kept at it, burrowing as he went. An energetic inchworm could have made better time—half a mile a day now, sometimes less—but not without the danger of being swooped on by a hawk: whereas, by Halleck's method, the risk was small, the casualties low, and the progress sure. The soldiers, digging and cursing under the summer sun, might agree with the disgruntled McClernand's definition of the campaign as "the present unhappy drama," but they would be there for roll call when the time came for the bloody work ahead. Besides, nothing could last forever; not even this. By the morning of May 28 — a solid month from the jump-off — all three component armies were within cannon range of Beauregard's intrenchments. After four weeks of marching and digging, Halleck had his troops where he had said they would be "tomorrow." He had reached the second stage, the one in which he had said he would "be governed by circumstances."

★ ★ ★   **E**ast and far northeast of Corinth, Halleck had two more divisions, both left behind by Buell when he marched for Pittsburg Landing. The latter, commanded by Brigadier General George W. Morgan, was maneuvering in front of Cumberland Gap, prepared to move in if the Confederates evacuated or weakened the already small defensive force. Morgan had further plans, intending not only to seize the gap, but to penetrate the Knoxville region — a project dear, as everyone knew, to the heart of Abraham Lincoln. However, the place was a natural fortress; Morgan reported it "washed into deep chasms or belly-deep in mud." So long as the rebels stayed there he could do nothing but hover and maneuver. The more substantial threat would have to come from the opposite direction, beyond the gap, and that was where Buell's other division, under Brigadier General Ormsby M. Mitchel, came in.

He was already in North Alabama, deeper into enemy country than any other Federal commander, having occupied Huntsville the day Halleck got to Pittsburg. From there he pushed on and took Bridgeport just as Halleck's army started south. A bright prospect lay before him. Once he had taken Chattanooga, thirty miles away, he would continue his march along the railroad and threaten Knoxville from the rear. This would cause the evacuation of Cumberland Gap, and when Morgan came through, hard on the heels of the defenders, Mitchel would join forces with him and make Lincoln's fondest hope a fact by chasing the scattered rebels clean out of East Tennessee. That was his plan at the outset, and it tied in well with another he had already put in motion, which resulted in what was known thereafter as the Great Locomotive Chase.

James J. Andrews, a Kentucky spy who had gained the trust of Confederates by running quinine through the lines, volunteered to lead a group of 21 Ohio soldiers, dressed like himself in civilian clothes, down into Georgia to burn bridges and blow up tunnels along the Western & Atlantic, the only rail

James Andrews (left) led an expedition deep into Confederate Georgia, intending to destroy communications lines along the Western & Atlantic Railroad between Atlanta and Chattanooga.

connection between Atlanta and Chattanooga. Andrews and his men infiltrated south and assembled at Marietta, Georgia, where — on April 12, the day after Mitchel took Huntsville — they boarded a northbound train as passengers. During the breakfast halt at Big Shanty they made off with the locomotive and three boxcars, heading north. The conductor, W. A. Fuller, took the theft as a personal affront and started after them on foot. Commandeering first a handcar, then a switch engine, and finally a regular freight locomotive, along with whatever armed volunteers he encountered along the way, he pressed the would-be saboteurs so closely that they had no time for the destruction they had intended. Overtaken just at the Tennessee line, where they ran out of fuel and water, they took to the woods, but were captured. Eight were hanged as spies, including Andrews; eight escaped while awaiting execution, and the remaining six were exchanged. All received the Congressional Medal of Honor in recognition of their valor "above and beyond the call of duty." Fuller and his associates received a vote of thanks from the Georgia legislature, but no medals. The Confederacy never had any, then or later.

Andrews' failure meant that the rebels could reinforce Chattanooga rapidly by rail. Advancing toward it, Mitchel found other drawbacks to his plan, chief among them being a shortage of supplies. Except for the fact that he could bring food and other necessities along the railroad, he told Washington, "it would be madness to attempt to hold my position a single day." Presently gray raiders were loose in his rear, capturing men and disrupting communications. "As there is no [hope] of an immediate advance upon Chattanooga," he wired Stanton, "I will now contract my line." He remained in North Alabama, doing what he could — mainly destroying railroad bridges which later Union commanders would have to replace — but on the day that Halleck halted within range of the Corinth intrenchments, Mitchel requested a transfer to another theater. "My advance beyond the Tennessee River seems impossible," he said.

Chattanooga was untaken, and though Morgan still hovered north of Cumberland Gap, Knoxville was spared pressure from either direction. Halleck could expect no important strategic diversion on his left as he entered the final stage of his campaign against Corinth.

★ ★ ★ I t turned out, simultaneously, that he could expect none on his right flank either. Farragut turned back from frowning Vicksburg, abandoning for the present his planned ascent of the Mississippi, and the descending fleet of ironclads, steaming south after the fall of Island Ten, received a jolt which gave the Confederates not only a sense of security on the river, but also a heady feeling of elation, long unfamiliar, and a renewal of their confidence in the valor of southern arms.

Midway between New Madrid and Memphis, Fort Pillow was next on the navy's list of downriver objectives, and Foote did not delay. With a burst of his old-time energy, he had the place under mortar bombardment within a week of the fall of Island Ten. The plan was for him to apply pressure from the river, while Pope moved in from the land side, a repetition of his tactics in Missouri. However, when Halleck took the field in person he summoned Pope to

Pittsburg Landing, leaving only two regiments to coöperate with the navy. Foote felt let down and depressed. Fort Pillow was a mean-looking place, with the balance of the guns from Columbus dug into its bluff, and he did not think the navy could do the job alone. Downstream there was a Confederate flotilla of unknown strength, perhaps made stronger than his own by the addition of giant ironclads reportedly under construction in the Memphis yards. The commodore was feverish — "much enfeebled," one of his captains wrote — still on crutches from his Donelson wound, which would not heal in this climate, and distressed, as only a brave man could be, by his loss of nerve. In this frame of mind he applied to Welles for shore duty in the North; which was granted with regret.

May 9 he said farewell on the deck of the flagship, crowded with sailors come for a last look at him. He took off his cap and addressed them, saying that he regretted not being able to stay till the war was over; he would remember all they had shared, he said, "with mingled feelings of sorrow and of pride." Supported by two officers, he went down the gangway and onto a transport, where he was placed in a chair on the guards. When the crew of the flagship cheered him he covered his face with a palm-leaf fan to hide the tears which ran down into his beard. As the transport pulled away, they cheered again and tossed their caps in salute. Greatly agitated, Foote rose from the chair and cried in a broken voice across the widening gap of muddy water: "God bless you all, my brave companions! . . . I can never forget you. Never, never. You are as gallant and noble men as ever fought in a glorious cause, and I shall remember your merits to my dying day." It was one year off, that dying day, and when the doctors told him it had come he took the news without regret. "Well," he said quietly, "I am glad to be done with guns and war."

His successor, Commodore Charles Henry Davis, a fifty-five-year-old Bostonian with a flowing brown mustache and gray rim whiskers, had been a salt-water sailor up to now, a member of the planning board and chief of staff to Du Pont at Port Royal, but before he had spent a full day in his new command he got a taste of what could happen on the river. His first impression had been one of dullness. Agreeing with Foote that the fleet alone could never take Fort Pillow — though in time, if ordered to do so, he would be willing to try running past it — he kept all but one of the gunboats anchored at Plum Run Bend, five miles above the fort. That one was stationed three miles below the others, protecting the single mortar-boat assigned to keep up a harassing fire by dropping its 13-inch shells at regular intervals into the rebel fortifications. "Every half-hour during the day," a seaman later wrote, "one of these little pills would climb a mile or two into the air, look around a bit at the scenery, and finally descend and disintegrate around the fort, to the great interest and excitement of the occupants." There was little interest and still less excitement at the near end of the trajectory. This had been going on for some weeks now, and as duty it was dull. The seven iron-clads took the guard-mount times about, one day a week for each.

While Foote was telling his crew goodbye, J. E. Montgomery, the river captain who had brought the eight River Defense Fleet gunboats up from New Orleans, was holding a council of war at Memphis. The bitter details of what Farragut's blue-water ships had done to the Confederate flotilla above Forts Jackson and St Philip had reached Memphis by now, along with the warning that Farragut himself might not be far behind; he was on his way, and in fact had captured Baton Rouge the day before. Montgomery's captains believed they could do better when the time came, but in any case there was no point in waiting to fight both Federal fleets at once. They voted to go upriver that night and try a surprise attack on the ironclads next morning, May 10.

It was Saturday. The ironclad *Cincinnati* had the duty below, standing guard while *Mortar 10* threw its 200-pound projectiles, one every half-hour as usual, across the wooded neck of land hugged by the final bend above Fort Pillow. The gunboat was not taking the assignment very seriously, however. Steam down, she lay tied to some trees alongside bank, and her crew was busy holystoning the decks for weekly inspection. About 7 o'clock one of the workers gave a startled yell. The others looked and saw eight rebel steamboats rounding the bend, just over a mile away — eight minutes, one of the sailors translated — bearing down, full steam ahead, on the tethered *Cincinnati*. Things moved fast then. While the deck crew slipped her cables, the engineers were throwing oil and anything else inflammable into her furnaces for quick steam. They were too late. The lead vessel, the *General Bragg*, came on, twenty feet tall, her great walking-beam engine driving so hard she had built up a ten-foot billow in front of her bow. The *Cincinnati* delivered a broadside at fifty yards, then managed to swing her bow around and avoid right-angle contact. The blow, though glancing, tore a piece out of her midships six feet deep and twelve feet long, letting a flood into her magazine.

Three miles upstream, around Plum Run Bend, the rest of the fleet knew nothing of the sudden attack until they heard the guns. They too were lazing alongside bank, steam down. By the time they got up pressure enough to maneuver — which they did as soon as possible, the *Mound City* leading the way — they were too late to be of any help to their sister ship below. When the *General Bragg* sheered off, the second ram-gunboat, *Sumter*, struck the *Cincinnati* in the fantail, wrecking her steering gear and punching another hole that let the river in. Next came the *Colonel Lovell*, whose iron prow crashed into the port quarter. Taking water from three directions, the proud *Cincinnati*, the fleet's first flagship and leader of the crushing assault on Henry, rolled first to one side, now the other, then gave a convulsive shudder and went down in water shallow enough to leave her pilot house above the surface for survivors to cling to, including her captain, who had taken a sharpshooter's bullet through the mouth. It appeared that one of the ironclad monsters could be sunk after all. And having proved it, the attacking flotilla proceeded to re-prove it.

The *Mound City* arrived too late for the *Cincinnati*'s good, and too early for her own. A fourth ram-gunboat, the *General Van Dorn*, met her almost head on, and punched such a hole in her forward starboard quarter that the *Mound City* barely managed to limp toward bank in time to sink with her nose out of water. Two down and five to go: but when the rest of the ironclads came on the scene, their 9-inch Dahlgrens booming, the river captains decided enough had been done for one day. They drew off downstream, unpursued, to the protection of Fort Pillow's batteries. Montgomery brought up the rear in his jaunty flagship *Little Rebel*.

After a full year of war, afloat and ashore, a contradictory pattern was emerging. In naval actions — with the exception of Fort Donelson — whoever

The gunboat C.S.S. Little Rebel took part in the May 10th attack on the Federal fleet as it came downriver toward Memphis.

attacked was the winner; while in land actions of any size — again with the same notable exception — it was the other way around. Montgomery was satisfied, however, with the simpler fact that an ironclad could be sent to the bottom. He knew because he had done it twice in a single morning. Returning to a cheering reception at Memphis he informed Beauregard that if the Federal fleet remained at its present strength, "they will never penetrate farther down the Mississippi."

★ ★ ★ The Creole had need of all the assurance and encouragement he could get. With Halleck knocking at its gate, Corinth was one vast groaning camp of sick and injured. Hotels and private residences, stables and churches, stores and even the railroad station were jammed, not only with the wounded back from Shiloh — eight out of ten amputees died, victims of erysipelas, tetanus, and shock — but also with a far greater number incapacitated by a variety of ailments. For lack of sanitary precautions, unknown or at any rate unpracticed, the inadequate water supply was soon contaminated. While dysentery claimed its toll, measles and typhoid fever both reached epidemic proportions. By mid-May, with the arrival of Van Dorn, Beauregard had 18,000 soldiers on the sick list, which left him 51,690 present for duty: well under half the number Halleck was bringing so cautiously against him.

He had done what he could to increase that caution at every opportunity. Many of the "deserters," for example, who had given the Union commander such alarming information as to the strength and intentions of the invaders, had been sent out by Beauregard himself, after intensive coaching on what to say when questioned. Valid prisoners were almost as misleading, for Beauregard had a report spread through the ranks that immediate advances were intended, and interrogated captives passed it on. Nor did the inventive general neglect to organize diversions which he hoped would cause detachments from the army in his front. Two regiments of cavalry were ordered to assemble at Trenton, Tennessee, then dash across western Kentucky for an attack on lightly held Paducah, meanwhile spreading the rumor that they were riding point for Van Dorn's army, which was on its way to seize the mouth of the Tennessee River and thus cut off Halleck's retreat when Beauregard struck him in front with superior numbers. A second, less ambitious cavalry project was intrusted to Captain John H. Morgan, who had shown promise on outpost duty the year before. He was promoted to colonel, given a war bag of $15,000, and sent to Kentucky to raise a regiment for disrupting the Federal rear. Though the former scheme was a failure — Beauregard blamed "the notorious incapacity of the offi-

★

cer in command"—the latter was carried out brilliantly from the outset. These were the gray raiders who caused Ormsby Mitchel to "contract" his line in North Alabama. However, it worked less well on the Corinth front. When Andrew Johnson protested that troops were needed to restrain Tennessee "disloyalists," the War Department referred the matter to Halleck, who refused to be disconcerted. "We are now at the enemy's throat," he replied, "and cannot release our great grasp to pare his toenails."

If Old Brains was to be stopped it would have to be done right here in front of Corinth, and Beauregard did what he could with what he had. His army took position along a ridge in rear of a protective creek, three to six miles out of town, thus occupying a quadrant which extended from the Mobile & Ohio on the north to the Memphis & Charleston Railroad on the east. Polk had the left, Bragg the center, and Hardee the right; Breckinridge and Van Dorn supported the flanks, being posted just in rear of the intersections of the railroads and the ridge. All through what was left of April and most of May, the defenders intrenched as furiously as the attackers, but with the advantage that while their opponents were honeycombing the landscape practically all the way from Monterey, their own digging was done in the same place from day to day. Even before Halleck started forward, the natural strength of the lines along the Corinth ridge had been greatly increased, and as he drew nearer they became quite formidable—especially in appearance. This was what Beauregard wanted: not only to give his men the added protection of solid-packed red earth, but also to free a portion of them for operations beyond the fortified perimeter, in case some segment of the advancing host grew careless and exposed itself, unsupported, to a sudden crippling slash by the gray veterans who had practiced such tactics at Elkhorn Tavern and Shiloh.

Pope was the likeliest to expose himself to such treatment, bristly as he was, and he had not been long in doing so. When he rushed forward in early May and took up an isolated position at Farmington, calling for the other commanders to hurry and catch up, Beauregard planned to destroy him by throwing Bragg at his front and Van Dorn on his flank. "Soldiers, can the result be doubtful?" he asked. "Shall we not drive back into the Tennessee the presumptuous mercenaries collected for our subjugation?" However, the result was worse than doubtful. Bragg hit Pope as planned, and hit him hard, but Van Dorn found the flank terrain quite different from the description in the attack order; Pope scurried back to safety before his flank was even threatened. In late May, when he returned to his old position—this time by more gradual approaches, allowing his fellow commanders to keep pace—Beauregard ordered the same trap sprung. Once more his hopes were high. "I feel like a wolf and will fight Pope like one," Van Dorn declared as he set out. But the results were the same as before, except that this time the Federals did not fall back, neither Pope nor the others alongside him.

★

*Through a massive hoax, Confederate
General Beauregard managed to fool the
advancing Federals and evacuate Corinth.*

The failure of this second attempt to repulse the Union host before it got a close-up hug on his intrenchments confirmed what Beauregard had suspected since mid-May. Outnumbered as he was, he would never be able to hold onto Corinth once the contest became a siege. In fact, if it came to that, he might not be able to hold onto his army. In addition to the water shortage and the lengthening sick list, there was now a scarcity of food. The arrival of a herd of cattle, driven overland from Texas, had already saved the defenders from starvation, but the herd was dwindling fast. Even if the Yankees failed, disease and hunger would force him out in time. So on May 25 he called a conference of his generals: Bragg, Van Dorn, Polk, Hardee, Breckinridge, and Price. Hardee, as became a student, had prepared a statement of primer-like simplicity: "The situation...requires that we should attack the enemy at once, or await his attack, or evacuate the place." To attack such numbers, intrenched to their front, "would probably inflict on us and the Confederacy a fatal blow." The only answer, as Hardee saw it, was to fall back down the line of the M & O while there was still a chance to do so unmolested, no matter how slim that chance appeared to be.

Beauregard and the others could do nothing but agree: the more so two days later, when Halleck got his whole Grand Army up within range of the fortified ridge and next morning — May 28 — opened a dawn-to-dusk cannonade, which paused from time to time to allow the infantry to probe for weak spots in the Confederate defenses. Fortunately, none developed; the wily Creole was left free to continue his plans for a withdrawal so secret that few of his officers suspected that one was intended. While the wounded and sick, along with the heavy baggage and camp equipment, were being evacuated by rail, the able-bodied men in the intrenchments were issued three days' cooked rations and told that they were about to launch an all-out attack: with the result that a timorous few — who indeed had cause to be frightened, being conscious of the odds — went over to the enemy with the news. Meanwhile the march details were formulated and rehearsed, the generals being assembled at army headquarters and required to repeat their instructions by rote until all had mastered their parts. No smallest detail was neglected, down to the final arrangements for bewildering the Federal pursuit by removing all the finger boards and mileposts south of Corinth.

Next afternoon, of necessity, the front-line troops were told of the planned deception in time to prepare for it that evening. They responded with enthusiasm, glad to have a share in what promised to be the greatest hoax of the war, and some proved almost as resourceful and inventive as their commander. When they stole out of the intrenchments after nightfall, they left dummy guns in the embrasures and dummy cannoneers to serve them, fashioned by stuffing ragged uniforms with straw. A single band moved up and down the deserted works, pausing at scattered points to play retreat, tattoo, and taps. Campfires were left burning, with a supply of wood alongside each for the drummer boys who stayed behind to stoke them and beat reveille next morning. All night a train of empty cars rattled back and forth along the tracks through Corinth, stopping at frequent intervals to blow its whistle, the signal for a special detail of leather-lunged soldiers to cheer with all their might. The hope was that this would not only cover the incidental sounds of the withdrawal, but would also lead the Federals to believe that the town's defenders were being heavily reinforced.

It worked to perfection. Beauregard would have been delighted if he had had access to the messages flying back and forth in reaction behind the northern lines. At 1.20 in the morning Pope telegraphed Halleck: "The enemy is reinforcing heavily, by trains, in my front and on my left. The cars are running constantly, and the cheering is immense every time they unload in front of me. I have no doubt, from all appearances, that I shall be attacked in heavy force at daylight." He turned his men out and did what he could to brace them for the shock, while Halleck alerted the other commanders. At 4 o'clock, mysteriously, the rattling and the cheering stopped, giving way to a profound silence which was broken at dawn by "a succession of loud explosions." Daylight showed "dense black smoke in clouds," but no sign of the enemy Pope expected to find massed in his front. Picking his way forward he came upon dummy guns and dummy cannoneers, some with broad grins painted on. Otherwise the works were deserted. So, apparently, was the town beyond. He sent back word of the evacuation, adding: "The whole country here seems to be fortified."

Halleck came out to see for himself. He had wanted a victory as bloodless as digging and maneuvering could make it; but not this bloodless, and above all not this empty. Even rebel civilians were scarce, all but two of the local families having departed with Beauregard's army. Seven full weeks of planning and strain, in command of the largest army ever assembled under one field general in the Western Hemisphere, had earned him one badly smashed-up North Mississippi railroad intersection.

In hope that more could yet be done, the order went out: "General Pope, with his reinforcements from the right wing, will proceed to feel the enemy on the left." Happy at being unleashed at last, Pope was hot on the trail with 50,000 men. At first there was little for him to "feel," but he reported joyfully: "The roads for miles are full of stragglers from the enemy, who are coming in in squads. Not less than 10,000 men are thus scattered about, who will come in within a day or two." This was mainly hearsay—like the information from a farmer that Beauregard, in a panic, had told his men to take to the woods and "save themselves as best they could"—but Halleck, anxious for a substantial achievement to put on the wire to Washington, was glad to hear it. Two days later, when Pope reported continuing success—a cavalry dash had destroyed an ammunition train and captured about 200 Confederate wounded—Halleck misunderstood him to mean that his former prediction had been fulfilled, and passed the news along to the War Department that 10,000 prisoners and 15,000 stand of arms had been seized because of the boldness of Pope's pursuit. Duly elated, Stanton replied: "Your glorious dispatch has just been received, and I have sent it into every State. The whole land will soon ring with applause at the achievement of your gallant army and its able and victorious commander."

Adjectivally, this was rather in line with Halleck's own opinion. The day after Corinth fell he informed his troops that they had scored "a victory as brilliant and important as any recorded in history," one that was "more humiliating to [the leaders of the rebellion] and to their cause than if we had entered the place over the dead and mangled bodies of their soldiers." However, this was a good deal more than any of his generals would say: except possibly John Pope. McClernand still considered the campaign an "unhappy drama," and not even Sherman, glad as he was to be out in the open, wearing his new major general's stars, praised it for being anything more than a "drill." Harsher words were left to the newspaper correspondents, who had never admired the elbow-scratching commander anyhow. "General Halleck...has achieved one of the most barren triumphs of the war," the Chicago *Tribune* asserted. "In fact, it is tantamount to a defeat." The Cincinnati *Commercial* extended this into a flat statement that, by means of his sly withdrawal, "Beauregard [has] achieved another triumph."

★ ★ ★ *T*hese verdicts, these ex post facto condemnations, were delivered before all the testimony was in. Hoax or no, the Confederate retrograde movement was, after all, a retreat; and as such it had its consequences. Fort Pillow, being completely outflanked, was evacuated June 4, along with the supplementary Fort Randolph, fifteen miles below. Now all that stood between the Federal ironclads and Memphis was the eight-boat flotilla which had been resting on its laurels since the affair at Plum Run Bend. Captain Montgomery had said then that the Yankees would "never penetrate farther down" unless their fleet was reinforced; but two days after Pillow and Randolph were abandoned he discovered, in the most shocking way, that it had indeed been reinforced.

Back in March — after years of failing to interest the navy in his theory — an elderly civil engineer named Charles Ellet, Jr., wrote and sent to the War Department a pamphlet applying the formula $f = mv^2$ to demonstrate the superiority of the ram as a naval weapon, particularly in river engagements, which allowed scant room for dodging. Stanton read it and reacted. He sent for the author, made him a colonel, and told him to build as many of the rams as he thought would be needed to knock the rebels off the Mississippi. Ellet got to work at once, purchasing and converting suitable steamers, and joined the ironclad fleet above Fort Pillow on May 25 with nine of the strange-looking craft. They carried neither guns nor armor, since neither had any place in the mass-velocity formula; nor did they have sharp dogtooth prows, which Ellet said would plug a hole as quickly as they punched one. All his dependence was on the two formula-components. Velocity was assured by installing engines designed to yield a top speed of fifteen knots, which would make them the fastest things on the river, and "mass" was attained by packing the bows with lumber and running three solid bulkheads, a foot or more in thickness, down the length of each vessel, so that the impact of the whole rigid unit would be delivered at a single stroke. Engines and boilers were braced for the shock of ramming, and the crews were river men whose courage Ellet tested in various ways, getting rid of many in the process. Perhaps his greatest caution, however, was shown in the selection of his captains. All were Pennsylvanians, like himself, and all were named Ellet. Seven were brothers and nephews of the designer-commander, and the eighth was his nineteen-year-old son.

★

Anxious to put $f = mv^2$ to work, the thin-faced lank-haired colonel was for going down and pitching into the rebel flotilla as soon as he joined up, but Flag Officer Davis had learned caution at Plum Run Bend. In spite of the fact that both sunken ironclads had been raised from their shallow graves and put back into service, the fleet was still under strength, three of its seven units having returned to Cairo for repairs. No matter, Ellet said; he and his kinsmen were still for immediate action, with or without the ironclads. But Davis continued to refuse the "concurrence" Stanton had told the colonel he would have to have in working with the navy.

The Confederates in Memphis, knowing nothing of all this, had assumed from reports that the new arrivers were some kind of transport. They relied on the guns of Forts Pillow and Randolph; or if the batteries failed to stop the Yankees, there was still the eight-boat flotilla which had given them such a drubbing three weeks back. Moreover, as at New Orleans, the keels of two monster ironclads, the *Arkansas* and the *Tennessee*, had been laid in the city's yards. The former, having been launched and armored up to her main-deck, was floated down to Vicksburg, then towed up the Yazoo River for completion in safety after the fall of Island Ten; but the latter was still on the stocks, awaiting the arrival of her armor. Like the city itself, she would have to take her chances that the enemy would be stopped.

Charles Ellet, Jr., designed and built the nine Federal rams used to take Memphis. He and eight relatives, all named Ellet, commanded the fleet.

Those chances were considerably thinned by the evacuation of Corinth and the two forts upriver. It now became a question of which would get there first, a sizeable portion of Halleck's Grand Army or the Federal fleet. The citizens hoped it would be the latter, for they had the gunboat flotilla to stand in its way, while there was absolutely nothing at all to stand in the way of the former. They got their wish. At dawn of June 6, two days after Fort Pillow was abandoned, the ironclads showed up, coming round the bend called Paddy's Hen and Chickens, four of them in line abreast just above the city, offering battle to the eight Confederate gunboats. The people turned out in tens of thousands, lining the bluffs for a grandstand seat at what they hoped would be a reënactment of the affair at Plum Run Bend. The first shot was fired at sunup, and they cheered and waved their handkerchiefs as at a tableau when the southern gun-boats, mounting 28 light cannon, moved out to meet their squat black bug-shaped northern opponents, mounting 68, mostly heavy.

Ellet had his rams in rear of the ironclad line of battle. When the first shot was fired, he took off his hat and waved it to attract the attention of his brother commanding the ram alongside his own. "Round out and follow me! Now is our chance!" he cried. Both boats sprang forward under full heads of steam and knifed between the ironclads, whose crews gave them a cheer as they went by. Ellet made straight for the *Colonel Lovell*, leader of the Confederate line, and when she swerved at the last minute to avoid a head-on collision, struck her broadside and cut her almost in two. She sank within a few minutes: brief, conclusive proof of the relation between force and mv^2. Meanwhile his brother had accomplished something different. Striking for the *General Price*, which held her course while the *General Beauregard* moved to aid her by converging on the ram, he darted between the two—which then collided in his wake. The *General Price* lost one of her sidewheels, sheared off in the crash, and while she limped toward bank, out of the fight, the ram came about in a long swift curve and rammed the *Beauregard* at the moment the rebel's steam drum was punctured by a shell from one of the ironclads. She struck her colors.

Four of the remaining five did not last much longer, and none ever managed to come to grips with an adversary. Montgomery's *Little Rebel*, the only screw steamer of the lot, took a shell in her machinery, then went staggering into the Arkansas bank, where her crew made off through the woods. The *Jeff Thompson* was set afire by a Federal broadside; the *Sumter* and the *Bragg*, like the flagship, were knocked into bank by the Dahlgrens. The whole engagement lasted no longer than the one at Plum Run Bend, which it avenged. One Confederate was sunk beyond raising; two were burned; four were captured, and in time became part of the fleet they had fought. *Van Dorn*, the only survivor, managed to get enough of a head start in the confusion to make a getaway downriver. Two of the gunless rams gave chase for a while, but then turned back to join the celebration.

The cheering was all on the river, where the rams and ironclads anchored unopposed, not on the bluffs, where the cheers had turned to groans. Smoke had blanketed the water; all the spectators could see was the flash of Union guns and the tall paired stacks of Confederate steamboats riding above the murk. Pair by pair, in rapid order, the crown-top chimneys disappeared. "The deep sympathizing wail which followed each disaster," one who heard it wrote, "went up like a funeral dirge from the assembled multitude, and had an overwhelming pathos." When the sun-dazzled smoke finally cleared away they saw that their flotilla had been not only defeated but abolished, and they turned sadly away to await the occupation which the Corinth retreat had made inevitable anyhow. There still was time to burn the *Tennessee*, sitting armorless on the stocks, and this they did, taking considerable satisfaction in at least making sure that she would never be part of the fleet whose destruction had been the aim of her designers. It was bitter, however, to surrender as they did to a nineteen-year-old medical cadet, Colonel Ellet's son, who landed in a rowboat with three seamen and a folded flag, the Stars and Stripes, which presently he was hoisting over the post office. Later that day the two regiments Pope had left behind marched in for the formal occupation. Thus was Memphis returned to her old allegiance.

Colonel Ellet himself did not come ashore. The only Federal casualty of the engagement, he had been pinked in the knee by a pistol ball while waving his hat on the hurricane deck of his flagship, directing the ram attack. The wound, though painful, was not considered dangerous; prone on the deck, he continued in command throughout the fight; but infection set in, and he died of it two weeks later, while being taken north aboard one of the rams. Before his death, however, he had the satisfaction of proving his theory in action and of knowing that his genius — in conjunction with the no doubt larger genius of that other civil engineer, James Eads — had cleared the Mississippi down to Vicksburg, whose batteries now would be grist for Davis's and Farragut's upper and nether millstones.

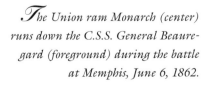

The Union ram Monarch (center) runs down the C.S.S. General Beauregard (foreground) during the battle at Memphis, June 6, 1862.

★ ★ ★   t Tupelo, where he called a halt fifty-two miles south of Corinth, Beauregard was infuriated by Halleck's widely circulated dispatch which glorified Pope at the Creole's expense by claiming a large bag of demoralized prisoners and abandoned equipment. He hotly replied, through the columns of newspapers guilty of spreading this libel, that the report "contained as many lies as lines." Far from being a rout, he said, or even a reverse, "the retreat was conducted with great order and preci-

sion, doing much credit to the officers and men under my orders, and must be looked upon, in every respect, by the country as equivalent to a brilliant victory."

Not all of his own countrymen agreed with him, any more than Halleck's had agreed with Halleck; but in the Southerner's case the dissenters included the Chief Executive. While the army was falling back, exposing his home state and the river down its western flank to deeper penetration, Davis told his wife: "If Mississippi troops lying in camp, when not retreating under Beauregard, were at home, they would probably keep a section of the river free for our use and closed against Yankee transports." The general had been sent west to help recover territory, not surrender more, and when it became evident after Shiloh that this was not to be accomplished, an intimate of the Davis circle wrote prophetically in her diary in reference to the hero of Sumter and Manassas: "Cock robin is as dead as he ever will be now. What matters it who killed him?"

As if in confirmation, soon after the loss of Memphis and its covering flotilla opened the river south to Vicksburg, the Tupelo commander received from the Adjutant General in Richmond a telegraphic warning that trouble was brewing for him there: "The President has been expecting a communication explaining your last movement. It has not yet arrived." Beauregard replied: "Have had no time to write report. Busy organizing and preparing for battle if pursued. . . . Retreat was a most brilliant and successful one," he added, maneuvering for solid ground on which to meet objections now that he had begun to see that the hoax might seem less fruitful and amusing from a distance. Next day, June 13, he forwarded a complete report, inclosing a clipping from the Chicago *Tribune* which showed that the enemy, at least, admired his generalship. He ended with a prediction that Halleck would find Corinth "a barren locality, which he must abandon as wholly worthless for his purposes."

If the document lacked his usual verve, there were more reasons than the melancholia resulting from lack of appreciation from above. Though the army's health was improving rapidly in the more salubrious Tupelo surroundings, the general's own was not. He had never entirely recovered from the throat operation he had undergone in Virginia, and the strain of long-odds campaigning had lowered his resistance even more. For months his doctors had been urging him to take a rest. Always he had replied that the military crisis would not permit it. But now that his army was out of contact with the enemy, he thought he might safely go to Bladon Springs, a resort north of Mobile, for a week or ten days of rest and relaxation before returning to take up the reins again. Bragg, the next ranking general, could hold them in his absence; Beauregard considered him fully qualified, having recommended him for the position just after Shiloh. Armed with a certificate of disability from his medical director, he was packing to leave on the 14th when he learned that Bragg had received, clean over his commander's head, a War Department order instructing him to assume command of the Vicksburg defenses.

★

Angry at having been by-passed, Beauregard wired that Bragg could not be spared. He himself was taking a short sick leave, he said, and was leaving the North Carolinian in charge of the army during his absence. Then, as if suddenly aware that this was the first he had told the authorities of his intended departure, he wrote a letter describing his run-down physical condition, quoting his doctors' insistence that he take a rest, and giving his travel schedule. He did not ask permission to go; he simply told the government he was going. Nor did he send the information by wire. He sent it by regular mail, and was on his way to Bladon Springs before the letter got to Richmond.

Bragg considered his position awkward, knowing the trouble that was brewing, and with Regular Army prudence wired Richmond for instructions as soon as his chief was gone. The reaction was immediate, perhaps because the wire arrived on the same day as news of another consequence of the retreat, the fall of Cumberland Gap. As far as Davis was concerned, the situation at Tupelo spoke for itself: Beauregard was Absent Without Leave. Accordingly, a telegram went to Bragg at once, assigning him to permanent command. The Creole first learned of the action from a telegram Bragg sent to intercept him in Mobile. "I envy you, and am almost in despair," Bragg said. Beauregard replied: "I cannot congratulate you, but am happy for the change."

He was not happy; he just said that to cover his anger and disappointment. Four months ago he had come west full of resentment at having been shunted away from the main field of endeavor into a vaster but relatively much less important theater. Since then, he had learned better. The war was to be won or lost as readily here as in the East. What was more, he had come to respect and love the western army, just as it loved and respected him, and he was bitter against the man who had taken it from him as abruptly as if by a pull on the trigger of a pistol already leveled at his head. Replying to a letter of sympathy sent by a friend, he wrote: "If the country be satisfied to have me laid on the shelf by a man who is either demented or a traitor to his high trust—well, let it be so. I require rest and will endeavor meanwhile by study and reflection to fit myself for the darkest hours of our trial, which I foresee are yet to come." Part at least of the study and reflection was devoted to composing other phrases which he considered descriptive of the enemy who had wronged him. "That living specimen of gall and hatred," he called Davis now; " 'that Individual.' "

★ ★ ★

Epilogue

In the opening months of 1862, the Confederates suffered a number of setbacks that spread gloom throughout the South. Delaware and Maryland were firmly in the Union camp. The border states of Kentucky and Missouri had come under northern sway and most of western Tennessee had been secured by the Yankees as well. The Mississippi River from Columbus, Kentucky, south to Memphis, and from the Gulf of Mexico, north past New Orleans and Baton Rouge to Natchez, was under Federal control. The Confederate invasion of New Mexico had been repulsed, leaving the Far West in northern hands. The virtual stalemate that had existed in Virginia following First Manassas was broken by events some distance away. The Federal capture of several Atlantic coast forts, coupled with a massive build-up of Union forces around Washington, D.C., forced the now isolated Confederates holding ground around Centreville to withdraw south toward Richmond. The threat posed to the Federal fleet by the C.S.S. *Virginia* at Hampton Roads had been greatly reduced with the appearance of the U.S.S. *Monitor.* In addition, Confederate emissaries in Europe had been rebuffed time and time again in their efforts to acquire recognition and support from abroad. And last, but not least, Union forces had landed on the York-James peninsula and were advancing on Richmond.

For Southerners, at this juncture of the war, the only hope was that, as they withdrew into a smaller and smaller area, forces and supplies could be more readily concentrated to fend off further attacks. While the Unionists might be greatly heartened by these apparent victories, there were drawbacks too. Northerners feared the concentration of Confederate forces. Also, with each advance into the South, garrisons had to be left behind to protect the gains, decreasing the size of the forces available for attack, and supply lines lengthened, giving greater opportunities for Confederate raiders. Even as news of one disaster after another reached Richmond, events were taking place that would seem to turn the tide. Southern hopes and northern fears were about to be realized.

Joe Johnston's Confederates were contesting the invasion by McClellan's Army of the Potomac at Yorktown and Williamsburg, but the Yankee juggernaut would not stop until it reached the Chickahominy River, a scant five miles from the Confederate capital.

While McClellan approached Richmond, Stonewall Jackson and his forces were stirring up things in the Shenandoah Valley, west of Washington. Jackson's "foot cavalry," so called for their ability to march longer and farther than anyone else and still have plenty of fight left in them at the end of the day, would fight four pitched battles, six formal skirmishes, and any number of minor actions, and win them all. Large numbers of prisoners would be taken and quantities of captured ordnance and commissary stores shipped to supply the army around Richmond. To meet this threat west of Washington, frightened officials in the Federal capital were to withhold reinforcements and supplies from McClellan's Peninsula campaign.

Meanwhile, Johnston would concentrate his forces for an all-out attack against the Yankees along the Chickahominy. He would bloody the invader's nose at Seven Pines/Fair Oaks, but would himself be severely wounded in the battle. His replacement, Robert E. Lee, would renew the attack — and, for seven long days, doggedly pursue McClellan's army as it "changed its base" to the James River, still within hovering distance of Richmond. Jackson, who had joined Lee's army for the Seven Days battles, would move north again and fight Pope's southbound Army of Virginia at Cedar Mountain.

The combination of the Shenandoah threat, the stalling of McClellan's invasion, and that general's apparent unwillingness to press the issue, along with the appearance of Jackson north of Richmond, would lead Lincoln to order the withdrawal of the Army of the Potomac back to the Washington area. The threat to Richmond was lifted for the present.

In the West, Halleck, in a doomed attempt to protect the gains made in Tennessee and along the Mississippi, would disperse his forces throughout the region. By scattering his armies, he would leave the door ajar for daring Confederate cavalry raids led by Morgan and Forrest. Union communications lines, supply routes, and confidence were shattered. These raids, coupled with bad weather and Federal General Don Carlos Buell's caution, would allow Braxton Bragg to win the race to Chattanooga and hold it, thus threatening most of eastern Tennessee.

Meanwhile, a single, hastily built Confederate ironclad gunboat, the *Arkansas*, would wreak havoc with the Federal fleet at Vicksburg, breaking the Union hold on the central Mississippi River. With the fleets withdrawn one moving north and the other returning to New Orleans, Confederate pressure would force the Federals to evacuate Baton Rouge, returning it to the southern fold. Just when things seemed so promising for the Union and so dark for the Confederacy, the tables would be turned.

★ ★ ★

★

Picture Credits

The sources for the illustrations are listed below. Credits from left to right are separated by semicolons, from top to bottom by dashes.

Dust jacket: Front, Library of Congress, Neg. No. B811-192; rear, Library of Congress, Neg. No. B8184-10006; flap, photo by Larry Shirkey. 8-10: Chicago Historical Society, Neg. No. 1920.1645. 15: Frank & Marie-Thérèse Wood Print Collections, Alexandria, Va. 18: From *The General's Wife: The Life of Mrs. Ulysses S. Grant,* by Ishbel Ross, 1959, published by Dodd, Mead & Company, New York—from *A Personal History of Ulysses S. Grant,* by Albert D. Richardson, American Publishing Company, Hartford, courtesy Library of Congress. 20: Library of Congress. 24, 25: Frank & Marie-Thérèse Wood Print Collections, Alexandria, Va. 29: Valentine Museum, Richmond. 33: The Museum of the Confederacy, Richmond. 35: Frank & Marie-Thérèse Wood Print Collections, Alexandria, Va. 36: Kentucky Historical Society, Frankfort. 38: Tennessee State Museum Collection, photographed by June Dorman, Artifact #73.17. 42, 43: Library of Congress. 44-46: Austin History Center, Austin Public Library, Austin, Tex., PICA 03674. 48: Library of Congress, Neg. No. USZ62-20438. 52: Library of Congress, Neg. No. USZ62-14089. 54: Library of Congress, dag. #185 by Mathew Brady. 57: Map by Walter W. Roberts. 62: Frank & Marie-Thérèse Wood Print Collections, Alexandria,Va. 65: George Wythe Randolph Print, Edgehill Randolph Papers (#1397), Special Collections Department, University of Virginia Library. 69: Library of Congress. 72: Massachusetts Commandery Military Order of the Loyal Legion and the U.S. Army Military History Institute (MASS-MOLLUS/USAMHI), copied by A. Pierce Bounds. 74-76: The Collection of Jay P. Altmayer, copied by Larry Cantrell. 80, 81: Library of Congress, Neg. No. USZ62-65326. 83: MASS-MOLLUS/USAMHI, copied by A. Pierce Bounds. 84: National Archives, B-4559. 88: Map by Peter McGinn. 93: Library of Congress, Neg. No. BH82-4023B; Chicago Historical Society, Neg. No. ICHi-22202. 98: Collection of The New-York Historical Society. 100: Library of Congress. 102, 103: From *Battles and Leaders of the Civil War,* The Century Company, New York, 1884. 105: The Mariners Museum, Newport News, Va. 109: Library of Congress, Neg. No. B811-1145. 110, 111: Library of Congress, Waud #375. 117: Courtesy Mark Katz, Americana Image Gallery. 118, 119: Library of Congress, Waud #696. 122-124: From *The American Soldier in the Civil War,* published by Stanley-Bradley Publishing Co., New York © 1895, courtesy Library of Congress. 127:

Chicago Historical Society, Neg. No. ICHi-12748. 128: Courtesy Dr. Thomas P. Sweeney Collection, Gen. Sweeny's Museum, Republic, Mo. 131: Courtesy Dr. William J. Schultz. 135: Courtesy Dr. Thomas P. Sweeney Collection, Gen. Sweeny's Museum, Republic, Mo. 137: Maps by Walter W. Roberts. 140: National Archives, Neg. No. 111-B-6144. 145: Map by R. R. Donnelley & Sons Co., Cartographic Services, overlay by Time-Life Books—Library of Congress. 151: Library of Congress, Neg. No. B8172-6574. 154, 155: Courtesy Colorado Historical Society, Denver, inset, courtesy Colorado Historical Society, Denver, photographed by David Guerrero. 157: Sketches by A. B. Peticolas, Arizona Historical Society, Tucson AHS#60,293. 161: Fine Arts Gallery of the University of the South, Sewanee, Tenn. 163: Frank & Marie-Thérèse Wood Print Collections, Alexandria, Va. 167: From *Battles and Leaders of the Civil War,* The Century Company, New York, 1884. 168, 169: U.S. Naval Historical Center, Washington, D.C. (Neg # NH 66752)—collection of The New-York Historical Society. 172-174: Cincinnati Historical Society, #1980.18. 177: National Archives, Neg. No. 165-JT-283. 180, 181: Western Reserve Historical Society, Cleveland. 184: R. R. Donnelley & Sons Co., Cartographic Services. 187, 191: Frank & Marie-Thérèse Wood Print Collections, Alexandria, Va. 194: Courtesy Byron J. Ihle. 196: From *The Life of Gen. Albert Sidney Johnston,* by William Preston Johnston, published by D. Appleton and Co., New York, 1878. 199: Library of Congress. 202: Frank & Marie-Thérèse Wood Print Collections, Alexandria, Va. 204: Map by Walter W. Roberts, overlay by Time-Life Books. 209: National Archives—Kentucky Historical Society, Frankfort. 211: Map by Walter W. Roberts. 214, 215: Miriam and Ira D. Wallach Division of Art, Prints and Photographs, The New York Public Library, Astor, Lenox and Tildon Foundations. 219: Map by Walter W. Roberts, overlay by Time-Life Books. 221: MASS-MOLLUS/USAMHI, copied by A. Pierce Bounds. 224-226: New Orleans Historic Collection (acc.#1982.32.1). 228: West Point Museum Collections, U.S. Military Academy. 231: Map by Walter W. Roberts. 235: National Portrait Gallery, Smithsonian Institution, Washington, D.C. 240: Chicago Historical Society, Neg. No. ICHi-11580. 243: National Archives, Neg. No. 111-B-513. 247: Collection of The New-York Historical Society. 250: National Archives, Neg. No. 111-B-4533. 252-254: MASS-MOLLUS/USAMHI, copied by A. Pierce Bounds. 257: Courtesy Meserve-Kunhardt Collection. 260:

★

Index

SHELBY FOOTE, THE CIVIL WAR,
A NARRATIVE
VOLUME 2 FORT DONELSON TO
MEMPHIS

ISBN 0-7835-0101-3

School and library distribution by Time-Life Education,
P.O. Box 85026, Richmond, Virginia 23285-5026.

TIME-LIFE is a trademark of Time Warner Inc. U.S.A.

OTHER TIME-LIFE HISTORY PUBLICATIONS

What Life Was Like
Voices of the Civil War
The American Indians
Lost Civilizations
Time Frame
The Civil War
Cultural Atlas
Myth and Mankind
Our American Century
World War II
Echoes of Glory
Living Wisdom

 Time-Life Books is a
division of Time Life Inc.

TIME LIFE INC.
PRESIDENT and CEO: George Artandi

TIME-LIFE BOOKS
PUBLISHER/MANAGING EDITOR: Neil Kagan
VICE PRESIDENT, MARKETING: Joesph A. Kuna
VICE PRESIDENT, NEW PRODUCT
DEVELOPMENT: Amy Golden
DIRECTOR OF EDITORIAL
ADMINISTRATION: Barbara Levitt

PROJECT EDITOR: Philip Brandt George
DIRECTOR, NEW PRODUCT
DEVELOPMENT: Elizabeth D. Ward
DIRECTOR OF MARKETING: Pamela R. Farrell
Design Director: Tina Taylor
Art Director: Ellen L. Pattisall
Marketing Manager: Peter Tardif
Copyeditor: Christine Stephenson
Photo Coordinator: Susan L. Finken
Editorial Assistant: Christine Higgins

Special Contributors: Susan V. Kelly (research),
Melanie Byas, John Drummond, Janet Dell Russell
Johnson, Monika Lynde, Kathleen Mallow, Alan Pitts
and Don Schaaf and Friends, Inc. (design and
production) Roy Nanovic (index).

Correspondent: Christina Lieberman (New York).

For information on and a full description of any
of the Time-Life Books series listed at left,
please call 1-800-621-7026 or write:

Reader Information
Time-Life Customer Service
P.O. Box C-32068
Richmond, Virginia 23261-2068